C000129856

LONGFORD.

HISTORY

OF

THE COUNTY LONGFORD,

ILLUSTRATED.

BY

JAMES P. FARRELL.

DOLLARD, PRINTINGHOUSE, DUBLIN.

1891

Price, Illustrated and Post Paid, Ten Shillings.

/0C 95 CB

PREFACE.

THE following pages will, I hope, throw a long-required light on the history of the most central county in Ireland. I have endeavoured to explain its ancient and modern formation; and no effort of mine has been spared to describe that transition stage when the land of Longford or Annaly passed away from the ancient to the planter owners. At very considerable expense I have secured an accurate copy of the Patent Rolls of James I., showing, as will be found on perusal, who the ancient owners of every townland in Longford County were, and to whom these lands were conveyed by Royal Letters Patent. If the reader is at all of an inquiring turn of mind, it will be very easy for him to fill up the space of two hundred and sixty years with the names of any old families in these townlands, and he has as accurate an idea as I can give of who are, and who are not, the "old stock" in Longford County to-day.

I am aware that many people, from whom better should be expected, have not hesitated to describe my previous publications on this subject as an attempt to laudate the O'Farrells, as they say, "because I am a Farrell myself." Such an idea can only be harboured by the ignorant. Anyone who knows me will not doubt me when I say, as I have said often before, that were the ancient possessors of Annaly any other family or name but that of Farrell or O'Farrell, I would take as much pains, and probably more than I have taken, to put their history before the world. The illustrations will, I hope, be found interesting—in any case they cannot but add to the interest of the volume

JAMES P. FARRELL.

LONGFORD.
Feast of St. Mel, 1891.

LANESBOROUGH.

HISTORY

OF

THE COUNTY LONGFORD.

HISTORY tells us that we Irish are directly descended from the Milesians, who were the sixth and last body of invaders that took possession of this island in the dark ages before the Christian era. Prior to their advent Ireland had been successively the prize of five different peoples— Partholans, Nemedians, Formorians, Firbolgs, and Tuatha-de-Danaans. The Partholans were the descendants of a chief named Partholanus, who was the first inhabitant of Ireland after the Deluge. They were expelled from the country by the Nemedians, who, after an occupation of nearly two hundred years, were driven out by a race of pirates called Formorians. One part of the Nemedians went to the south of Europe, where they were put into slavery as bag-carriers, from which they were called Firbolgs. Another part went northwards, and became the powerful race subsequently called Tuatha-de-Danaans. The Firbolgs were the first to turn with a longing eye to the isle they had lost, and two hundred years had not passed away until they reconquered this country, driving the Formorians into the sea. Almost immediately after the Tuatha-de-Danaans began to think of returning to the home of their forefathers, and before their cousins had been thirty years in their reconquered homes, the Tuatha-de-Danaans swooped down from the north and expelled them from the country. Even at such a remote period we see this striking example of the affection with which these rude sons of the forest and the sea regarded "the woody isle," as

B

Ireland was then called. For one hundred and ninety years the Tuatha-de-Danaans reigned supreme in the land, during which time they organized a system of government, and divided the country into kingdoms. But in the year B.C. 3,500 a new race appeared to claim the island in the persons of the Milesians, who had been long established as a considerable nation in Spain. The Milesians were descended from Ghaedhal or Gatelus, who was the sixth in direct descent from Noah, and Noah being the ninth patriarch from Adam, Ghaedal was, therefore, the fifteenth patriarch in direct descent from the first man. Ghaedal gave his name to his posterity, who were therefrom called Gadelians, and the ancient records of the world prove that the twelfth king of the Ghadelians was Milesius, who was the father of the three sons that headed the Milesians in the sixth and last pre-Christian conquest of Ireland. When the Milesians arrived at Inver-Scene in the present County of Kerry, the Tuatha-de-Danaans complained that they were taken at a disadvantage, and were unprepared to offer the Milesians battle. They proffered, however, if the invaders would retire the distance of nine waves from the shore to give them battle on returning, and to yield up the island peacefully if the issue was against them. To this the Milesians consented; but when they had retired the required distance, the Tuatha-de-Danaans, who were skilled in the art of necromancy, caused a great storm to arise which dispersed the Milesian ships and sunk many of them. Such of them as escaped were driven to the mouth of the Boyne, where they landed, and marching to Teltown, in the County Meath, a great battle was fought, in which the Tuatha-de-Danaans were entirely defeated, and the Milesians became masters of the island.

The new masters were commanded by three chieftains—Heremon, Heber Finn, and Ir, and the latter having been killed in the battle, his son, Heber Donn, became co-heir with his uncles to the new possession. Heremon was the elder brother, and scarcely had the difficulty of beating the enemy been got over until Heber Finn and he quarrelled, whereupon, as in the case of Cain and Abel, Heremon slew Heber

Finn, and became sole ruler himself. He then made a distribution of the land, retaining the fair portion of Leinster to himself, giving Ulster to the son of Ir, Munster to the son of Heber Finn, and Connaught to two of his most trusted chieftains. Thus then was the Milesian invasion of Ireland accomplished five hundred years before the birth of Christ. It will now be our duty to confine ourselves to the particular fortunes of the house of Ir; because, as we shall see, it was from him that were descended the families who occupied what, two thousand years later, became the County of Longford.

It is not the purpose of this volume to give a history of Ulster. That, indeed, would be a herculean task, although in itself scarcely as difficult as to give a history of those ancient days in what became and now is the County Longford. Men, and things, and places were in those days known by names which have undergone so much change, that few there are who can accurately trace the history of any one spot in Ireland. In general it may be safely supposed that the same things which happened elsewhere in Ireland in those days happened in Longford; that there were wars, and raids, and ravages between many contending factions in each generation, as when we read in the "Four Masters": "A.M. 3790. After having reigned eighteen years as monarch of Ireland, Aengus Olumchaidh fell in the battle of Carmen (now in County Wexford). Aengus gained several battles, amongst which was the battle of Ardachaidh, in which fell Smiorgall, the son of Smeatha, king of the Formorians."

The Irian race became owners of the' land of Ulster, and their chiefs kings of that province, dwelling with great splendour at Emania, near the present city of Armagh. The twenty-sixth king from Ir was a monarch called Fergus the Great. He had reigned but seven years when he was overcome in battle by the famous Connor MacNessa, and had to fly into Connaught for safety. At this time there lived there the celebrated Queen Maud, or Mave, whose name is connected with so many legends in Ireland. Maud gladly received the exiled prince, and hospitably entertained him, the result being that Fergus

married her. Of this marriage three sons were born, two of whom
became founders of the O'Connor family of Kerry, whilst the third,
who was the eldest, and whose name was Conmac, received all his
mother and father's inheritance. This included, on his mother's side,
all of the present Counties of Galway, Mayo, and part of Roscommon,
whilst by his father he came into possession of the southern portion of
the dominions from which Fergus Mor had been driven   Conmac
erected this large inheritance into the kingdom of Conmacne, over
which he and his descendants ruled ; but after the lapse of years the
kingdom was divided into principalities and chieftaincies according as
the race of Conmac increased in numbers.   In the course of centuries
a chieftain ruled all that part of the territory of Conmacne bounded on
the west and north-west by the Shannon, and the south and east by the
Inny.   This man's name was Anghaile, and after his time the land he
ruled was called " the land of Anghaile," or, as it was afterwards
Anglicized, Annaly.   Aughaile's grandson was a chieftain named Fearghail, who, with his sons and clansmen, fought against the Danes at
Clontarf, A.D. 1015.   So distinguished and powerful did he become,
that his descendants were called O'Fearghails, which was Anglicized
O'Ferrall, the family name of the old inhabitants of Annaly to this
present day.

It is right to mention that there is a diversity of opinion as to the
exact location of old Annaly. ' From the following extracts from a com-
mentary on the Tripartite Life of St. Patrick, it would seem as if the
O'Farrells derived possession of the County Longford from force of
arms.   Thus it appears that—

"Teffia, which fell to Mann and his posterity, was formerly a very
extensive country in Meath, comprising five baronies in Westmeath—
viz., the country of the Foxes, Calrigia, Bregmania, Cuircina (besides
the lands assigned to the Tuites, Petits and Daltons), and the County
Longford, divided into North and South Teffia.   North Teffia is Cabra-
gaura, the possession of Carbry, son of King Niall, where the sons of
Carbry, apprehensive of the curse pronounced against them by Patrick,

were converted, and entertained him in a friendly spirit, to whom they gave the beautiful place called Granard. South Teffia, in the County Longford, being divided from Westmeath by the River Eithne (Inny), belonged to Mann and his posterity. St. Patrick regenerated this Mann in the waters of baptism, and built a church in a place called Ardachadh, which to this day is the See of Ardagh, and consecrated Melus, his sister's son, bishop, with whom he left Milchuo, his brother, co-bishop."

From this it would appear that Mann, who, according to O'Hart, was the progenitor of the O'Keareys, inhabited Longford County. But this account is obscure and unreliable, whereas all modern commentators agree that the County of Longford was the principal part of the ancient patrimony of the O'Farrells

Writing on this subject quite recently, a learned divine of the Diocese of Ardagh says :—

"The 'O'Ferrall' Sept, Princes of Annally, is an illustrious family of Milesian origin ; descended from Milesius, who was king of Galicia, Andalusia, Murcia, Castile and Portugal, and who is known as Milesius of Spain. The Milesians came into this country several centuries before the birth of Christ. The three sons of Milesius who left any issue were Heber, Ir and Heremon. From *Ir* descended Fergus Mor, who (by Meavre, or Mab, Queen of Connaught) was the father of three sons, respectively, Conmac, Ciar, and Corc ; from Ciar are descended the O'Connors of Kerry, who were kings *Agri Kerriensis* (the O'Connors of Connaught being descended from Heremon); from Corc, the O'Connors of Corcomroe, and the O'Loughlins of Burren, both territories being situate in the County of Clare; and from the eldest son, Conmac, the O'Farrells, Kings of Conmacne (this word signifying 'the posterity of Conmac'), which contained all that territory which we now call *the County of Longford*, a large portion of the Counties of Leitrim, Sligo and Galway, and that part of the County of Westmeath anciently called *Cuircneach*, but more lately, 'Dillon's Country.'

"From Angall, a direct lineal descendant of Conmac, that part of

Conmacne, now known as the County of Longford, and *Cuircneach*, in Westmeath, was called 'Upper Annally;' and the adjacent part of the County of Leitrim was called Lower Annaly; and his posterity, after they lost the title of Kings of Conmacne, which his ancestors enjoyed, were upon their submission to the Crown of England, styled Princes or Lords of both Annalies until a recent period.

" Third in descent from Angall was Feargal (*a quo* ' O'Ferrall') who was King of Conmacne, and was slain fighting on the side of Brian Boru at the Battle of Clontarf, A.D. 1014.

" About that time the O'Farrels conquered Cairbre the Incredulous (upon whom, for his incredulity, the malediction of St. Patrick swiftly descended), and dispossessed the O'Kearys, whose tribe was *Hy-Cairbri;* and they changed the name Hy-Cairbri to ' Annaly,' their *own* tribe name."

From this it would seem that the territory of the O'Farrells lay prior to the tenth century more eastwards, and that the major part of Teffia, which was the Irish name for Meath, belonged to them. Be that as it may, it is undisputed that the County of Longford was included in the ancient patrimony of Conmac, who was the direct pro-genitor of the O'Farrell family. We will now look through that excellent book, the " Annals of the Four Masters," for references to Hy-Cairbre, or, as it was called at a later period, Annally.

EXTRACTS FROM THE " ANNALS OF THE FOUR MASTERS."

" A.D. 236. This year Cormac, the grandson of Conn, who was King of the Lagenians (Leinster), overthrew the Ultonians (Ulstermen), in a great battle fought at Granard. Their defeat was so great that many of them fled to the Isle of Man and the Hebrides, and Cormack was ever after known as Cormack Ulfoda.

" 476. In this year a battle was fought between the Granardians and the Leinstermen, in which Eochaidh, who was descended from Enda Madh, King of Leinster, was defeated and slain in the battle.

"480. In this year a battle was fought between the Lagenians themselves, in which Fionchadd, Lord of Hy Kinsellagh, was slain by the Granardians."

(The references which are found in the Annals relating to St. Patrick's visits to the County of Longford will appear further on.)

"742. Fiachra, son of Gabran of Meath, was drowned in Lough Ree.

"747. Conang, grandson of Dhubhan, Lord of Carbry of Teffia (Granard), died.

"751. The fleet of Dealbua-nudat was wrecked on Lough Ree.

"761. At Shruthaire a great battle was fought between the rival clans of Conmacne and Hy Bruin. In this battle the Conmacians were routed, and many of them killed, including Hugh Dub, the son of Toichleach. The victory in this battle was gained by Dubindracht, the son of Cathal.

"766. Artgal, son of Connell, Lord of Carbry of Teffia, died.

"842. Torlorg, son of Aileladh, Chief of Fealla (Faly), was slain by the Danes in Lough Ree, and Findacan, his brother, escaped from them

"843. There was a hosting on Lough Ree by Turgesius, Lord of the Danes, and they plundered Connacht and Meath, and all the churches they could reach.

"858. An army composed of Lagenians, Connacians, and the southern Hy Nialls, marched to Fiachla, under the conduct of Mael-saghlin, the son of Maelrony, and encamped at Moydumha, in the vicinity of Ardagh.

"902. Cormac Mac Culeman and Flaithberthach marched with an army against the Hy Nialls of the south and against the Connacians, and they took the hostages of Connaught in their great fleets on the Shannon, and plundered the islands of Lough Ree.

"913. An attack was made on Flann Sionna by his sons, Donagh and Connor, and they plundered Meath (Annaly) as far as Lough Ree.

"920. Clonmacnoise was plundered by the Danes of Limerick, and they went on Lough Ree and plundered all the islands.

"921. The Danes were on Lough Ree, and they slew Eachtighern, son of Flamchad, Lord of Breghmaine.

"927. A naval engagement took place on the Shannon between Conmacne and Tuath Ella, in which were slain Cathal, grandson of Mael, and Flaghertagh, son of Tuathaile, and others besides.

"929. The Danes of Limerick took up on Lough Ree.

"934. Amlaff *the Scabby-headed*, with his Danes, came from Lough Erne across Breffny, and as far as Lough Ree, on Christmas Day, where they remained seven months, and plundered the country.

"935. Auliffe, son of Godfrey, Lord of the Danes, came from Dublin about the 1st of August, and brought away with him Amlaff the *Scabby-headed* and his Danes, having destroyed his ships.

"960. Inismore, on Lough Ree, was taken by Murchadh O'Kelly from Ceallach, son of Rorke, Lord of Siol Ronan (Clan Ronan), whom he brought with his fleet in captivity to Hy-Maine

"987. The men of Munster and the Danes of Waterford came in vessels on Lough Ree. The Connacians assembled against them, and a battle was fought between them. Great numbers of the Momonians and Danes were cut off with slaughter, and, amongst others, Dulaing, the heir-apparent to the crown of Munster, and many others along with him. The heir-apparent to the crown of Connaught also fell by them in the heat of the engagement.

"992. A new fleet was brought by Brian, the son of Kennedy, and he plundered the territory of the men of Breffny.

"1030. The kingdom of Meath was obtained by O'Melaghlin after he had been banished on Lough Ree by Gott O'Melaghlin (the Stammerer).

"1069. In this year Murchad, the son of Diarmuid, marched into Meath and burned a large amount of property, lay and ecclesiastical. He also burned Granard and Ardbraccan, the lord of which met and slew him.

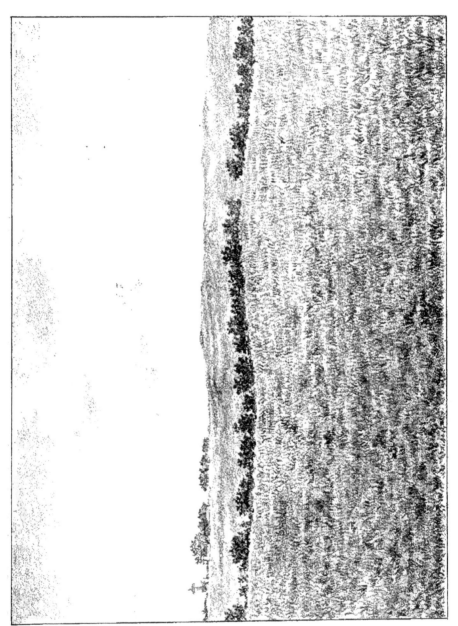

VIEW OF THE SITE OF THE ANCIENT TOWN OF GRANARD.

"1082. A great number of the inhabitants of Westmeath and of Delvin were slain on Lough Ree by Domnhall, and their defeat was called 'the defeat of the ships.'

"1095. The Dalradians gave the Ultonians a great overthrow in a battle at Ardagh, in which fell Lochlen O'Carroll, heir-apparent to the Kingdom of Ulster, and Giolla Comghall O'Carroll, and many others.

"1103. Cathalan, son of Seanan, was slain by the people of Capra Gaura (Granard).

"1108. Donnell, son of Donnell O'Rourke, Lord of Breiffney, was slain by the people of Granard.

"1133. The sons of Cuconnaught O'Connor were drowned in Lough Ree.

"1135. The fleet of Morogh O'Melaghlin was brought on Lough Ree; and the O'Connors with their king, and the O'Kellys with their lord came, and each party left hostages with Morogh. (Morogh O'Melaghlin was this year Ard Righ of Ireland, hence the giving of hostages to him.)

"1137. Turlogh O'Connor brought a fleet on the Shannon and on Lough Ree. That was a valiant expedition for him indeed against the fleet of the men of Breiffny under Tiernan O'Rourke, and against the fleet of the men of Meath under the King of Tara, which consisted of 200 vessels, although Turlogh had only twenty.

"1161. Matudan, grandson of Cronan, Lord of Carbry Grabha (Granard), fell by the sons of MacComgall at Granard.

"1162. Carbry-na-Ciardha (Granard) was plundered by Maolsaochlin O'Rorke. He was, however, defeated, and many of his men were killed.

"1172. The sons of Annadh O'Rourk and the English treacherously plundered the inhabitants of Annally. They drove off many cows and took many captives. They afterwards made another incursion into Ardagh, and during the expedition ravaged the County Longford, and slew Donnal O'Farrell, Chieftain of Annally.

"1189. After Connor Moinmoy had been slain by a party of his own people, the O'Connors of Connaught came to Roderick O'Connor, once King of Ireland, to restore him to his kingdom and give him hostages, for the hostages given to Connor Moinmoy were left in Lough Ree on Inisclothrann.

"1190. A meeting took place between Charles *the Red-handed* and Charles Carrach O'Connor to conclude a peace. The Archbishops Connor MacDermott and Arteach O'Reddy were also present. No agreement could be come to, and O'Connor and his clan came that night to Clonmacnoise. Afterwards they sailed up the Shannon to Lough Ree, where a great storm tossed their fleet. O'Connor's ship became unmanageable and foundered, and but six others and himself were saved.

"1183. Auliffe (Oliver) O'Farrell assumed the Lordship of Annaly, and Hugh was expelled.

"1196. Hugh O'Farrell, Lord of Annaly, was treacherously slain by the sons of Sitric O'Quinn.

"1207. Auliffe O'Farrell, Chief of Annaly, died.

"1209. Donogh O'Farrell, Chieftain of Annaly, died.

"1210. The sons of Roderic O'Connor, and Tiege, the son of Connor Moinmoy, accompanied by some of the people of Annaly, crossed the Shannon, and making an incursion into some of the territory east thereof (Meath), carried a spoil with them into the wilderness of Kenel-Dobhtha. Hugh, the son of Charles the Red-handed, pursued them, and a battle was fought between them, in which the sons of Roderic were defeated and driven again across the Shannon, leaving some of their men and horses behind them.

"1232. Hugh, the son of Auliffe, son of Connal O'Farrell, Chieftain of Annaly, was burned on the island of Inislochacuile (Lough Owel), by the sons of Hugh Cialach, son of Morogh O'Farrell, having been nine years chieftain of Annaly, from the death of his predecessor, Moroch Carragh O'Farrell.

"1262. A great pillage was committed by the English of Meath on Giolla-na-Naomh O'Farrell (the Just), Lord of Annaly. His own tribe also, forsook him and placed themselves under the protection of the English, afterwards they deposed him, and bestowed the lordship on the son of Morogh Carragh O'Farrell. In consequence of this, Giolla committed great devastations, depredations, spoliations, and pillages upon the English, and fought several fierce battles upon them, in which he slew vast numbers. He also defended vigorously the lordship of Annaly, and expelled the son of Murrough Carrach O'Farrell from the country.

"1274. Is recorded his death, having achieved the victory of penance. He was son of Auliffe.

"In the year 1271, it is related that Donall O'Flynn was slain by the son of Robin Lawless at Shrewne.

"1282. Cathal, his son, who succeeded him in the lordship, died in Iniscuan, and Jeffry O'Farrell, his brother, succeeded him.

"1318. Jeffry, the grandson of Giolla-na-naiomh O'Farrell, Lord of Annaly, died.

"1322. Moragh, son of Giolla and Lord of Annaly, was treacherously slain by Seonnin (Little John) O'Farrell at Cluainlisbeg.

"1328. Connor Mac Brennan was slain by the inhabitants of Annaly.

"1345. Brian O'Farrell, worthy heir to the lordship of Annaly, died.

"1347. Giolla-na-Naomh, the son of Jeffry, who was son of the other Giolla, died at Cluanlisbeg, having held for a long time the lordship of Annaly.

"1348. Cathal O'Farrell, lord, died.

"1353. Mahon, the son of Giolla, Lord of Annaly, died.

"1355. Donall, the son of John O'Farrell, Lord of Annaly, died.

"1362. Dermot, son of John, Lord of Annaly, died.

"1364. Melaghlin, son of Morogh, son of Giolla, son of Hugh, son of Auhffe, Lord of Annaly, died.

"1373. The English of Meath made an incursion into Annaly, in the course of which they slew Roderic, the son of Cathal O'Farrell, his son, and numbers of his people. Donagh O'Farrell pursued them with all his forces, and slew great numbers of them; but whilst following the English he was killed by the shot of an arrow, whereupon his people were defeated.

"1374. Melaghlin, son of Dermot O'Farrell, went from Annaly to Muntır Maolmordha, to wage war with the English. A fierce and determined conflict ensued, in which O'Farrell and many others were slain.

"1375. Geoffrey O'Farrell, a man of many accomplishments, died.

" 1377. The Castle of Lıos-ard-ablha (now only marked by the moat of Lisserdowling) was erected by John O'Farrell, Lord of Annaly.

"1383. John dıed, and was interred at Abbeylara.

"1384. Cuconnaught, son of Hugh, and Jeffry O'Farrell, dıed.

"1385. Cathal O'Farrell, worthy heır to the lordship of Annaly, died.

"1398 Morogh O'Farrell, a very renowned man, died a month before Christmas, and was buried in Abbeylara; and Thomas, son of Cathal, son of Morogh, also a renowned man, was slaın at his residence (at Killeen in Legan), by the English of Meath and the Baron of Delvın. He had been elected Lord of Annaly in preference to John, hıs elder brother. John was then inaugurated as his successor.

" 1399 John O'Farrell, Lord of Annaly, dıed.

"1411. Murtogh O'Farrell, son of the Lord of Caladh, ın Annaly, died.

" 1417. Mathew, son of Cuconnaught, Lord of Magh Treagh, dıed.

" 1430. Owen O'Neıll, accompanied by the chiefs of his provınce, marched with a great army ınto Annaly. He went first to Sean (old) —Longphort (now the town)—and from that to Coillsallach (Kilsallagh), where he resıded for some tıme. He went afterwards to Meath, and returned home ın triumph, bringing the son of Donall-boy O'Farrell with hım to Dungannon, as a hostage to ensure O'Farrell's submıssion to him as his lord.

" 1443. Brıan, the son of Ever, who was son of Thomas, son of Cathal O'Farrell, was slain as he was endeavouring to make his escape by force from the island of Inis-purt-an-gurtin, where he had been detaıned ın confinemont two years by Donnall Boy O'Farrell.

"1445. William, the son of John, who was son of Donall O'Farrell, Lord of Annaly, died after a long and virtuous life; and two chieftaincies were then set up in Annaly. Rossa, the son of Murtough the Meathian, who was son of Brian O'Farrell, was called The O'Farrell by all the descendants of Morogh O'Farrell and the sons of the two Hughs— the sons of John O'Farrell and all his other friends proclaimed Donall Boy, the son of Donall, who was son of John, as chief of the tribe. The territory was destroyed between the contests of both, until they made peace and divided Annaly equally between them. (Here the division of Annaly into Upper and Lower is clearly defined—Granard and Longford being the respective seats.) In this year also, in which two chieftaincies were set up in Annaly, John, son of Brian, son of Edmond O'Farrell, and eight others along with him, were slain by John O'Farrell and the sons of Donnell Ballach O'Farrell, on the mountain which is now called Slieve Callum Brigh Leith (Slieve Galry), in Ardagh.

"1452. The Earl of Ormond and the Lord Chief Justice of Ireland marched into the territory of Annaly, where O'Farrell made submission to the Earl, and promised him beeves as the price of obtaining peace from him. The Earl and Lord Chief Justice then proceeded to Westmeath.

"In 1461, The MacGheogan of Westmeath, committed great depredations on the Baron of Delvin, and plundered the County Longford as far as Shrewle.

"1462. Thomas, the son of Cathal, who was son of Cathal O'Farrell, Tanist of Annaly, was slain at Bail-atha-na-Pailse (now Palles, Goldsmith's birthplace) at night, whilst in pursuit of plunder which a party of the Dillons, the Clan Chonchabar, and the sons of Murtagh, were carrying off. They carried away his head and his spoils, having found him with merely a few troops, a circumstance which seldom happened to him.

"1467. Donnell Boy O'Farrell, Chieftain of Annaly, and Lewis, the son of Ross, who was son of Cathal O'Farrell, died; Iriel O'Farrell was elected to his place, and John assumed Iriel's place as sub-chief of Annaly.

" 1474 John O'Farrell was appointed to the chieftainship of Annaly in preference to his brother, who was blind (and so incapacitated).

" 1475. John O'Farrell, Chief of Annaly, died at Granard, after the feast of his inauguration had been prepared, but before he had partaken thereof; he was interred at Lerrha. At the same time O'Donnell, son of Niall Garve, at the head of his forces, accompanied by the chiefs of Lower Connaught, marched first to Ballyconnell, with intent to liberate not only his friend and confederate, Brian O'Reilly, but also to conclude peace between The O'Rorke and O'Reilly; O'Reilly repaired at once to Ballyconnell, where a peace was ratified between him and O'Rorke. After this he marched to Fenagh, and from thence he directed his course to Annaly, in order to assist his friends, the sons of Iriell O'Farrell. He burned and destroyed Annaly, except that part of it which belonged to the sons of Iriell, whom he established in full sway over the County of Annaly.

"In 1476 the English of Meath made an excursion into East Roscommon, during which they demolished the village of the O'Quinns, occupied Pallas (then called Baile-an-atha-Pailse), the scene of Goldsmith's boyhood days, and burned the monastery of Shrewle and the fields of corn in that country.

" 1486. Teigue MacEgan, Ollave of Annaly, was slain by the descendants of Iriel O'Farrell—an abominable deed.

" 1489. A great intestine quarrel arose among the inhabitants of Annaly, during which they committed great injuries against each other, and continued to do so until the Lord Chief Justice made peace among them, and divided the chieftainship between the sons of John and the sons of Cathal.

" 1490, Edmond Duff, the son of Ross, Lord of Calahnah-Angaile, died, and Phelim, the son of Giolla, who was son of Donnell, assumed his place.

" 1494. Cormack O'Farrell, the son of John, son of Donall, the second chieftain of Annaly of that day, died.

" 1497. A great battle was fought between the rival parties for the chieftaincy, in which Donnell, son of Brian, Lord of Clan Auliffe, and Gerald, son of Hugh Oge, Lord of Magh Treagh, were slain, and a great many others.

" 1516. William, the son of Donogh O'Farrell, Bishop of Annaly, who assisted the Lord President to subdue The MacWilliam Burke, and thus prevented him ruining The O'Kelly of Hy Maine, in 1504, died.

" 1572. The sons of the Earl (of Roscommon, I think) next plundered the district lying between the River Suck and Shannon, and pillaged every person who was on friendly terms with the English as far as the gates of Athlone. Afterwards, keeping the Shannon on the right hand, they marched directly outwards to Slieve Baghnad-tuath, crossed the ferry of Anghaile, and burned Athleague.

" 1576. Brian O'Rourke committed great predatory outrages this year in Annaly

" 1595. Red Hugh O'Donnell marched an army into Connaught, plundering the parts of the country that he passed through. On his arrival in Leitrim, near Mohill, his enemies thought he would return thence into Ulster, but this he did not do, but privately despatched messengers to Hugh Maguire, of Fermanagh, requesting that he would meet him in Annaly. He sent scouts before him through that country, and ordered them to meet him at an appointed place. He then marched onwards secretly and expeditiously, and arrived with his troops at the dawn of day in the Annalies, then the territories of the O'Farrells, though the English had some time previously obtained some power there. The brave troops of O'Donnell and Maguire marched from Sliabh Carbry to the River Inny, and as they passed along they set the country in a blaze, which became shrouded under a black and dense cloud of smoke. They took Longford, and set fire to every side and corner of it, so that it was only by a rope that Christopher Browne, his brother, and their wives, were conveyed in safety from the prison of which he was marshal."

This concludes the references in the Annals of the Four Masters relating to this county. As the readers will see, Annaly was invaded by the Danes in the eighth, ninth, and tenth centuries, during which many battles were fought on both the Danish and Irish side, principally in Lough Ree and Lough Gowna. The creation of the two chieftaincies in 1445, is dealt with so fully by the Annalists, that the extract given is sufficient to describe that eventful period which marked the beginning of the end of native rule in Annaly.

In the year 1553 the good Queen Mary ascended the English throne, and appointed as her principal lieutenant in Ireland the famous Sir Henry Sidney, who first visited Annaly in 1553, and subsequently had the ancient patrimony of the O'Farrells styled the County of Longford. No one who has read this history can find in any of the extracts quoted a precedent for this action; and, as we shall see, it was the opening act of a drama, in which the unfortunate natives of Annaly were the chief sufferers.

I presume it is now clear to the people of Longford that (1) it formed at one time portion of the ancient kingdom of Conmacne, and (2) that it was subsequently called Anghaile, which was in turn Anglicized Annaly, and was known by this title until the advent of Sir Henry Sidney, as Queen Elizabeth's Lord Deputy, in 1570. I have discovered in the State Papers of the years 1540 to 1580 a number of very interesting extracts relating to his dealings with what I may truly describe to be the unfortunate inhabitants of Annaly. Sir Henry Sidney thus writes to the council at Dublin Castle, under date 1553 :—

"Between the Shannon and O'Reilly's country is the Annale, a strong country, where the Ferralls dwell, men of good obedience, who pay yearly to the king 100 marks rent, and find 240 galloglas for a quarter of the year after the rate of 4d. sterling the spear by the day. Lately, in the absence of my Lord Deputy, I being there for the order of their contentions, they obeyed my letters."

It would seem from this extract that Annaly was subjected by the Tuites, &c., early in the thirteenth or fourteenth century, and that at this period the English were able to levy blackmail on the inhabitants of Annaly, which was always open to the inroads of the enemy, not being protected by any natural barriers, whose friendly aid the inhabitants could use to advantage.   In addition to this natural disadvantage under which they laboured, we find them also labouring under a more unnatural and decidedly more disastrous one, namely, that of disunion. For, in 1445 (that is one hundred years before), " two chieftaincies had been set up in Annaly," as the Four Masters tell us, and the quarrels and dissensions which arose out of this state of things, of course largely helped the invader in his evil purposes.   What a moral does not the treatment of our forefathers contain for us, Irishmen ?   Let us examine any phase of Irish history—let us search up to its source the true reason of the failure of any combination against the progress of our enemies, and we will find invariably that Irishmen themselves were either to blame from ambitious causes, or were made the dupes of their more cunning and less scrupulous opponents.   The progress of Irish industry, even in those days, did not please the so-called Parliament sitting in Dublin ; for according to the State Papers for 1452, we find that it was passed as a law :—

" Cap 3—That no English merchant carry any goods or merchandise to any of the merchants of Cavan, Granard, or any other Irish county out of the English pale, or bring any goods from the said marches, upon pain to forfeit the same goods, and their bodies to be at the king's pleasure.   It shall be lawful to any of the king's subjects to attack or arrest such as attempt to do the contrary, and to commit them to gaol.   One moiety of the goods forfeited to be the king's ; the other his that makes the seizure ; wine, ale, and bread always excepted."

We now come to the time when the wholesale confiscations begin. Sir Henry Sidney made a second tour of Ireland in 1570, and visited Annaly, which he erected into the County Longford.

According to the State Papers of Sir Henry Sidney's tour in Annaly in 1570, we find it set forth :—

" On February 11th, 1570, the following indenture was made

between the O'Farrells, of the County Longford, and Sir Henry Sidney, President of the Council of Wales and Lord Deputy of Ireland, of the one part; and Faghne O'Farrell, otherwise called O'Farrell Bane, of Tully, in the County Longford, sometime called the Annale; William Fitzdonnell O'Farrall, of the Moat, John O'Farrell, of the Glane, captain of William's sept; Donnell O'Farrell, of the Reen, now called McMorge, in Tleeve; Melaghlin O'Farrell, of Moneylogan; Felyn Boye O'Coyne, of the Brewne, called O'Coyne, and O'Donnell O'Farrell, of Kilgrease, captain of Gillernow's sept in the said county, gentlemen, of the other part.

" 1. The said Faghne O'Farrell, and the rest above-named, promise and bargain to surrender in the Court of Chancery in Ireland to the use of the Queen, when they shall be required to do so, all their possessions in the said country, sometimes called the Annally, and now the County Longford; and the Lord Deputy promises that they shall receive the same by letters patent from the Queen, to hold to them and their heirs for ever by Knight's service, and that they shall be exonerated from the Bonaught accustomed to be paid out of the said country to the Queen's Gallowglasses, and from all other cesses and impositions, In consideration thereof, they grant to the Lord Deputy and his heirs, for the use of the Queen, and her successors, a yearly rent-charge of 200 marks, Irish, payable at the feasts of Michaelmas and Easter, from Michaelmas next. For lack of money to be paid in the Exchequer, the Treasurer or Receiver General is to receive kine to the value of the rent unpaid, as kine shall be worth, and sold in the market of Athboye and Navan. If the rent be behind unpaid in part or in all by the space of six months next after any of the said feasts, it shall be lawful to the Lord Deputy, or to the Treasurer, or Receiver-General to enter a distrain on all the lands.

" 2. They promise to answer to all general hostings, roads, journeys, and risings out as they have been accustomed, and to pay yearly for ever the ancient rent due to the Queen's Majesty out of the said portion of the said country, now being under the rule of the said Fahny Farrell, that is to say, 50 kine or 6s., Irish, for every cow.

" 3. That the captainship of that portion of the said county called Annalye, which heretofore had been used by the said O'Ferrall Bane, shall from henceforth be utterly destroyed, abolished, extinguished, removed, and put back within the said county for ever ; and that the said Fahny O'Ferrall shall receive and take up by letters patent from the Queen's Majesty for the term of his life, an authority in the said county called Blentane, in the said County Longford, by the name and stiles of Seneschal, and not otherwise, together with all such customs, duties, and charges as has been accustomed to be yielded yearly, and paid into the said Tague O'Farrell, as captain of the said county, and indorsed on the back of said indentures, and the said O'Farrell not to be removed from his captaincy till such time as he have in patent the Seneschalship. After his death, like letters patent to be made out to one of the O'Farrells within the said county, such as the governor for the time being shall choose.

" 4. None shall be sergeant nor petty sergeant within the said county but of the said county birth.

" 5. The said Seneschal shall apprehend all traitors, felons and other malefactors, and commit them to the common shire gaol of the said county, and prosecute them according to the laws. For this (his travail) he shall have the moiety or half-hendel of the lands of persons attainted, and of the goods and chattels of such felons as shall be executed within his rule, the other moiety to remain to the Queen. The Seneschal shall also have all frays, batteries and bloodshed that shall happen within his rule, according as his predecessors have used to have by the name of O'Farrell.

" 6. The County of Longford shall henceforth pay yearly the subsidy of 13s. 4d. yearly upon a ploughland, granted of late by Parliament to the Queen, when it shall be divided into ploughlands. For the first three years next after the division into ploughlands, wastes shall be allowed as in other places of shire ground. The lands of the Geraldines and Nugents and others of the English Pale, shall all be contributors, and bear to the said Seneschal all such lawful customs and duties as heretofore they used to receive by the names of captain or tanist. If the same be obstinately refused, the Sheriff of the said county will distrain.

" 7. None of the gentlemen freeholders, or others of the same county, shall take any goods or chattels, one from the other, on any account, but only for rent service, rent charge or damage fesant, and none of them to seek to revenge their private quarrels, one upon another, for anything, but by order of the Queen's laws or arbitraments, with consent of the parties, upon pain of double the thing received to heirs quotiens, to him or to them who shall so offend.

" 8. Neither the Seneschal nor Sheriff shall levy or exact upon the said county any money, cattle or other things for expenses in coming to the council and governor to Dublin or elsewhere in their own private business, unless they be appointed by the said county for the common profit thereof, and then such expenses as they shall have shall be first condescended by the said county and afterwards cessed indifferently.

" 9. The said county shall be discharged of soldier, horse, horse-boy, and all other cesses and exactions, unless when they shall have occasion to travel for the prince through that country.

" Sealed by the parties above-named, and signed and delivered in the presence of Richard Tailor, Fergus O'Ferrall, Richard Staine and William MacDonnell, 11th February, 1570."

It would be well for the reader to carefully study the nine articles under which the O'Farrells surrendered their lands, and to observe how those articles were subsequently upheld. It would be also well to remark here, that in order to create disunion all the more readily amongst the inhabitants of Annaly, Sir Henry Sidney elevated one family to the chieftaincy, whilst, as will be seen, his successors elevated a different family, and hence the creation of a clan feud which placed the O'Farrells at the entire mercy of the invader.

After having carefully perused the foregoing articles, the reader will perceive that the so-called Seneschalship was to be vested first in Faghney Farrell, and afterwards to be elective amongst the other chieftains of the name in the county. We shall soon see how, after Sir Henry Sidney had bargained thus with the chieftains, Sir John Perrot, whose name is well known in the pages of Irish history, set this arrangement aside, and in order still further to place the deluded owners at his mercy, set up a chieftain, whose claim was forcibly disputed by the rest of the name. In 1571 the following indenture was signed by all the O'Farrells.—

"Indenture betwixt Sir Henry Sidney of the one part, and Faghy O'Ferrall, otherwise called O'Ferrall Baye, of the Pallise, in the County of Longford, sometime called the Annale, Kedagh O'Ferrall of Raharavey, Fergus O'Ferrall, of the Bawn, Edmund O'Ferrall, of Criduffe, Irriel O'Ferrall, son to the said O'Ferrall, of Mornin, Teige Duffe McCormicke O'Ferrall, of the Killyn Crubock (Killeen Legan), O'Ferrall, of, the Camace, Bryan McRory O'Ferrall, of Drumvinge, Shane M'Garrot O'Farrall, of the Corrigeen, Tirrelagh O'Barden of Drombishen, Wm. O'Bardan, of the same, Rory Mackrose O'Farrell, of Kilmacshane, Teige Bay O'Ferrall, of Tyrlicken, Iriell MacWilliam O'Farrell, of Ballyishaun, Bryan McHebbard O'Ferrall, of Kilmacommoge, Murrough McDonnell O'Farrell, of Athadonnell, Rosse MacDonnell O'Farrell, of Ballyringan, Moragh McTeige O'Farrell, of Ballyclare, Cathal McHebbard Farrell, of Devyclyne, Murcho McOonyck O'Ferrall, of Corrigglagan, Ruran McGerrot O'Ferrall, of Clonfower, Teige Duffe O'Ferrall, of the same, Connell MacShane O'Ferrall, of Drommeded, Gillernewe MacFaghne O'Farrell, of Raclyne, Cowke McHebbard O'Ferrall, Bellallyng, Felem MacDonnell O'Ferrall, of Keramkeyll, Connor MacRossa O'Farroll, of Cashell, Beage Hebbard MacRossa O'Farroll, of Furkeyll, Teige McMoryarty O'Farroll, of Cornyll, Jeffry Oge O'Farroll, of Cornageurk, Moyertagh O'Farroll, of Liveny, Hugh McDonogh O'Farroll, of the Carygn, Shane McDonnell O'Farroll McDonnell, of the Curry, Felem O'Cuyne, of the Arcwranake,

Jeffry O'Cuyne, of Rathcline, William M'Donkey O'Farroll, of Dare-more, Donnell McColle O'Farroll, of Crulaghte, in the said county, gentlemen, of the other part.

" The said Faghna O'Farrell and the rest above named covenant to surrender in the Court of Chancery in Ireland to the use of the Queen, when they thereunto shall be required, all their possessions in this country, sometime called the Annally and now the County of Longford, with the like covenants and conditions as in the former indentures are mentioned."

This is the consequent document of the previous one, and, in my opinion, was framed so as to render the articles therein contracted for open to suspicion, by subsequent deputies, who could, of course, more easily question the validity of two than one document. The reader will perceive by it that in this case the surrender was made without any such stipulations as were made in the first one.

On April 27th, 1576, Lord Deputy Sidney wrote :—

" As to Annalye, or O'Ferrall's country, and East Brenye (Breffny), or O'Reille's country, they all attended upon me during my abode in the Counties of Roscommon and Westmeath. At my being at Athlone I sent commissioners thither to hold sessions. This country was made shire ground by me by the name of the County Longford, and the chief lords are bound to pay 400 marks by the year of increase of revenue, whereof albeit they were in arrear for several years, yet immediately upon my demand they paid part, and took short days for the payment of the rest "

"1588, December 2.—A grant made to Faghna O'Ferrall, of the Palace, County Longford, alias O'Ferrall Bay, and his heirs, of divers lands, tenements and hereditaments, in the townlands of Moybravain, Clanawly, Clangillemewe, Mountirgelgan, Callon, and elsewhere, in the County Longford."

This grant was the beginning of the dispute between the O'Ferralls, because here is given to another family that which Sir Henry Sidney previously gave to the O'Ferralls, of Tully, and was in direct violation of one of the articles of the indenture.

July 15, 1588 —Lord Deputy Fitzwilliam wrote to the Privy Council that complaints were made by the chiefest gentlemen of O'Farrell Boy's country, the indenture made in Sir Henry Sidney's deputation not to be infringed by the patent which the present O'Farrell Boy has sent his son Iriell to have confirmed in England.

Kedah O'Ferrall, Connell O'Ferrall and others wrote to Queen Elizabeth against Faghna O'Farrell and Iriell, his son, who seek the confirmation of a patent contrary to an agreement made by Sir Henry Sidney between Faghna, Iriell and all the other O'Farrells for the quiet government of the County Longford.

In 1588 it was " objected against Sir John Perrot " that—

" He hath lately within this twelvemonth passed a patent under the great seal of Ireland to Faghnagh O'Farrell, Iriell O'Farrell, his son, and their heirs, of certain lands, as also the Seneschalship in the County of Longford, which patent is very prejudicial to Kedagh O'Farrell, and a number of others besides, and contrary to certain indentures passed in the tenth year of Her Majesty between both the septs of the O'Farrells and Sir Henry on Her Majesty's behalf, by which indenture after the death of the said Faghna, the Seneschal is to be nominated by the Lord Deputy from any of the name O'Farrell during his life only. This is likely to cause great disquietness in the O'Ferrall's country." The cause of the dispute from this extract would seem to be that the Seneschalship was at first vested in Faghne O'Ferrall for his lifetime; and after his death the office was not to be hereditary, but to be given to any other of the name O'Ferrall. The wily Sir John Perrot, well knowing the fiery temperament and proud disposition of the Irish chieftains, conferred the office on Faghne's son, which immediately set the country aflame, and was the means of giving the invader a stronger hand over it. This has always been the invader's best card to play, because when he had set the Irish against each other, he knew their enmity was enough to leave him, nothing more to wish for.

We now come to the advent of the informer on the scene in the person of one Patrick Fox, who (like the vulture that hovers over the battlefield) scenting the plunder, which by clever and artful lying might be his, approaches the Lord Deputy and council with plausible tales of the treachery and treason of the O'Ferralls. From the context it appears that this Fox was either a lawyer or a scrivener of some description, and that having no recourse with which to earn an honest living but on the ruin of honest men, took to this method to build up for himself and his successors a name and a fame in the country. A poor name and fame, indeed, is such!

On January 28th, 1589, Patrick Fox, of Dublin, wrote to Lord Walshingham *inter alia* :—

" One Hubert O'Ferrall, son to Fergus O'Ferrall, him that withstands the patent of Mr. O'Farrell, now in England, had been lately with Feagh MacHugh O'Byrne, and had of him a chief horse, and is with a great number of idle knaves ranging up and down the County of Longford, and meaneth to do some mischief to some of Her Majesty's subjects there."

On February 4th, 1589, the sept of the O'Farrells wrote to Walshingham, praying "that in case it be not meant to refer the determining of the controversy between them and Iriell O'Farrell for the captaincy of Annally, they may have license to repair to England with their evidences, Iriell O'Farrell not to be made sheriff."

1589. February 13th.—Sir Henry Harrington wrote to Lord Walshingham, informing him that one of Fergus O'Farrell's sept is now at the court a suitor for the captaincy of Annally. " Fergus O'Farrell has been always ready and willing to serve Her Majesty, and has had the good opinion of all governors. General report says the right is in Fergus and in the rest of his sept according to the compositions made in the time of Sir Henry Sidney."

Memorandum.—The controversy between the O'Farrells to be referred to the Lord Deputy with advice for the division of Annaly.

March 31, 1589.—" The matter of the O'Farrells groweth daily worse and worse."

April 29, 1589.—Walshingham to Burghely — " Wishing the

DISTANT VIEW OF THE CASTLE OF ARDANDRA.

O'Farrells to be satisfied and contented lest the action of the governors and council be discredited when people perceive that matters of this weight having been, upon good deliberation, concluded and established by one deputy for a public good, shall afterwards be dissolved and disannulled by another for the benefit of any private family."

June 24.—"The O'Farrells of Tenelike wrote to Burghely that their agent, Edward Nagle, may be returned in safety with the despatch of their suit."

June 24.—"Petition of Edward Nangle to Burghely that the patent lately granted of certain lands to O'Farrell Boy may be speedily revoked."

October 24th, 1589.—Patrick Fox, of Dublin, wrote to Lord Walshingham a letter containing the following "articles of treason and disloyalties committed by Fergus O'Farrell and his adherents to the prejudice of the state, as shall be sufficiently proved":—

"1. When O'Rorke received the Spaniards into his protection, he sent Fergus O'Farrell a fair Spanish cloak of great value, and a pair of gilt spurs, which were very thankfully received by the said Fergus in the said dangerous time in which O'Rourke was in rebellion.

"2. He sent letters and messages daily to O'Rourke, and gave him intelligence of the movements of the Queen's troops whilst O'Rorke was in rebellion.

"3. A priest named Connor O'Kenny often took messages between O'Rourke and Fergus, and with a view to join O'Rourke's daughter in marriage with Hubert, his son.

"4. He advised and caused O'Rorke not to come to the Lord Deputy upon the safe conduct which the Lord Deputy sent by Sir Henry Harrington and Lord Thomas Lestrange.

"5. He received a letter from O'Rourke by the hands of Cahil Keogh, one of O'Rorke's footmen, and a follower of Fergus's wife.

"6. He sent Bryan McMortagher, a priest brought up in his house, to Spain for some bad purpose, and afterwards he also sent his son, Brian O'Farrell, to Spain.

D

" 7. He sent a harp as a token to Feagh MacHugh, by one Richard O'Quinn, a priest, well knowing MacHugh to be a bad member.

" 8. The said Fergus's son, called Hubert MacFergus, repaired to Feagh MacHugh, and remained with him a week to establish friendship betwixt Feigh and O'Rorke and his own father. At his deparure the received a dog from Feigh MacHugh and a chief horse as a bond of his devotion, which horse, with eight others, was forcibly and feloniously taken with much goods and other cattle from Hugh Duffe, one of the Earl of Ormonde's tenants, about 14 days before, at which time Feigh MacHugh sought Hugh Duffe to kill him.

" 9. The said Fergus being High Sheriff of the County Longford, went to the house of Bryan O'Reilly, and became his gossip, he knowing O'Reilly to be a notorious traitor, whose overthrow was sought for by the State, as may appear by the £20 that was paid for cutting off his head.

" 10. It is to be remembered that in Ireland there is no greater proof of friendship than to become the gossip of any man.

" 11. Fergus and his sons were of great acquaintance and familiarity with the traitor, Hugh Roe O'Donnell, and while he was prisoner in the Castle of Dublin they often visited him, and after his escape Fergus sent him messages by his servant, Cormack O'Hanly. For this Cormack received a large horse from the said Hugh, and he called it O'Donnell, and having brought the said horse to the house of Fergus, the Sheriff of Longford requested Fergus to keep Cormack prisoner till the Lord Deputy did send for him, but Fergus would neither deliver him to the said sheriff nor keep him in his castle; but thinking that he might escape from the sheriff, sent him out of his castle with his sword and target, and willed him not to submit himself to the said sheriff, but rather revenge his death, whereupon the sheriff pursued him, and was shot by a bullet."

October 29, 1589.—The sept of the O'Farrells—Kedagh Connell and Fergus—wrote to Burghely for licence to prosecute their cause against Iriell O'Farrell in England, or have a hearing in Ireland.

October 31, 1589.—The sept of the O'Farrells wrote to Walshingham, asking that the cause between them and Iriell O'Farrell may be referred to Lord Deputy and Council, or that they may be licensed to go over to England to prosecute the same at court; but their agent was intimidated and driven away by J. William Mostyn.

December 15.—In a docket of Irish suits that of the O'Farrells occurs.

December 22.—The Privy Council wrote to the Lord Deputy to license Fergus O'Farrell to repair over to England about the difference between him and Iriell.

1590. Letter from Sir Lucas Dillon to Sir John Perrott, informing him that Fergus O'Farrell is Sheriff of Longford for this year. Sir Lucas was Lord Chief Justice about this time.

February 20.—A letter from the Lord Deputy, informing the Council that Fergus O'Farrell will repair over to England to answer Iriell O'Farrell in the end of March.

March 26.—The Baron of Delvin wrote to Burghely, commending Fergus O'Farrell to him as one inclined to civility and good life.

April 10, 1589.—Letter from Queen Elizabeth ordering O'Farrell Boy, and Iriell, his son, to be strengthened in their position by a regrant on surrender.

April 18.—Letter from Gerald Birn to Sir John Perrot, informing him how Fergus O'Farrell's son and another horseman, well furnished with armour, and a harper riding upon a hackney with them, tarried certain days at the house of the traitor, Feagh MacHugh O'Byrne.

About same date a petition was received from Iriell O'Farrell, asking the Privy Council to forbear ordering anything against the O'Farrells, his adversaries, till he be made privy and heard.

December.—Iriell O'Farrell, of Mornyne, asks that £40 per annum be settled on him for sixty years, as his estates have reverted to Sir Nicholas Aylmer and Sir Patrick Barnewall, also a letter from Sir J. Perrot, recommending the tanistries to be abolished, and citing the O'Farrells' cases.

In 1590 the cases instituted by the O'Farrells against the jurisdiction

bestowed by Sir Henry Sidney on Faghney O'Farrell and Iriell, his
son, against which they rebelled, having been submitted to the Lord
Delvin, he reported on 10th May, 1590, as follows:—" The O'Farrells
never enrolled the indenture between themselves and Sir Henry Sidney.
They never surrendered their lands according to the covenant made
20 years past, but held them by the tanist and captaincy granted
by Sidney. As the indenture ties none but those that be living, I doubt
much whether the grant to Mr. Malby be good enough or not.
It is covenanted in Sir Henry's indenture that the Lord Deputy
may grant an estate to them and their heirs of such lands as they
will surrender. In the grant made by me I have performed that
covenant, so that all who allege that I have varied from that covenant are much deceived, and I am greatly misused in the report of the
Deputy's letters. I see no reason why the rest of the O'Farrells now
living, and privy to the indenture, may not surrender their lands as
O'Farrell Bane and Faghny O'Farrell (Boy) have done, notwithstanding
anything in my patent to the Faghny. Where they say that they saw
O'Farrell Bane, who surrendered his lands at one time with the said
Faghny O'Farrell, being the greater lord of both, against whom nothing
is said, and the said Faghny, with the rest of the O'Farrells, do pay
£200 sterling yearly to her Majesty, they pay the said £200 now to
Malby; but the same is gotten with great difficulty, for I made many
warrants whilst I governed there to the sheriffs to distrain them with
force for the payment thereof, and they got from her Majesty above 500
marks yearly when they granted to pay her Majesty the said £200; for
the O'Farrells were bound to find her Majesty 200 galliglasses for a
certain time, whereby her Majesty gained nothing by that covenant, but
lost. Faghny was appointed captain by Sidney, and was afterwards to
become seneschal of his county, but I never thought fit to perform
that covenant. No captain or seneschal should be appointed, because
they have justices, sheriffs, and other officers. Fergus has no reason to
find himself grieved, as Kedagh is before him; nor either of them so
long as Faghny O'Farrell is alive. To find fault to my letters patent

to Faghny would be a dangerous example. When they were issued we could not get a sight of the said indenture, which was consequently exempted from their influence."

Thus we see that whilst Fergus O'Farrell was supported by the Lord Delvin, Iriell, the son of Faghne, who was first seneschal, was supported by the lying tales of Fox. This is a pretty medley of affairs, to find two Irish chieftains fighting against each other for a mere empty honour, and backed each by the deceitful and pretended support of two Saxon adherents. Later on we shall see how both Fox and Delvin had the spoil, in the shape of large grants of land taken from the very men they encouraged to fight on!

1591. September 21.—Sir Richard Bingham writes to the Privy Council informing them that he "has been requested to give his opinion of Rory O'Farrell and his brother, Iriell, who is now in England. Their adversaries are Lisagh O'Farrell, the Bishop of Ardagh, and Fergus O'Farrell. The former has always been dutiful in her Majesty's service since Sir Nicholas Malby's time, whilst the latter have been severally accused and touched both before and after his banishment."

In certain accusations made against Sir Robert Dillon, Chief Justice of the Common Pleas in 1593, several references are made to Longford. One of these is of Christopher Brown, who escaped from Longford when it was burned by Red Hugh O'Donnell in 1595. From informations delivered to the Lord Deputy and Council on 13th August, 1593, by an informer, named Shawn McCongawny, the following references to the town and neighbourhood of Longford appear :—

"This is the service which I have opened against Sir Robert Dillon, that O'Rourke sent the constable of Longford, Christopher Brown, to Sir Robert Dillon and Sir Lucas Dillon, to know what course they would advise him to hold, or whether they were able to do him good, and to espy about the Lord Deputy and Council what disposition they bare to him. And John Garland related to the Lords of Delvin and Howth, in the Easter term, 1593, that 'when I was sent from Sir John

Perrot with letters to O'Rourke, by the direction of her Majesty's Privy Council in England—within a month or two after my arrival here—I set forward upon that service attended by my brother, Richard Garland, and my horseboy, Richard Neile; and being come as far as Mr. Rory O'Farrall's house in the Annally, he sent one with me to be my guide. Having travelled so far as to the wood beyond Longford, we overtook three men on foot, whereof one carried a bottle of aqua vitæ, the other a small barrel of gunpowder, and the third, who wore a hat (query, had the others no hats?) bore in the skirt of his mantle some heavy things which to our seeming should be lead. We made no long tarrying with those fellows, misdoubting the danger of the way by reason that O'Rourke was not long before fallen into rebellion. This was on Tuesday, and we held our way towards O'Rourke, to whom we came the morrow after upon Loughguire. Upon Thursday the three men arrived also; and being at dinner, O'Rourke called out for Christopher Browne's men, whereof he that carried the gunpowder stood up and answered.' "

Sir W. Russell's Journal.—1597. February 5th.—Fergus O'Farrell sent in the heads of Farrell O'Bawne's son, and another rebel.

1597. June 20th.—The Lord of Delvin sent in one of the O'Farrells, a notable rebel, who was taken and wounded by the Nugents. He died of his wounds.

1597. September 6th.—The Lord of Delvin sent in three of the O'Farrells' heads

    *   *   *   *   *   *   *   *

In the year 1603 James I. ascended the English throne. Bad as were the persecutions under which the Irish suffered up to that, they were nothing to what followed during his rule. He had not been long on the throne before that remorseless system of confiscation for which his reign is famous in Irish history was planned. The following extracts will show how it was carried out. Nothing that plotting could devise was left undone to afford the necessary excuse to the royal robber. He first ordered a survey of the lands of Ireland to be made, in the report of which Longford figures as follows:—

July 6, 1606.—Return of chargeable and free lands in the County Longford.—" Com. Longford.—I find as well by the view of some records as by mine own experience and knowledge in part, as also by the conference and consent of some of best antiquity and knowledge of the county, that there are 700 cartrons and upwards of chargeable lands in the County Longford, and near 200 cartrons of free land; and that the quantity of the land of these cartrons is very uncertain—some of them containing 30 acres of arable land, some 25 acres, some 15 and some 10 acres, and some less, besides bog and mountain; and that every one of the cartrons aforesaid are in respect of the rents and services payable to the Manor of Granard, and to Mr. Malby, who is charged with 10s. 6d. old money, besides his Majesty's rent."—Datum at Dublin, 6th July, 1606.

" Having examined the complaint of Rosse and Brian O'Farrell, and others of their kindred and name of the sept of O'Farrell Bane, against a grant made unto the Baron of Delvin and the lady dowager, his mother, of certain lands possessed by them before their attainders in the County of Longford, they have now at last, after much debating of the matter, prevailed with the Lord of Delvin and his mother voluntarily to surrender all, one patent, which is cancelled, containing not only the O'Farrells' escheated lands in fee-simple within the said county, but also certain divers other parcels of lands in the Counties of Cavan and Longford, besides some of their own ancient inheritance, and purchased lands in fee-simple within the said counties, which they had since rendered up and taken again of his Majesty, reserving thereon a small rent, the better to assure to themselves a better protection against the O'Farrells and all others. Some other parcels of the O'Farrells' lands which they had passed in another patent, which parcels they have by deed surrendered, so that all of the O'Farrells' lands granted unto them are now resumed and revested to His Majesty.

" Their lordships understand for what consideration his Majesty was pleased to pass to the Lady Delvin and the Baron, her son, in fee-farm for ever, so much escheated and concealed lands in Meath, Westmeath, Cavan, and Longford, at their election, as should amount to the clear yearly rent of three score of pounds of lawful money of England, above all reprisals; but they think it their duty to set down what they find in this particular of the O'Farrells' lands. The lands passed by the Lord and Lady of Delvin, although surveyed at £21 per annum, contain a great scope and extent of land in that country; and they further learn from the Lord of Delvin that there remains yet a good portion of the said O'Farrells' lands which may be reduced by the Crown by their attainders, though hitherto there hath been no inquisition taken thereof, and is not included within their grants, but is yet at his Majesty's disposition. It is alleged that both Rosse and Brian claim more lands by far than ever properly belonged to them or their ancestors, and that they aspire to a greatness and superiority over their rest, after the manner of lords of this country. We think this necessary to be prevented. The disproportion between the lords of counties and the rest of the King's poorer subjects that dwelt under them, is the cause of all the disorders and jars that have at any time, or ever will happen in this realm. Wherefore, if his Majesty shall restore to these O'Farrells any part of the said lands, provision should be made that they, together with some other inhabitants there of best quality, shall repossess only such portion of lands in freehold as any of them now living were repossessed of before the wars, and no more. And the rest of the lands whose owners are dead or slain in rebellion, or otherwise extinguished, shall remain to the Baron of Delvin, and his mother, to fill up their book withal, or otherwise to be disposed of to persons of best merits. We may not forget to say that Rosse O'Farrell, in the time of the late rebellion, had conveyed his interests in that country unto Connocke O'Bawn, the Earl of Tyrone's brother, and made him absolute lord thereof if their general design had succeeded; and this voluntary, without any compulsion on his part, or fear of the rebels, whereby it appears how worthy such a one is to repossess the land which he had yielded up so readily to the enemy of the Crown.

" For this reason, and for the consideration of the great cost incurred by the Lady of Delvin and the Baron, her son, in possessing these lands, as may appear by the enclosed petition, at least of that land which they so much affect (cherish)—feeling confident that they shall deserve the same when there will be occasion to serve his Majesty—the rest they leave to the Baron's own relation.

"Signed by Privy Council, and enclosing petition from the Delvins for compensation for the O'Farrells' land which they had yielded up to the King."

In May, 1611, the Lord Deputy asked the Solicitor-General for Ireland "(1) how much of the Farrells' land in the County Longford could be passed to the Baron of Delvin. The latter replied that no lands could be passed to him. (2) How much land are they to re-obtain other than that mentioned in Lord Delvin's book?—All the residue, except such as is required for the better establishing of the county. (3) To whom shall the lands escheated be granted?—To the ancient possessors, and the Lord Deputy and Council are to take care to give them contentment."

We have seen up to this the very disgraceful intrigue carried on by Lord Delvin on the one hand, and Patrick Fox on the other, whereby Iriel O'Farrell's claims to the seneschalship of the county were disputed by Fergus O'Farrell and all the others of the name in the county. We can also gather from the extracts before us that both parties proceeded to England to have their respective claims decided upon by her Majesty's Privy Council. Thus matters went on between both sides, neither being content at the other's success, until 1603, when the Queen died, and James I. succeeded, and when "the wholesale confiscation" mentioned commenced. Then it was that the intrigues of Delvin and Fox were successful; and too late the unfortunate ignorant chieftains saw their possessions handed over to the very men who had been encouraging them to fight on. It was the old story of the dogs fighting over the bone which the third party walks in and carries off without a struggle. The following record will show the true state of affairs about the year 1607, after which will be found a petition against the grants made at the expense of the litigant chiefs.—

"1607. July 16th.—The King wrote to Sir Arthur Chichester, Lord Deputy, as follows.—'The controversy long depending between the Baron of Delvin and the O'Farrells being now ripe for settlement, by reason of the entire lands being in his Majesty's hands through the surrender made by the said Baron and his mother, the King declares it to be his wish generally as regards the O'Farrells, that they and some of the chief inhabitants shall repossess such portions of the lands as they held before the war in freehold at the rents payable before the rebellion, and for the Lord of Delvin and his mother, in consideration of their surrender and of a former promise, escheated lands are to be found in Meath, Westmeath, Cavan or Longford, to the value of £60 a-year; and for some recompense of their hopes by their late suit he is to have lands of the value of £20 yearly for ever in fee-farm, which was the value of the O'Farrell's lands passed to him in his book, and now surrendered, and also £7 yearly more of his warrants unfilled, and an increase of £20 yearly more, amounting in all to £48 of lands; and if he will he may have as part thereof any of the lands in O'Farrell's country which are not to be restored to Rosse or Bryan O'Farrell and their name, but belonged to men slain in rebellion, paying the King, however, such rents as upon survey shall be thought meet.

"'Datum apud Westminster, 16th July, in the fifth of our reign.'"

1607.—The humble petition of Rosse O'Farrell, called O'Farrell Bawn, and of Bryan O'Ferrall, against the claims of Lady Dowager Delvin and the new Baron—

"Praying for letters patent to them and their kinsmen of the lands in the County Longford.

"The O'Farrells state that they have been, chiefly through Lord Delvin's procurement, attainted and outlawed under the late Queen; Lord Delvin (having) sought to obtain their lands by virtue of a grant of lands value £100 per annum, by her late Majesty."

"The O'Farrells submitted to the State under promise of pardon and remission of forfeiture; nevertheless, the Lord Delvin having died, the present Lord Delvin and his mother have obtained a warrant to pass to them the lands, their lands being, with the O'Farrells', lands, half the County Longford. On the O'Farrells objecting, Lord Delvin appeared willing to take lands of like value elsewhere. The King having ordered that Lord Delvin's patent should be cancelled, and the O'Farrells restored, the Lord Deputy and Council cited Lord Delvin, and having heard him, recommended the renewal of his patent under certain amendments; and after some further litigation it was ordered that a *scire facias* should issue to prove the invalidity of Lord Delvin's patent."

" On this order the position of the O'Farrells now is—" That as they suppose the Lord Delvin hath passed two patents since the King's coming of several parcels of the O'Farrells' lands, they may have a *fieri facias* (inquiry) against the one as against the other—otherwise, the one patent being overthrown, they have no remedy against the other. That as his Majesty's first letter to the Lord Deputy was upon information that Lord Delvin would surrender, directing the Deputy upon that surrender to pass the lands to the O'Farrells—now he having refused to do so, but standing upon the validity of his patent in law, the O'Farrells may have another letter with more sufficient assurance to authorize the Lord Deputy to pass the lands to them upon the overthrow of the Lord Delvin's patent. That his Majesty would please to signify his pleasure that the O'Farrells, with their kindred, be restored in blood the next Parliament to be holden in the realm.

" Dated December 5, 1607."

" In the previous month of June, the Lord Delvin went into England, when the Archbishop of Dublin gave him a letter to Lord Salisbury, recommending him to him, and informing him that when Lord Delvin was joined to Ormond, Rosse O'Farrell, who is now in England, having revolted from his duty, being demanded what moved him to enter into that desperate course, had nothing to answer or excuse, but that he had given up all his lands to Cormocke, Tyrone's brother "

" January 27, 1609.—James O'Farrell being in London on behalf of his estate and other poor inhabitants in Ireland, and being impeded in his movements in that behalf by the heirs and executors of Sir Nicholas

Malby, and also Sir Francis Shaen, presents a petition to Lord Salisbury, showing that the inhabitants of the County Longford are heavily charged for beeves and taxes, and having already paid £400 out of £600 arrearages, prays that the King may be pleased to discharge further arrearages and growing rents, and promising to yield to the King as much as will be yielded out of any ploughland in Ireland."

Things went from bad to worse with the unfortunate inhabitants of Annaly, during which ten years slowly rolled by, until the scheme which James had long conceived to totally confiscate the lands of Ireland was complete, as the following article, appearing in the *Dublin Review* of 1846, on a then recent work by Thomas Carlyle, will show :—" The king, elated with his success in Ulster, determined to extend his paternal spoliation to the other parts of the kingdom. On this occasion it was not necessary to forge a plot. The new and more ingenious device of pleading the king's title to ALL THE LAND in the kingdom was resorted to.   .   .   .   All grants of the Crown from 1307 to 1495, embracing nearly two centuries, were RESUMED by Parliament, and the lands of all absentees and of all that had been expelled by the Irish, were, by various Acts, again vested in the Crown, which IMPEACHED NEARLY EVERY GRANT of land made previous to 1600.   .   .   DISCOVERERS were everywhere busily employed in finding out men's titles to their estates. In 1614 James issued a Special Commission to Lord Deputy Sir Alexander Chichester, to inquire into his title in the King's and Queen's Counties, and in those of Longford, Leitrim, and Westmeath, the result being the seizure by the Crown of 385,000 acres. This confiscation was carried on with such inhumanity, that in the small County of Longford twenty-five of one sept alone (the O'Farrells) were deprived of their estates *without any compensation whatever, or any means of subsistence being assigned them.*"

The following extracts have been taken from Dr. Erck's edition of the Patent Rolls of James I. From the previous few extracts the reader has learned that "the work of devastation was begun." The extracts to follow will show how it was completed. Nothing in the whole course of the history of our county will repay attentive perusal more fully than these few extracts. The names of the townlands confiscated, the old owners and the new planters, will afford the reader a pleasant study in tracing the families in the same place at the present day. We will preface the extracts with the full text of the commission issued to Sir Alexander Chichester and the rest, directing them how to proceed in the laudable mission of their royal master.

" 1620.—Commission directed to Oliver St. John, Knt., Lord Deputy; Sir Adam Loftus, Chancellor; Christopher, Primate of Armagh; Arthur Lord Chichester, High Treasurer; Richard Lord Powerscourt, Marshal of the Army; Sir Arthur Savage, Knt., Vice-Treasurer; Sir Henry Doccura, Knt., Treasurer at Wars; Sir William Jones, Knt., Chief Justice King's Bench; Sir Dominick Sarsfield, Knt, Chief Justice Common Pleas; Sir William Methwolld, Knt., Chief Baron Exchequer; Sir Francis Aungier, Knt., Master of the Rolls; Sir Toby Caulfield, Master of the Ordnance; Sir John King, Knt., Muster Master General; Sir Dudley Norton, Knt., and Sir Francis Annesley, Principal Secretaries of State in Ireland, and Sir Thomas Hibbotts, Knt., Chancellor of the Exchequer, *all* for the time being; and to the Bishops of Meath and Raphoe, Sir James Balfour, Knt., Sir Hugh Montgomery, Knt., and Sir James Hamilton, Knt., Commissioners; seven to be a quorum, whereof the Deputy, Chancellor, Primate, High Treasurer, Lord Powerscourt, Bishop of Meath, Chief Justices, Chief Baron, Muster Master General, and Principal Secretaries, to be five, and the Lord Deputy to be always one.

" Whereas in the right of our Crown, the lands in the County of Longford, and territory of Ely O'Carroll, in this our Kingdom of Ireland, are lawfully come unto us, We, as well in regard of our zeal to Almightie God, which in the whole course of our government hath been and is our chiefest care, as our gratious and tender respect to this kingdom, where we desire that civility and goodness should be known and imbraced by those which as yet are ignorant thereof, have resolved to conferr a fourth part of the said lands upon such British undertakers as shall be conformable to the religion established in the churches of our other kingdoms.

and every way dutiful and obedient to our laws ; yet have we *not* for
these pretenses, how fair soever, any purpose to leave our other subjects,
the ancient inhabitants of those parts, destitute of sufficient means to
support them according to their several qualities and degrees, as may
appeare by the favorable regard we have had of the better sort of them
in our instructions for that plantation, and the large quantity of the said
lands, which, for the convenient settling of all of them in generall, we
have been pleased to assign unto them, and to the end that our royal
intentions and directions concerning the said plantation may be the
better performed, know ye, that we, reposing special trust and confidence in your care, diligence, and circumspection, have assigned and
appointed you to be our Commissioners of the said plantation of the said
County of Longford, and territory or country of Ely O'Carroll, and by
these presents we doe give and grant full power and absolute authoritie
to you, or any seaven or more of you, whereof you, the Deputie, Chancellor, Primate, High Treasurer, Viscount Powerscourt, Bishop of
Meath, Chief Justices, Chief Baron, Muster Master General, and
Principal Secretaries for the time being, to be five, and our Deputie
for the time being to be always one, during our pleasure to dispose and
make severall effectuall grants from us, our heirs and successors in due
forme of lawe, by the advise of some of our learned counsell there, by
letters patents under the Great Seale of this our realme of Ireland, unto
such person and persons, natives and undertakers, their heirs and
assignes, according to the tenor and effect of our letters, signed with
our royal hand, and dated at Rufford, the eighth day of August last past,
and according to the instructions in that behalfe shall receave from us,
or the Lords of our Privy Counsel in England, or otherwise, as you or
any seaven or more of you, as aforesaid, in your discretions shall think
fit, for the better settlement of the said plantation, and likewise signed
with our royal hand, of *all* the lordships, manors, castles, lands, tenements, rents, and hereditaments whatsoever, within the said Countie of
Longford, and country of Ely O'Carroll, and under such rents, tenures,
services, conditions, and covenants, as by our said instructions are

appointed. And we do hereby further give unto you, the said Sir Oliver St. John, Knight, our Deputie Generall, and to everie other Deputie for the time being, and the other before-mentioned persons, which hereafter for the time shall be, our full power and absolute authority to hear and determine all such questions, doubts, and controversies, as shall from time to time arise or grow concerning our said intended plantation, or the lands within the same, either in generall or particular, according to your discretions, and to take special care and order from time to time, as occasion shall be offered, that no trial be had by course of law or equity to the crossing or prejudice of our said now intended plantation, but only before you, our said Commissioners, or any seaven or more of you as aforesaid. And we do also hereby give full power and authority to you, or any seaven or more of you as aforesaid, to give present order and direction to our excheators, and all others whom it may concern, that no offices be found or returned of any lands within the said County of Longford, and country of Ely O'Carroll, which shall or may hinder and impeach the credit of any office or offices already found, or to be found, entitling us to the said lands. And further, we do hereby authorize you, or any seaven or more of you as aforesaid, to do and perform all other things tending to the advancement and settlement of our said plantation from time to time, according to the instructions now sent or hereafter to be sent by letters from us to the Lords of the Council in England to you. And we do hereby will and require you and every of you to be careful and diligent in the execution of this our commission.—30th September. 17th year."

Under the authority of this commission, the following grants from 1620 to 1627 were either confirmed or annulled. James's dealings with the estates commenced in 1606, but it was not till fourteen years later the full measure of his iniquitous schemes was formulated, according to the tenor of the foregoing document. We will, therefore, lead the reader up step by step to the time when "the tender respect to this kingdom" was made manifest:—

"Grant of lands to William Taeffe.—The towns of Gallid

Ballinlagh, Camroan, and Sunnah, and all the lands, &c., in the town and fields of Gallid aforesaid, containing 2 cart. of waste land, at a rent of 5s. *irish*. In Ballinlagh, 2 cart. of waste land. In Camroan and Sunnagh, 2 cart. of waste land, at a rent of 5s. irish (i). In Aghuemore, 2 cart., at 5s. rent, in County Longford; parcels of the possessions of Shane O'Farrell, late of Inchnegrane, slain in rebellion; in Ballinmullin, *alias* Ballinmulvey, in Clanconnor, one cart, at a rent of 6s. 8d. irish. The rectory of Ratherogh, with the tithes, glebes, etc., at a rent of 4s. irish, in County Longford, late the lands of M'Patricken, *alias* Patrick O'Quine, of Lesseghalie, attainted; and late in the tenure of Pat Fox, belonging to the late Abbey of Clarie, or Loughsewdy; in Tibber, 1 cart., at a rent of 2s.; in Kilmore, ¼ of a cart., at a rent of 1s. In Boneherve, 1½ cart., at a rent of 3s.; in Aghnecorskie, 1 quarter, at a rent of 6s. 8d., in County Longford, late the lands of Rorie McRosse O'Ferrall, late of Tibber, slain in rebellion."

"Grant of lands, &c., to Theobald, Baron of Castleconnell.—One cartron in Ballevickenomac, near Forgny, containing 25a. in County Longford; the Rectory of Agherie, with all its tithes, oblations, &c.; parcel of the late Abbey Shroill, *alias* Shroyr; valued above reprises, at 5s. per annum."

"Grant of lands, &c., to Lady Delvin and her son, Lord Delvin.—King's letter for a grant of lands, &c., to the Baron of Delvin (Richard), his heires and assignes, to the clere yerely value of £60, Engl.— The site and precinct of the late priorie of channons of the Holy Island, with all houses and edifices and 2 quarters of land within said site, 2 quarters called Durrenye and Dirrenegellagh, each quarter estimated to contain 30a. arable, 10a. pasture; in Sruhir, 1 quarter, estimated at 30a. arable, 10a. wood and underwood; in Clarue, 2 quarters, estimated at 60a. arable, 30a. bog and pasture; in Keroushegg, 1 quarter, estimated at 30a. arable, 15a. underwood; in Kerowmone, 2 quarters, estimated at 60a. arable, 30a. wood and pasture; in Cashell, 1 quarter, estimated at 30a. arable, 10a. wood and pasture; in Kerovantie, the whole rectories

The supposed Priory of Moydow,

and vicarages of Rathline and Casshell, with all their tithes, alterages, &c., spiritual and temporal, the vicarages of Sruhir, Killire, Killnomer, and Kilronen, with all their tithes, alterages and profits, together with all the tithes of the lands of Dirreine and Dirrenegealagh, in County Meath or Longford, being parcel of the possessions of said priory of Holy Island, demised in reversion to Christopher Lord Delvin, on 10th June, in 28th Elizabeth, for 30 years, at £21 9s., Irish; a castle and certain lands, containing 1 cartron, or the fourth part of a carucate; in Monilagan, half a cartron of land; in Aughengor, the castle of Newton, and a moiety of 3 cartrons; in Corbally and Newton, the moiety of 1 cartron; in Newton and Corbally, an island and half a cartron, called the Cloninge, the castle of the Moate, and 5 cartrons in the fields of Moate, in which castle and 5 cartrons one James O'Farroll, of Clonarde, claims a proportion by custom of gavelkind; the castle and 2 cartrons of Lisnevoa; 4 cartrons in Killenlassaragh; 8 cartrons in Ballymakarmick; 1 cartron in Bealamore, and the lough of Mill-heade, nigh Granardkille, in County Longford; parcel of the lands of the late Abbey of Larha, in County Longford, valued at 6s. 8d., Irish."

Page 228.—" Grant of lands, &c., to John Kinge.—Two cartrons in Corpovelagh, each containing the fourth part of 1 carucate; 1 cartron in Cordarragh; half a cartron in Leighcartronekellry, near Rathreogh, in County Longford; and all castles, messuages, mills, houses, structures, orchards, gardens, shops, cellars, lands, tenements &c., belonging to the premises, all of which are extended to the clear annual value of £52 17s. 4d., Irish; to hold the advowsons of churches, rectories, lands, and all other the premises, to John Kinge, his heirs and assigns, for ever, as of the Castle of Dublin, by fealty only, in free and common soccage, at the rent of £52 17s. 4d., Irish, making £39 13s., English, and this grant to be valid in law, notwithstanding, *inter alia*, the statute of 18 Henry VI."

Page 269.—" Grant of lands, &c., to John Wakeman.—One carucate in the town and fields of Palles, with a certain fishing and a weare upon the Enny; 1 caruc. in *Ballievicknamae*, valued above the

E

composition and other charges, at 23s. 4d. per annum, in the County Longford."

Pat. 3, LX. 8.—" King's letter to revoke a grant of lands made to the late Baron of Delvin, and the lady dowager, his mother, and to make a new grant of the same to O'Ferrall bane and Bryan O'Ferrall, the former proprietors."

Do. CXIII.—" Grant from the King to Sir Richard, Lord Delvin.— Longford County. Licence to hold a Thursday market and a fair on the 1st of August, and two days at Longford, with the usual courts and fees; rent, 6s. 8d., English —7 Dec. 3rd."

Pat. 4, VII.—" Grant from the King to John Wakeman, Esq.— Longford County. In the town and fields of Pales, 1 cartron, with the fishing, and a weir upon the Enny; rent, £1; in Ballivicknamae, 1 cartron; rent, 3s. 4d.; extended in all at £1 3s. 4d. Total rent, a red rose at the Feast of St. John the Baptist. To hold in fee-simple, as of the Castle of Dublin, in common soccage.—18 May. 4th."

Pat. 4, IX.—" Livery of seisin to Sir Richard Nugent, Knt., of Delvin, son and heir of Christ. Nugent, Knt., late Baron, deceased, for a fine of £6.—13 May. 4th."

Pat. 4, Pat. III.—" Grant from the King to Theobald Boorke, Baron Bowrke, of Connell, or Castleconnell.—Lissechit, otherwise Lissekitt, ½ cart., parcel of the estate of Hugh McDermott O'Ferrall, attainted; value, 1s. 6d. Listrine, ½ cart., parcel of the estate of Rory McGerrott O'Ferrall, slain in rebellion; value, 1s. 6d. Kilhnes, otherwise Killine, ¼ cart., parcel of the estate of Donough, in Iriell, slain in rebellion; value, 9d. Aghenevedogh, ½ cart, parcel of the estate of Cahill McShane Oge, slain in rebellion, value, 9d. Dune, ½ quarter, and Knockan, Eleggle, ½ quarter, being each the eighth of a cartron; parcel of the estate of Pholime McJames, slain in rebellion; value, 9d.; total value, 5s. 3d."

Pat. 5, page 104.—" Surrender by Sir Richard Nugent, Knt., Lord Baron of Delvin, and Lady Maria Nugent, Lady Dowager of Delvin.— Longford County. A castle and 1 cart., containing ¼ caruc., in Monilagan, parcel of the land of Rory bane M'Laughlin, attainted; Aghengor, ½ cart.; the castle of Newton, and half of three carts. in Corbally and Newton; ½ cart. in the same; a small island and ½ cart., called the Cloning; a castle and 5 carts. in the Moate, in which James O'Ferrall, of Clonard, claims one part by custom of gavelkind; a castle and 2 carts. in Lisvenoa; in Killinasragh, 4 cart.; in Ballinmackarmicke, 8 carts.; in Bealamore, 1 cart.; a mille-head near Granardkille.—3 May. 5th."

Pat. 5, page 115.—"Grant from the King to Pat Fox, of Dublin, Esq.—Longford County. All the land, tenements, and hereditaments in Gallide, containing 2 cartrons; in Ballinelagh, 2 cartrons; in Camrowan and Sunoagh, 2 cartrons; the estate of Shane O'Ferrall, late of Inchenegran, gent., slain in rebellion, annual value, 10s.; the two cartrons of Aghvenmore, 2 carts., parcel of the estate of Ferdorough M'Conwicke, late of Killincrobagh, gent., attainted, value 5s.; in Lissiguhie, or Lissiduffie, 1 cart., parcel of the estate of Patrick O'Quine of Killincrobagh, gent., attainted, value 2s. 6d ; Leighçartronenekelry, near Rathreogh, ½ cartron, the estate of Morrough McConnocke O'Ferrall, attainted, value 1s. 3d.; in Aghnegore, ½ caruc. and a fishery weir, called the weir of Suawowlie, upon the Shennen, parcel of the estate of Rory McAwlie, late of Aghnegore, attainted, value 8s.; Termon-Ianaigh, or Corby of Ballyroddy, containing a ruinous castle, 2½ cartrons, value 6s. 4d.; Ballinmullvy, 1 cart., parcel of the estate of Gerald McHubert Boy O'Ferrall, attainted, value 6s. 8d ; the rectory and tithes of Agherie, parcel of the estate of the late Abbey of Shruel, otherwise Shrowell, in O'Ferrall Boy's country, value 5s.; the rectory and tithes, &c., of Rathreogh, parcel of the estate of the late priory of Loughsewdy, value 4s."

Pat 6, XXII., page 132.—" General pardon to Richard Nugent, Knt., Lord Baron of Delvyn —26 September. 6th."

LIX. 8.—" King's letter for an inquisition to ascertain the several former estates of the O'Ferralls, and other inhabitants of Longford County, and for a re-grant of the same to them respectively, reserving a rent of £23, English, mentioned in the grants of these lands, formerly made to Lord and Lady Delvin, which grants have been surrendered; and reserving such other rents, services, etc., as are due to the Crown for said lands; also reserving, for the defence of the Castle of Bellabeg, such portion of land as shall be thought meet, and for settling the controversy between, Sir Francis Shaen, Knt., and the O'Farralls and said other inhabitants of Longford, concerning the rent of 120 beoves, payable by them to said Sir Francis, as farmer of the Manor of Granard; Sir Francis to receive for the arrear of 1½ years, 20s. for every beef; for every beef due before that time, 10s., English, in satisfaction of all arrears. Said Sir Francis Shaen being but lessee for years, the Lord Deputy to further him in the future collection of said rent.— 16 May. 6th."

LX.—"King's letter for a grant of lands, &c., in fee farm to Sir Francis Shaen, Knt., which he now holds by lease for years.—13 July. 6th."

LX. 9.—"King's letter for a grant of lands, &c., in fee farm to Sir Francis Shaen, Knt., which he now holds by lease, for years.—13 Jul. 6th."

LXI.—"King's letter, directing the Lord Deputy to assist Sir Francis Shaen in recovering the arrears of rent due to him by the inhabitants of Longford County, and to use expedition in passing grants of the Manor of Granard and other lands to said Shaen; also that in grants of escheated lands or otherwise, in the County of the Annaly, his Majesty's composition and rent beoves of Granard, and all other services appertaining to the Crown, may be reserved.—16 Jul., 1608."

LXXIII. 18.—"King's letter for a grant of lands to the Baron of Delvin, and the lady, his mother, to the yearly value of £48; also to confirm a former letter for a grant of lands to the yearly value of £60. —29 Nov. 6th."

CI. 34.—"General pardon to Lawghlin McFagny O'Ferrall, of Rathlime, in Longford County, yeoman; * * * to Connell O'Ferroll, of Dierie, in Longford County, gent."

CV. 40.—"* * * General pardon to Teige O'Farrell."

CVII. 43.—"Grant from the King to Thomas Ledsom of three-fourths of the several intrusions, alienations without licence, and wardships of the land of Edward Nugent, of Ballibrenagh, in Westmeath County, son and heir of Sir Gerald Nugent, late of the same, Knt., or of any of his ancestors; of Melaghlen McBrian of Runroe, in Longford County, son and heir to Brian McShane Vane, late of the same, or by any of his ancestors; of Ferdorogh O'Farroll, of Kiltaffine, in the same county, or by any of his ancestors."

Pat. 7, page 140.—"Grant from the King to Adam Loftus, &c — The vestry, tithes, &c., of Killoe, in the Anneley, Longford County."

VII.—"General pardon to Sir Robert Nugent, of Ballibrevaghe, in Westmeath Co., Knt.—27 May. 7th."

XXV. 28, page 142.—"Grant from the King to Sir James Dillon, Knt.—Westmeath and Longford Counties. In Gortmore, 1 caruc.; in Cloncullen, 2½ caruc.; in Sheulez, 2 caruc.; certain lands in Clanconnor, called the Lature; Clonekenlesmajor, otherwise Gregagh, and Clogher; in the Kill, 1 caruc   Total rent, £6 12s., Ir.; to hold to the heirs male of his grandfather, Sir Robert Dillon, Knt.—'habend., &c., pfato. Jacobo Dillon, milit. hered mascul de corpore Robti. Dillon, militis avi ipsius pfat. Jacobi Dillon, legattime pcreat. et pcreand. ad sobit et ppim. opus et usu. ipsius pfat. Jacobi Dillon, hered mascul. de corpore dci. Robti.   Dillon, milit. pcreat. et pcreand.;' by the twentieth part of a Knight's fee for a fine of £22, Ir., and in virtue of the commission for remedy of defective titles.—15th July, 1609."

Pat. 7, Dorso. LXXXIII 17.—"Grant from the King to Mary Lady Delvin, widow, and Sir Richard Nugent, Lord Delvin, her son.—Longford County.   The site, &c., of the late monastery of Inchemore, otherwise Inismore, in the Annalie; a cemetery, containing ½ an acre in the island of Inismore; 6 cottages and 6a of pasture in the said island; 5 messuages, 80a. of arable, 130a. mountain pasture, 20a. wood, and 24a. bog, in Castle Richard, the demesne of said monastery; 5 cottages, 90a. arable, 60a. mountain pasture, and 12a. underwood, in Ballintoll; rent, £6 14s. 8d., Ir.   *   *   *   in Cargaghclyevan, Cavan County, 3

pottles, lately in the occupation of Ferrall Oge McFerrall McPrior and Tirlagh Mantagh McFerrall, of Garrimore, attainted. * * *
The castle, bawne, town and lands of Liserdawle, otherwise Lisserdowle, with 8 cartrons of land surrounding the same ; rent, £1."

Pat. 7, pt. 2, Dorso. p. 154, LVI.—"Grant from the King to Henrie Pierse, Esq.—The King's great lough, called Loughree, in the river of Shanyne, lying between Connaught province, Westmeath County and Longford County; the whole fishings thereof, and all islands therein, and all messuages, lands, fishings and hereditaments within the circuit of the said lough, except those heretofore granted by patent; the estate of the Crown ; rent, £1."

Pat. 7, Pt. II.—LXVII.—" In Camagh and Gorreynagh, 1 cart. ; in Smeare, or Smeare, 2 cart. ; in Rathmore, 1 cart. ; in Enkinroe, 1 cart. ; in Tawlaght, or Breaghtwoy, ½ cart. ; in Sunagh and Camroyane, 1 cart., parcel of the estate of Shane McPrior O'Ferrall, attainted ; rent, 16s. 3d."

Pat. 8, Pt I.—"Grant from the King to John Bathe, of Balgriffen, in Dublin County, Esq.—In Fornoy, otherwise Forgney, 1¼ caruc."

LI. 13.—"Livery of seisin and pardon of intrusion for Edward Nugent, cousin and heir of Edward Nugent, late of Braclin, in West-meath and Longford Counties, gent., deceased, for a fine of £61 3s. 4d. —9 May. 8th."

LXVII. 21.—" General pardon to Robert Nugent, of Balline-brenagh, in Westmeath County, Knt.—12 Jul. 8th."

Pat. 8, Pt. II.—" Grant from the King to James Ware, Esq., trustee for the provost, fellows and scholars of Trinity College, Dublin.—Nine cartrons, called the termon-irinagh, or corbie, in Clonlogh ; rent £1 1s 6d. ; 4 cart., called the termon-irrinagh, or corbie, Clondoragh ; rent, 9s. 6d ; 8 cart. of Clonbrony ; rent 19s. 3d. ; 2 cart., called the same, of Granard ; rent 4s. 9d. ; 2 cart., called the same, of Ardagh ; rent, 4s. 9d. , parcel of the estate of the late priory or monastery of Connall ; Cartron ; Eloghan, 1 cart., with 8 cottages or houses in Moneskallighan, 1¼ cart. ; Etworboy, with 10 cottages, 1 cart. ;

Moneard, 1 cart; Killenbea, 1 cart.; in Clonemackerry, 1 cart., rent £2 0s. 6d.; parcel of the estate of the late monastery or house of St. Peter de Rabio, otherwise Monasterick, or Monasterdirgie, in O'Ferrall boy's country; total rent, £7 17s. 8d.; to hold for ever, as of the Castle of Dublin, in common soccage.—1 Oct. 8th."

" King's letter to accept of a surrender from Walter White, and to make him a re-grant of the office of General Escheator and Feodarie, in the County of Longford, and all other counties in Leinster province."

LVII. 29.—" Assignment by Thomas Read to Walter White, of his share of the office of Escheator in the County of Longford, and all other counties in Leinster province.—25 Jul. 1608.—Pat. Off."

IX. 2.—" Surrender by Mary Lady Nugent, Lady Dowager of Delvin, late wife of Christopher Nugent, Baron of Delvin, deceased, and Richard Nugent, now Baron of Delvin, of lands in Longford County, escheated to the Crown by the attainder of the O'Ferralls, and granted to the said Lady and Lord Delvin.—14 June. 2nd.—7 Dec. 3rd.—15 Feb. 8th."

Pat. 8, Pt. V.—" Grant from the King to Patrick Foxe, of Dublin, Esq.—Longford County. In Taghssynatt, otherwise Taghseni, 1 cart., parcel of the estate of the priory of Loughseudie, or manor of Bally-more, Loughsewdie; rent 7s.

" Aghnecrosse, otherwise Dromnecrosse, 1 caruc. or cart.; rent, 6s. 8d. Ir.; Corrobehy, 1 cart.; Lissomine, 1 cart.; Cartron Reagh, ½ cart. or caruc.; rent, 13s. 4d. Ir.; Carhrye, 1 caruc. or cart; in Ballinrodde, ½ cart.; the estate of Kerdagh McShane O'Ferrall, rent 6s. 8d. Ir.; in Croghillen, ½ caruc. or cart., the estate of Murrough McComvicke O'Ferrall, of the same, attainted; rent, 4s. Ir.; in Killne-moddagh, 4a., parcel of the estate of Owen Roe McEdmond O'Ferrall, of the same, attainted; rent, 1s. 4d. Ir.; in the same, 4a., parcel of the estate of Melaghlin Moyle O'Ferrall, of the same, attainted; rent, 1s. 4d. Ir.; Cowlaurte, 1 caruc. or cart.; Killenawesh, ½ caruc. or cart., parcel of the estate of Murrough McComvicke O'Ferrall, aforesaid; rent, 6s. 8d. Ir.

" The rectory of Shrowell, otherwise Urre, parcel of the estate of the monastery of the B. V. Mary of Shrowell, in O'Farrell Boye's country, in Balliwilly, 1 qr., containing 60a. arable meadow, wood and pasture; parcel of the estate of Gerald McHubbert boy O'Farroll, attainted. 18th June. 9th."

" LXVII. 30.—Grant to Patrick Fox, Esq., of the wardship of Faghney O'Ferrall, son and heir of James Ferrall, late of Castlereogh, in Longford County, Esq , deceased, for a fine of £5, Ir., and an annual rent of £2; the amount of the annual allowance for his maintenance and education is omitted, apparently through inadvertency.   20th May. 9th."

" Grant from the King to Patricke Foxe, Esq., Longford County.— Two cartrons, each containing ¼ plowland in Correpoblagh; in Carradeira, 1 cartron, parcel of the estate of Cormac O'Farroll, attainted; rent, 7s. 6d. Ir. Liskitt, otherwise Lissechit, half a cartron.; rent, 1s. 6d.; Listrime, ½ cartron. ; rent 1s. 6d.; parcel of the estate of Rorie McGerrott O'Farroll, slain in rebellion ; Aghenevedocke, ¼ cartron; rent, 9d ; parcel of the estate of Cahill McShane Oge, slain in rebellion ; Killins, otherwise Killine, ¼ cartron; rent, 9d.; parcel of the estate of Donough M'Ireill, slain in rebellion; Downe, ½ qr.; Knockanetgell, ½ qr.; rent, 9d ; parcel of the estate of Phelym McJames, slain in rebellion; in Cammagh and Corrennagh, 1 cartron; in Smeare, 2 cartrons; in Rathmore, 1 cartron; in Evkineroe, 1 cartron; in Tawlaght and Breighwoy, ½ cartron, in Sonnagh and Camroan, 1 cartron; rent, 16s. 3d."

XXVIII.—" Grant from the King to Patrick Foxe, Esq.—The site, &c., of the friary of Ballinesagart, with a cottage, 34a. arable, 2a. bog, and 6a. pasture, in the town and fields of Ballineseggard; rent, £1 6s. 8d."

XXIX.—" Lease from the King to Richard Hardinge, Esq.—In the *Anelie.* One ruinous church, 3 messuages, 40a. arable, and 30a. pasture ; parcel of the lands of the hospital of St. Patrick, called Granard-kille, in O'Ferralls' country ; rent, £1 10s., besides the King's composition ; in

Clonemore, 2 carews; the moiety of the tithes of Granard Rectory; rent, £12 3s. 4d.; parcel of the estate of the abbey of Granard."

Dorso.XXXIII.—"Grant from the King to Captain Roger Atkinson— The manor of Lissardoyle, otherwise Lissardawly, and 8 cartrons, parcel of the said manor; except all the lands, &c., granted by patent to Henry Pierce and John Cusake, gent., the ancient inheritance of the Crown; rent, £1 10s. The fruits and profits, spiritual and temporal, of the church and town of Macestrine and Ballinesagart; rent, £2; parcel of the priory of Little Melverine, England

" The rectory of Shrowell, otherwise Urre, the estate of the monastery of the B. V. Mary of Shrowell, except 3 couples of corn, and all the alterages for the stipend of the vicar, yearly gathered by six couples of acres of corn; rent, £2 4s 4d , Irish. To hold for 81 years, from 10th March last; in Ballywilly, 1 quarter, containing 60a.; rent, 6s. 8d. To hold for 77 years from 20th March, last.—19 June. 9th."

Pat. 10, XXVII. 12.—" Grant from the King to Sir Francis Shane Knt.—Aghowmore, Aghownehae and Aghowfrey, each 1 cartron, in the country of O'Quyn in the Annely , the wood of Killevrench; a parcel of meadow called Sraghfine; Teaghsinat, 1 cartron; in Sare, otherwise Sruher, 3 cart.; the rectories of Sare, otherwise Sruher, and Killihamock; of Clongisse; of Killshie, otherwise Killneshie; of Ballymaccormick ; Moygowe, otherwise Moydowe; Tessenert, otherwise Teighsinatt; Teaghshinney, otherwise Tessynie; Killglasse; St. Michael; Rathrewgh; all which, with their tithes, belong to said priory of Loghsewdie; rent, £34 16s. 11¼⅛d. Ir.; and one able archer for the defence of the kingdom; all the tithes, great and small, of all the towns and lands in the territory of Maghery-granard; parcel of the estate of the abbey of the Blessed Virgin Mary of Larha, otherwise Granard; rent, £8; the rectory of Strade, and 20a. of glebe land thereto belonging; rent, £8; the advowson and right of patronage of the vicarages of Granard and Strade; all the tithes, great and small, late in the tenure of Donogh O'Herra, farmer to the abbot and convent of Larha, viz., half of all the tithes of Tully, 1 cart.; Tonybarden, 2 cart.; Ardechullin, 2 cart.; Monytgoven and Lien, 2 cart.; Eycharda, 1 cart.; Muckersagh, 2 cart; Cullenmeragan, 1 cart.; Kilnenavis and Sian, 1 cart.; Clonfyn, Culartie, Killyne, Blightoge, Moniskribbagh, and all the other tithes; parcel of the estate of the said abbey of Larha; rent, £1 6s. 8d.; the castle and town of Cloneswote, otherwise Castleton, containing 1 cart.; rent, 2s. 3d.; Annagh, 1 cart., rent, 2s.; Boherboy, 1 cart.; Clonedderda-Inver, ½ cart.; rent, 3s.; Ballagheconelan, otherwise Balliaghychonell, 1 cart.; rent, 2s.; Leitrom in Moytra, 2 cart.; rent, 4s. The north cartron of Leitrom, near Drohednegalliogh, which parcel of Leitrom, contains 2 cart.; half of the cart. of the Windmill, near Granard; rent, 3s.; Lagan, otherwise Listosty, or Lislosty, otherwise Killmackanan, 1 cart.; rent, 2s.; the castle and cart. of Robinston, Ballinecross, 2 cart.; Ballihiggin, 1 cart.; rent, 2s.; Ballibrien, 1 cart.; rent, 2s.; the parcels of Alidermod, Cowletrim, Quivishin, Monegane, Tonekilly, Clonenreagh, and Corrynallan, containing ½ cart., lying in Ballimacbrien; rent, 1s.; the south cart. of Ballynegall; rent, 2s.; the castle and south cart. of Monilaggan; rent, 3s.; the ruinous castle and cart. of Bealamore; a mill-head and site of a water-mill near Granard Kill; rent, 2s. 6d."

Pat. 10, XLI 30.—" Commission to Sir John Blenerhassett, Knt., Sir John Elliott, Knt., both barons of the Exchequer, John Beere, Esq., serjeant-at-law, and others, to inquire what were the ancient limits and bounds of Longford County; how many cartrons, qrs., and other proportions of land were therein, with their names; the chiefest or ancientest tenants, inhabitants, owners or possessors of the said lands; or how much thereof had been subject to the composition of £200 per annum, lately granted to Sir Nicholas Malby, Knt., and the heirs male of his body; or to the rent of 120 beoves, heretofore due or payable to the Crown as parcel of the manor of Granard, or to any other charges, and what lands were holden as free lands, with their owners or possessors; what other lands the Crown ought to be seized of, and by what title, expressing their particular names, and, if church lands, with the occupiers or possessors thereof, and by what title they held the said church lands; the yearly value of all the lands beyond reprises; to accept the surrenders of all such persons as claimed any estate in the said county, and to return same into the chancery; to appoint so many cartrons to be conveyed to Sir Francis Shane, Knt., and his heirs, as may countervail the yearly rent of £100, Eng., which he had in lieu of the said 120 beoves, to be laid in the most convenient places for Granard and the abbey of Longford; to plot the yearly rent of £230, Eng., to be reserved to the Crown, upon the rest of the lands intended to be granted to the natives of that county; to limit, appoint, and set out in particular 300a., to be laid out with the foot of Ballilegg next adjoining thereto; to divide and allot how much of the residue of the lands every one of those natives which they should think fit to be freeholders should have for his portion, and to do all other things for the setting of Longford County.—22 Mar. 9th.

" The execution of this Commission as to the ancient bounds of the county, the names of the lands which were subject to the said rent and beoves, and what church lands were in the county, was found by the inquisition annexed, taken at Ardagh, 4th April, 1612; but as for execution of the other parts of the Commission, the Commissioners could not proceed therein, partly for that the heir of James O'Ferrall, lately deceased, chief of the sept of the O'Ferrall Boyes, was within age, and his lands were in his Majesty's hands during his minority; and partly for that the rest of that sept which were *not* attainted, did refuse to make surrenders of their lands, but upon such conditions as the Commissioners had no authority to allow of.— No date."

XLII. 31.—" Inquisition, taken at Ardagh, in Longford County, 4th April, 10th, setting out the mearings and bounds of Longford County, and other matters as directed in the preceding commission. Note.— The contents of this inquisition are to be found in full in the Repertorium Inquisitionem Hiberniæ, Vol. I, published 1826, by order of his Majesty's Commissioners of Public Records in Ireland, to which the reader is therefore referred for particulars."

Pat. 5, XXIX 18.—" King's letter for a grant to Richard,

Baron of Delvin, of so much lands of the late monastery of
Fower as shall amount to the value of the 24 poles of land which
the said Baron is to surrender to the Crown, for the plantation of
the County of Longford."

XLVI. 27.—"King's letter to issue a commission to Sir Robert
Jacob, Knt., the King's Solicitor, the Surveyor-General, and others,
to enquire as to the King's title to the country of *Carbry*, County
Longford, and the islands belonging thereto, and to make grants of the
same to Sir James Fullerton, Sir James Carroll, and Eusebius Andrews,
or to such persons as they shall nominate; also, instructions in favour
of Sir James Simple, and for inquiring into the state of the inhabitants
of Carbry, and their intercourse with foreign parts.—10 Jul.   10th."

CXLI. 48.—"The monastery of Learray, with the appurtenances,
Killen Lassaragh, Breaklone and elsewhere."

Pat. II.—LXIII. 24.—"Grant to Daniel Birne and Charles Heitley,
gent., of authority to seize all Irish mantles and bendells dyed with
saffron which may be worn in Longford and the other counties of
Leinster, &c., together with two-third parts of all fines incurred for the
wearing thereof, contrary to the statute, during seven years, yielding
to the Crown the other one-third of such fines.—19 Apr.   11th."

Act. Reg.—LXX. 35.—" Grant from the King to James Ware, Esq.—
The towns and lands of Coolenegor and Fiamore, 1 cartron; Bonaclea,
Ballicor, each 1 cartron; Ballimore, ½ cart.; Tonein and Aghoinbillie,
or Aghowbilhe, 1 cart.; Aghowraha, ½ cart; Garvagh and Bonowen,
1 cart.; Leytrim and Kellyn, 2 cart.; Aghownewre and Aghownecree-
day, 1 cart.; all which were lately called the termon-irrenagh or corbe-
land of Cloneogher, otherwise Clonogherie; rent, £1 15s. 6d. Ir.; the
4 carts. or parcels called the termon-irrenagh, or corbe-land of Clondoragh; rent, 9s. 6d.; Clonbrony, 1 cart.; Feymore and Clonemullen,
1 cart.; Ballinreaghan, 1 cart.; Leytrim, ½ cart.; Cloncoose, 1 cart.;
Clongormegan, ½ cart.; Laghall, ½ cart.; Cullefadde, ½ cart.; Rowe,
1 cart.; Corlagh, ½ cart.; Aghmore, ½ cart.; all which were the termon-
irrenagh or corbe-land of Clonbrony, and contain 8 carts.; rent, 19s.

3d.; Granardkill, 2 carts., called the termon-irrenagh or corbe-land of Granard, otherwise Granardkill; rent, 5s. 9d.; Ardagh, 2 cart., called the termon-irrenagh or corbe-land of Ardagh; rent, 4s. 9d.; Elogham, otherwise Eloghan, 1 cart, with 8 cottages thereon; in Moniskallaghan, 1¼ cart; Etworboy, 1 cart., with 10 cottages thereon, Moneard, Killenbea, Clonemuckerie, 1 cart. each; rent, £2 0s. 6d.; parcel of the estate of the late Monastery of St. Peter de Rabio, otherwise Monasterrick, otherwise Monasterdirgie."

Pat. II., Pt. 2, page 260.—"Grant from the King to Henry Piers, Esq.—Leitrim and Longford Counties, or one of them. Cartron—Aghnecrosse, otherwise Dromnecrosse, 1 caracute or cartron; rent, 6s. 8d."

Page 264.—"The rectory or parish church of Dermore, otherwise Demore, parcel of the estate of the late Monastery of Granard, otherwise the B. V. Mary, of Learagh; rent, £2 13s. 4d."

Pat. 12, XLI. 49, page 275—"King's letter to receive a surrender from Richard, Lord Baron of Delvin, of all his lands and possessions in Longford County, and to re-grant the same to him by letters patent.—12 Jun. 12th."

Pat. 13, page 284, LXI. 19.—"King's letter concerning the plantation of Longford, Leitrim, and other Irish counties.—12 Apr. 13th, Act. Reg."

Page 287.—"Grant from the King to Francis Annesley, Esq., as assignee of Edmond Middhopp, gent.—The monastery of Loncourt, otherwise Longford, ½a., a house, a cottage, 28a. arable, 6a. pasturage, being the demesne lands of said monastery, with common of turbary in the great moor thereunto pertaining; the premises had been granted 2 Jul., 21st Eliz., to Sir Nicholas Malby and his heirs male. Total rent, £32 1s. 10d., Ir. To hold for ever, as of the Castle of Dublin, in common soccage.—29 Jan. 13th."

Page 298, Pat. 13, XVII. 30.—"Grant from the King to Patrick Foxe, William Crowe, Esq., and Robert Caddell, gent, Longford County.—The rectories, churches, or chapels of Sare, otherwise Srure,

Killockmocke, otherwise Killacomocke, Clonglisse, Kilsie, otherwise Kilnesy, Moygow, otherwise Moygowll, Tessenert, otherwise Taghsynatt, Tessynny, Kilglasse, and St. Michael of Rabuck, all being parcel of the estate of Loughsewdy Priory. Total rent, £14 3s. 4d., Ir. To hold for ever, for a fine of £10, Ir.—15 Aug. 9th."

Dorso. Pat. 13, p. 300.—"King's letter for a surrender and re-grant to Richard Waldron, Esq., of the Lord of Delvin's land in Longford, and other lands.—16 Aug. 12th."

P. 303, Pat. 14, Pt. I., XXVI. 19.—"Power of Attorney from James Turnor, of Kishock, in Dublin County, Esq., to Francis Edgworth, Esq., of Longford County, to make a surrender of the office of Second Engrosser and Comptroller of the Pipe in the Exchequer.—14 Aug. 14th."

P. 306, LXXXIII. 14.—"King's letter for a surrender and re-grant of lands in favour of Sir Patrick Fox, of Dublin, Knt.—11 Jul. 14th."

XLIV. 13.—"Licence to Sir Richard Nugent, Knt., Baron of Delvin, to hold a Tuesday market at Fina, in Westmeath County, and two fairs there, one on 8th September, unless that day should occur on Sunday, in which case the fair is to be held on the Monday following, and the other on Whitsun-Monday ; with courts of pie-powder and the usual tolls ; rent, £1, Ir. ; also a fair at the abbey of Fower, in Westmeath County, to be held on 15th August, except on Sundays, *as before ;* rent, 13s. 4d. Ir.—12 Feb. 14th."

P. 342, Pat. 15, LXVII. 27.—"Deed, whereby dame Mary Shane, widow of the late Sir Francis Shane, Knt., and Henry Fynnings, of Ballymore, gent., son and heir of William Fynnings, late of London, barber-surgeon, assign to Edm. Humfrey Richard the manor of Granard, in the Annalie, in Longford County, with its appurtenances, which had been demised to Sir Francis by Queen Elizabeth, 20th Nov., 36th of her reign, to hold for 45 years after the termination of the leases then in being ; also, the tithes of such lands as the heirs of Morough O'Ferrall held in Longford County, and the tithes of Magheri-granard, in the same county, and of the rectory of Strade, and the fields thereof, with 20a. arable thereto belonging in Westmeath County, demised to Henry Sheffield by Queen Elizabeth, 25 Nov., 33rd of her reign, for 31 years after the expiration of a prior demise by the said Queen, 10th May, 20th of her reign, to Thomas Plunket, of Loughgowre, gent., and Thomas Cosgrowe, of Dublin, merchant, for 21 years, and afterwards demised by the said Queen, 20 Nov., 36th of her reign, to the said Sir Francis, for 45 years after the expiration of Sheffield's lease. To hold during the residue of the term, to the use of Sir Francis Aungier, Knt., paying thereout all rents and reservations stated in the former grants thereof.—4 Jul. 15th."

P. 45, Pat. 15, p. 348-9, V. 45 —"The King having, by letter dated 8th Sept., 1617, required the Lord Deputy to grant to such person as the Lady Mary Shane should nominate the following lands—Longford County, the manor and castle of Granard, and 120 rent beoves, payable yearly by the inhabitants of the Annaly, with all the lands, rents, work-days, works, customs, services, and other hereditaments, at a rent of £36, Ir., and to maintain two able horsemen for the defence of the kingdom; which lands had been demised by Queen Elizabeth, 20th November, 1594, for 45 years, to Francis Shane of Killane, in Westmeath County, Esq., in reversion of *all* leases then in being; having also required him to grant the tithes of Maghery-Granard, and the rectory of Strade, *all* the tithes, within the territory of Maghery-Granard, and the tithes of *all* the lands which the heirs of Murrough O'Ferrall lately held, at a rent of £8, and of £1 for O'Ferrall's lands; which, together with those of Strade, had been demised, 25th Nov., 1591, to H. Sheffield, gent., for 31 years in reversion after a lease thereof, made for 21 years to Thomas Plunkett, of Loughgowre, gent., and T. Cosgrowe, of Dublin, merchant, from 10th May, 1578. Also, p. 349, Westmeath and Longford Counties—The rectory and tithes of Strade, and 20a. of the glebe of the said rectory; the advowson, &c., of the vicarages, &c., of Granard and Strade, at a rent of £8; parcel of the estate of the abbey of the B. V. Mary of Larrha, otherwise Granard; and she having, by two deeds, 4 July, 1617, together with Henry Fynninge, of Ballymore, gent., son and heir to William Fynninge, of London, barber-surgeon, deceased, sold the said premises to Sir Francis Aungier, Knt., Master of the Rolls, for the sum of £850, Eng., the King confirms the same to him and his heirs by this patent, with power to hold courts leet and baron within the manor of Granard, and to hold a Tuesday market at Granard, and two fairs there on 23rd April and St. Matthew's day, and the day after each, unless such days occur on Saturday or Sunday, in which case the fairs are to be held on the Monday and Tuesday following; with courts of pie-powder and the usual tolls; rent, £1, Ir.—30 Jan. 15th."

P. 361, XXXVI. 13.—"Grant from the King to Sir Thomas Rotherham, Knt.—Longford County. The castle and fort of Ballyleigg, otherwise Bealaleig, and 300 acres then or late in the tenure of Sir Richard Greame, Knt., lying about said castle, and next adjoining to the River Shannon. Total rent, £2, Ir. To hold for 21 years, from last Michaelmas, for a fine of £3, Ir—2 Mar. 15th."

Pat. 16, XXI. 46.—"Grant from the King to William Crowe, of Dublin, Esq, assignee of David, Viscount Fermoy, by deeds dated 20th Feb., 1614, and 22nd Jul, 1615.—Longford and Cavan Counties, or one of them. The tithes of the parish church of Dromlonan, otherwise Dromloman; parcel of the estate of the monastery of Granard, otherwise Larrha; rent £3, Ir. Longford and Cavan Counties. The tithes of the parish church of Ballimachewe, otherwise Ballimack, parcel of the estate of the said monastery of Granard; rent, £2 13s. 4d., Ir."

P. 401, Pat. 16.—"Longford, &c. &c. Deed between the most high and mighty Prince James of the one part, and Sir Robert Jacob of the other part, whereby, in consideration of faithful services, the King granted to the said Sir Robert, Longford, &c. &c., the tithes of Bally-managh, alias Ballynemanagh, and the tithes of certain lands in the lordship or country called McGermon's country, parcel of the possessions of the monastery of Granard; rent, £3 6s. 8d."

P. 420, Pat. 16, XXIV. 39.—Proclamation against giving shelter or assistance to Richard, Baron of Delvin, who escaped from Dublin Castle

The Ancient Moat of Granard, showing Steeple of St. Mary's Church.

where he was confined on a charge of high treason, Dublin. 23 Nov., 1607.

Facie II. 2.—" Lease by the King to James Ware, of Dublin, Esq., and Will. Plunkett, of same city, gent.—Longford County. The late monastery of St. Peter of Rabio, otherwise Monastererick, or Monasterderge (Abbeyderg); the site, ambit, and circuit of said house; the town and lands of Monastererick, otherwise Rerick, containing 14 messuages, 130a. arable, 60a. pasture and underwood; common of pasture in the great moor of Monasterkerry; all the lands, tenements, and hereditaments, temporal and spiritual, of said house; the cartron and ¼ cartron of Moniskallaghan, the cartron of Etworboy, the cartron of Moneard, the cartron of Killenbea, and 1 cartron in Clonemockery, all in said county, always excepted; the rectory of Rerick; the tithes, great and small, arising out of the lands above excepted (two couple of corn and the alterages belonging to the vicar only excepted); rent, £6, Ir. The tithes of 4 granges near Granard, of the grange of Tonaghmore, of the grange of Rincoll or Rincoole, and of the 3 granges of Golldony, otherwise Coldonny; Cloncrall, otherwise Clonecraw, and Deragh, parcel of the late monastery of the B. V., of Larha, otherwise Learah, or Granard; rent, £6, Ir.; the tithes of Montecarbry or Slewcarbry, parcel of the last-named monastery; rent, £5 3s. 4d."

P. 423, IX. 21.—" Living of Seisin to James Nugent, son and heir of Christopher Nugent, late of Clonlost, in Westmeath County, deceased; for a fine of £25, Engl.—20 Nov. 16th."

* * * * * * * *

XCIX. 18.—" Regulation as to the mode of passing grants of land to be observed by the two auditors and the surveyors-general, and fees to be paid, submitted to the Lord Deputy, by Sir Will. Jones, Sir Will. Methwold, and Sir Fra. Aungier, of the Longford County.—No date."

C. 19, p. 434.—" Approval of said regulations by the Lord Deputy.—20 April, 1619."

CI. 19.—" King's letter for a grant to Lord Cromwell, of lands to the yearly value of £400, Engl., in consideration of his having relinquished the benefit of the King's promise of 3,000a. of the escheated lands in Longford, such lands not being any part of the plantations in Ulster or in other parts, now in hand; regard also being always had of the English fee-farmers in Leyx, who are conformable to the King's laws and religion.—14 Apr. 17th."

P. 435, CXVII. 30.—"Grant to Will. Crofton, of Dublin City, Esq., for a fine of £10, Engl, of the wardship and marriage of Owin McSwyne, son and heir of Erevan McSwyne, of Longford County, gent., deceased.—5 July. 17th."

CXXIX. 36.—"Assignment by Thomas, Lord Cromwell, to Sir Will. Brabazon, Knt., of lands of the yearly value of £8 6s. 8d., Ir., being part of a grant of lands to the amount of £400, Engl., from the Crown to Lord Cromwell, in consideration of his having relinquished the benefit of the King's promise of 3,000a. of escheated lands in Longford County.—22. Aug. 17th."

P. 448, CXXIX. 37.—"Presentation of Daniel O'Farrall to the prebend of Termonbary, Elphin dioc., vacant, and in the gift of the Crown, of full right or otherwise, with a stall in the choir and a voice in the chapter.—25 November. 17th."

CXXIII. 34.—"King's letter to grant to Jonas, Bishop of Ossory and King's chaplain, and his successors, 1,000a. of escheated lands, in the territory of Ely O'Carroll.—7 August. 17th."

P. 450, Pat. 17, Pt. III.—III. 5.—"Grant from the King to Donnell Mac Teig Owne O'Farroll, King's or Longford.—In Ely O'Carroll's country, Clonmore, Monnirahin and Islandmore, 80a. arable and pasture, and 30a. bog and wood; Breekenagh and Ballinvorrin, containing the hamlet of Rakeeragh, Farrinnswagh, Dirrinesallagh, Granaghan and Lissahagh, 236a. arable, 342a. pasture, and 52a. bog and watercourse; in the two Kinnaghans, containing the hamlet of Clonyncabla, Bela-gaddy, Gortinribbin, Shanvally, Ferecheny, Gortvally and Tirlaghan; Feigh, containing the hamlet of Killinefeagh and Monyhairy, 200a., excepting thereout 20a. of pasture adjoining the church of Serkeran, *alias* Serkerine, out of Clonmore, as a glebe; rent for the 858a. pasture land, £8 18s. 9d. English; for the 82a. wood and bog, 3s. 5d. To hold in free and common soccage. O'Farroll covenants not to grant or demise any of the aforesaid premises to any person, but according to the law of England, and not to reserve or take any uncertain rent or Irish exaction; to cause his several tenants in fee-farm, and the tenants for the term of life, lives, or years, or in fee-tail, to erect their dwelling-houses contiguous to each other, in "town *reeds*," and not scattered or single, as well for the mutual defence and safety of the said O'Carroll, and of his tenants, as for the erection of several villages, for the public good and service of the kingdom of Ireland; and if the tenants act to the contrary, that the said O'Farroll shall forfeit in every case £5, English, per annum, for every house so built. The Deputy and Commissioners reserve a right within 3 years to give liberty to any person to carry away sand, slates, stones and timber from the lands in Longford and Ely O'Farroll. That he will sow every year one acre of English standard measure with hemp, on and upon every 100 acres of land; not to alien in fee-simple or fee-tail, or for any greater estate or term than 3 lives or 41 years, to any person being " mere Irish," and who be *not* of the English race and name; and if the said O'Farroll enter into actual rebellion, or commit any treason, or if he, his heir or assigns, assume or take the style or title of 'the Great O'Farroll,' or maintain or use the said name, by giving or paying any rent, taxation, or service, or divide the afore-said lands according to the Irish custom of gavelkind, that it may be lawful for the King to re-enter into all and singular the premises, and resume and repossess the same, with a clause of exoneration, acquit-tance and assurance.—10th January. 17th."

The several conditions of the plantation in the preceding patent mentioned are also contained in every grant from the Crown to the undertakers and the natives of the King's and Longford Counties, with the exception alone that the natives are prohibited from assuming or recognising the ancient titles, distinguishing the chiefs of their families, or to divide their possessions according to the ancient Irish custom of gavelkind.

III.7.—"Grant from the King to William McBrian Murtagh O'Farrell
—Longford County. The castle and town or cartron of Donclone, 138a.;
Corylachclone, 58a. of pasture and 92a. of bog and wood; Cartrone-
clagh, 163a. of pasture and 35a. of bog and wood, Laghclone, 2 cartrons, 113a. of pasture, and 39a. of bog and wood; Ballmknock, 38a. of
pasture and 11a. bog and wood, in the castle and fields of Knockivagan
and the 2 Ardes; Kilmacaylan and Aghonehonen, 75a. of pasture and
68a. wood and bog; 2 parcels of wood, called Derryoghil and Derri-
glogher, 60a., in the barony of Moydow. Total, 585a. pasture, and
305a. bog and wood. Total rent for the pasture lands, £6 1s. 10½d.
Engl.; and bog and wood, 14s. 4½d. To hold in free and common
soccage, with a provision that if the said William McBrian Murtagh
assume the name, style, or title of 'the Great O'Farrell,' by giving or
paying any rent, taxation, or service, or divide his lands according to
the Irish custom of gavelkind, this patent to be wholly void; with other
covenants.—29 January. 17th."

VII.15.—" Grant from the King to Bryan Duff McConnell O'Farrell
—Longford County. The lands of Cloneshoge, Aghowgarve, and Berry-
dabegg, 214a. pasture, 66a. moor and bog, except 14a. of pasture
adjoining the lands of Agholcassa and Burrin, in Muntergerrin, in the
barony of Granard; rent for the pasture land, 50s. Engl.; bog and wood,
2s. 9d.—12 Feb. 17th."

VIII. 17.—" Grant from the King to Richard, Lord Baron of Delvin.
—Longford County. The lands of Smere, 215a. of pasture, 147a. bog
and wood, and 282a. of mountain; Cornedronee, 92a. pasture, and 206a.
bog and wood; Rosseduffe, Drumshanaly, and Faghowry, 1,000a. pasture, and 332a. bog and wood; Doonbeggan, 69a. pasture, and 66a. bog
and wood; Cleynragh, 137a. pasture, and 100a. bog and wood; Bir-
renagh and Crott, 265a. pasture, 75a. wood and bog, and 197a. mountain; Aghagagh and Dromowry, 1 cartron and quarter, 230a. pasture,
Aghekine and Lisgarry, 228a. pasture, and 106a bog and wood;
Agherclogh, 78a. pasture, and 55a. bog and wood, with a common and
a mountain belonging to the above lands, 212a. pasture and 638a.

mountain; Ballyranell and Coolegawen, 50a.; Ballyneraghan, 111a.; Portegurtenwoghtragh, 50a.; Portegurtenyeightragh, 50a.; Cartronvore, 27a. pasture, and 84a. bog and wood; also the lands of Creeve, adjoining the lands of Ballyneraghan; total, 2,970a. pasture, 2,288a. bog, wood, and mountain; rent, pasture lands, £30 7s. 8½d., Engl.; bog and wood, £4 15s. 4d.   To hold *in capite*, by military service, with a provision that the said Richard, Lord Baron of Delvin, is *not* to assume the name, style, or title of ' the Great O'Farrall,' in giving or paying any rent, taxation, or service, or divide the lands before mentioned according to the Irish custom of gavelkind, otherwise this patent to be wholly void.—All the lands granted under the commission for the plantation of Longford and Ely O'Carroll's territory, are subject to the covenants set out in Art. No. 11.   17th."

P. 452, XIV. 30.—" Grant from the King to Francis Edgworth.— Longford County.   In Ely O'Carroll's country, the castle and lands of Crenelaghmore, Crenelaghbegg, Lissane, and Groote, 300a. arable pasture, and 276a. wood and bog, excepting thereout 80a. arable and pasture, adjoining the lands of Ringanny and Coolemeregin; rent, for the arable and pasture land, £3 15s., Engl.; for wood and bog, 11s. 6d. To hold in free and common soccage, with power to create tenures, to enjoy *all* waifs and strays, with free warren and chase.—28th Feb. 17th."

XV. 31.—" Surrender by Sir Francis Aungier, Knight, a privy counsellor; Dame Margaret, his wife; George St. George, and Henry Holcroft, of the City of Dublin, in furtherance of the settlement of the plantation in that county, which cannot well be performed without surrenders for the patentees.—The castle, town, and lands of Granard-Shehan, *alias* Cartron-Caslane, Racronan, and Teemore, with their appurtenances, containing 3 cartrons, and also the annual rent of 120 beeves, which he receives from the inhabitants of the Annaly.—18 Feb. 17th."

XVI. 32.—" Grant from the King to Sir Francis Aungier, Knight, and Lady Margaret, his wife.—Longford County.   The 2 *Ballynegalls

*Knockslaune, and *Lissegaddery, 139a. arable and pasture, and 4a. wood and bog; half of *Mullynegie, 82a. arable and pasture, and 5a. wood and bog; Aghaboy, 54a ; *Kankilly, *alias* *Kinkilly, 106a.; *Lisneant, 40a. *Higginstown, Tenefoble, 79a.; *Ballymorris, 119a. arable and pasture, and 114a. wood and bog; half of *Cartrongeragh, 72a.; *Aghabrack, 42a. arable and pasture, and 77a. wood and bog; 2 *Leytrims, 214a. arable and pasture, and 77a. wood and bog; Galid, 162a.; *Bally-nehowne, 110a. arable and pasture, 22a. bog and wood; Ballybryne, 83a. arable and pasture, 13a. wood and bog; *Ballymacgillechriste, 131a.; *Tromroe, 160a. arable and pasture, 35a. wood and bog; *Shrareogh 40a. arable and pasture, 9a. wood and bog; *Killosoenyetra, 144a.; *Granard-killy, 183a. arable and pasture, 34a. wood and bog; half of the town and lands of †Longford, 3 cartrons lying south of the river of Longford, 91a. arable and pasture, 104a. wood and bog; Ferran Tungan, *alias* Cartrondowgan, 29a. arable and pasture, 119a. wood and bog; and Car-trongarrow, 109a. arable and pasture, 18a. wood and bog; †Mornyn, 10a. arable and pasture, 69a. wood and bog; Clogher, 153a.; Clon-turke, 77a. arable and pasture, 43a. wood and bog; Cartronegeragh, 80a. arable and pasture, 77a. wood and bog; Cloneny, 45a. arable and pasture, 149a. wood and bog; Clonelerhin, 129a. arable and pasture, 144a. wood and bog; the half of the town and lands of Longford, 3 cartrons lying on the north side of the said river, 196a. arable and pasture, 63a. wood and bog (except the abbey of Longford, and 1 cartron of demesne land). Total, 3,000a. arable and pasture, 1,298a. wood and bog; also the castle, town, and lands of Granard-Shehan, *alias* Car-tronecaslane, Racrenan, and Teemore, 3 cartrons; with all the tithes both great and small, all glebes, oblations, &c.; rent, £36, Ir. To hold to the heirs male of the said Francis and Margaret, and in default, to the right heirs of the said Francis, in free and common soccage; to maintain two able horsemen of the English nation, well-furnished for the defence of the country. In the lands marked thus * power to hold courts leet and baron, appoint seneschals, with a jurisdiction under 40s., Ir.; the lands marked thus † a power to hold courts leet and baron, appoint seneschals, with a jurisdiction under 40s., Ir.; to enjoy all waifs and strays, to hold a Saturday's market at the town of Longford, and 2 fairs there, one on the Thursday next after the Feast of the Pentecost, and the day following; also a Monday's market at the town of Granard, and 2 fairs there, one on the 23rd April and the next day, and the other fair on the festival of Saint Matthew the Apostle and the next day, with courts of pie-powder, and the usual tolls and customs.—4th March. 17th."

For the authority of the following wholesale grants, see commission set out in full at page 49.

Pat. 18, James, I., p. 466, (Facie) I. 1.—" Grant from the King to Robert Dillon, under the commission for the plantation of Ely O'Carroll's country.—Longford County. The lands of Ballymulvey-eightra, 76a. arable and pasture, and 52a. moor and wood; Ballymulvey-moghtra, 48a. arable and pasture, 22a. wood and moor; Cloonkine and Garriloske, 160a. arable and pasture, and 47a. bog and wood; Bally-branegan, 122a arable and pasture, 57a bog and wood, and a certain parcel of wood called Derrymaccarr and Dirrybegg; moor and wood lying in Mointaghcallow, excepting thereout all other woods and under-woods in Mointaghcallow, in the barony of Rathclyn; rent for the pasture lands, £4 5s. 7d. Engl., and for the bog and wood, 10s. 9d. To Hubert Dillon—The town and lands of Annagh, 165a. in the barony of Shrowle; Dirry, alias Dirrynebane, 188a. arable and pasture, 75a. wood and moor, and a parcel of wood called Edderra, in Mointagh-callow, 60a., excepting all other wood and underwood in Mointagh-callow, in the barony of Rathclyn; rent of the pasture land, £3 13s. 6d. Eng.; and of the bog and wood 3s. 9d. To Gerald Murtagh—The castle and lands of Creevaghmore 212a. arable and pasture, and 25a. wood and moor; Cloncallow, 35a. arable and pasture, 64a. bog and wood, adjacent to Creevaghmore, and the river Enhy, and half of Canenore-wear in said river, with the bottom and soil of said river; and a parcel of wood called Derrygraige, Dirrinesky, and Derryloghbane; 20a. in Mointaghcuilme, aforesaid, barony of Rathclyn and Moidowe; Corleagh, 151a.; Rynvanny, 85a. arable and 244a. bog and wood; Lehard, 4a. adjacent to Corleagh, barony of Ardagh; rent of the arable land,

£5 1s. 5½d. Engl.; and of the bog and wood, 15s. 9½d. To hold in free and common soccage, but subject to forfeiture on assuming the name, style, or title of the Great O'Farrall, or on paying any rent, taxation, or service, or to divide the lands according to the Irish custom of gavelkind, and subject to the other conditions of the plantation as set out in Art. II., p. 450. All ancient glebe lands, rectories and vicarages excepted.—27 March. 18th."

II. 3.—"Grant from the King under the same commission, to John Ferrall.—Longford County. The lordship, castle, town and lands of Ardenagh, viz., Upper and Lower Ardenagh, Faymore, Cloonmackelly, Aghowdrissagh, Parke, Cloancullen, Turry, Aghevonyn, and Belaburgh, 261a. arable and pasture, and 27a. bog and wood; Tullagh, 85a. arable, and 24a. bog and wood; Tobbernerye, 55a. pasture, and 7a. wood and moor; Leggan and Lisseclet, viz., Aghowinluigg, Radayne, and Aghowinroane, 71a; Agharrowe, and Lissevarrowe, 276a. arable, and 125a. bog and wood, excepting 20a. adjacent to the church of Agharow as a glebe for said church, barony of Shrowle; and also the wood of Derryodneskeny, 30a. lying in Mointaghcallowe; rent for the 728a. pasture, £7 11s. 8d., and for the 230a. bog and wood, 8s. 10½d. To hold in free and common soccage to the heirs male of the said John, and in default thereof to the heirs male of Iriell O'Farrell, his father, and in default thereof to his right heirs. To Carbry McShane O'Ferrall—Derrygawne, 207a.; the wood of Derryglasse, 30a. in Mointaghcallow, barony of Rathclyn; rent for the pasture lands, £2 3s. 1½d. Engl.; and for the wood, 1s. 3d. To Morgan, *alias* Morrogh Ferrall—The town and lands of Skehechan, viz., Tenebane, Lisschoile and Lissechogill, 99a. arable, and 21a. wood and moor; Ballymacshane, *alias* Kilmacshane, viz., Lughim and Aghenhorne, 99a.; Cartron McRory, 20a.; Laggan, 45a., and a parcel of wood called the 2 Derryshanvoges, *alias* Derryshanmuck, 10 acres arable, and 50a. wood in Mointaghcallowe, barony of Shrowle. To hold in free and common soccage, to the heirs male of the said Morgan, and in default thereof to the heirs male of Iriell O'Farrell, his father, and in default thereof to the right heirs of Morgan; rent for the 273a. pasture, £2 16s. 10½d., Engl.; and for the 71a. wood, 2s. 11½d. To Thadeus, *alias* Teige McConnell Ferrall—Clonryn, 90a. arable, and 92a. wood and moor; Aghenra, 20a arable and pasture, 9a. bog and wood, adjoining Clonryn; rent for the pasture lands, £1 2s. 11d., Engl.; and for the wood and moor, 4s. 2d. To Shane McRichard Ferrall—Ballinry, 59a; Killoges, parcel of Lisanedew, 40a. arable, and 20a. wood and moor, barony of Ardagh; rent for the pasture lands, £2 1s. 5½d., Engl; and for the bog, 10d. To James McWilliam Ferrall—The castle, town and lands of Ballymahon, 109a. pasture, and 44a. bog and wood, with the water mill; Drynan, 109a. arable, and 25a. bog and moor, barony of Rathclyn; Moy, *alias* Moyeth, 39a.; Beladrome, *alias* Baladrome, 48a. arable, and 30a. wood and moor, and a parcel of Grillaghmene, barony of Moydow; rent for the pasture lands, £3 5s. 2½d.; and for the wood, 4s. 1½d. To Nicholas McEdmund Ferrall—Clonine, 92a. arable, 24a. bog and wood, barony of Shrowle; rent for the pasture lands, 19s. 2d.; and for the bog and wood, 12d. To Patrick McHubert Ferrall—Cloghanbeddy, Dromune, and Bealakip, 99a. arable, and 30a. bog and wood, barony of Shrowle; rent for the pasture lands, £1 0s. 7½d; and for the bog and wood, 1s. 3d. Engl. To Cahell McHubert Ferrall—Clanany, 100a. arable, and 10a. bog and wood, lying to the east, in the barony of Moydowe; rent for the arable land, £1 0s. 10d., Engl.; and for the bog and wood, 5d. To William McDonogh Ferrall—-Upper Granard, 38a. arable, and 30a bog and wood; Lissiarrielleightra, 118a. arable, and 12a. bog and wood, barony of Ardagh; rent for the pasture land, £1 12s. 6d., Engl., and for the bog and wood, 1s. 9d. To Edmond McConnock Ferrall—Faslonfert, *alias* Royldrinagh, 74a. arable, and 128a. bog and wood; Tonechurry, 56a.; Killyvyan, 43a. arable, and 50a. bog and wood; Lisnegomock and Curraghytean, 57a., Clonbreny, 48a. arable, and 48a. bog and wood, and a parcel of wood, 10a., called Dyrrevehey, in Moinytaghcallowe, excepting 20a. in Clonbreny, adjacent to the church of Kildakmoge, as a demesne for said church, barony of Rathclyn; rent for the pasture land,

£2 17s. 11d., Engl.; and for the bog and wood, 9s. 10d. To Daniel McConnick Farrell—The lands of Dowry, 30a. arable, and 3a. bog and wood, adjacent to the townland of Aghencarm, Ahowcharran, and Aghmevedoge, 34a., barony of Shrowle; a parcel of wood called Carrelagh and Derregile, in Mointaghcallowe; 20a. bog and wood, and the liberty and common of turbe, in the bog of Listibbott and Aghownoran, and free ingress and egress to said bog; rent for the pasture lands, £1 10s. 4d., and for the bog, wood, and turbary, 11½d.; *all* ancient glebe-lands, rectories, and vicarages excepted. To hold in free and common soccage, and *not* to alienate the above lands to any person but of the race or name of an Englishman, nor to take or assume the style or title of the Great O'Ferrall, or to give or receive rents, taxation, or services, or to divide lands, tenements. and hereditaments, according to the Irish custom of gavelkind.—6 April. 18th."

P. 467, VI. 15.—"Surrender to the Crown, by Nathaniel Fox, of *all* his interest, claim, and demand in his lands and premises in Longford County.—9 May. 18th."

VII. 16.—"Grant under the same commission to Nathaniel Fox.— Longford County. The castle, town, and lands of Rathreagh, Corfobrelaghes, 106a. arable and 60a. bog and wood; Rosart, 100a. pasture and 50a. bog and wood; Aghencoshlane, *alias* Coghegen, *alias* Silhanreagh, 87a. pasture, 9a. bog and wood; Aghdrissagh, *alias* Corrickstannell, 86a. pasture and 6a. bog and wood; Clonfermock, 37a.; Agheneshioge and Cloghamore, *alias* Clonaghmore, 39a. pasture and 15a. bog and wood, Treely, 38a. pasture and 10a. bog and wood; Kinard, 184a.; Lorge, *alias* Lurge, 47a.; Tanebegg and Skarvan, 44a.; Cargin, 100a. pasture, 12a. bog and wood, Aghevenchor, 52a. pasture, 127a. bog and wood; Agheneveloge, *alias* Aghaneveloge, 95a. pasture and 20a. bog and wood; Killincrobagh, Aghnekelly, Aghanderry, Cloghgare, and Rath, 90a. pasture and 84a. bog and wood; Cordarragh, 95a. pasture and 12a. bog and wood; Silhanmagoy, 71a. pasture and 37a. bog and wood, barony of Ardagh; Clonarde, 113a. pasture and 138a. bog and wood, barony of Rathclyn; excepting 20a. of the lands of Rathreagh and the Corfobulagh, adjoining the church of Rathreagh, as glebe land, and also excepting 20a. adjacent to the church of Kilglass, as glebe land; rent for the pasture land, £6 16s. 3½d., and for the bog and moor, 7s. 6d., with power to alienate as in former patent. To hold in free and common soccage, and to enjoy *all* the tithes of hay, corn, flax, hemp, wool, and lambs.—10 May. 18th."

VIII. 17.—" Grant under the same commission to Thomas Clerke, —Longford. The town or quarter of Killineganagh and Gardaragh, and a parcel or cartron of land called Fiermore, Cordarragh, Aghene-voushin, and Aghoward, *alias* Lislea, 69a. ; Cashebegg, and a parcel or cartron called Liscormack, Aghenehowlemoyle, Aghelurganchapnill, and Curraghfine, *alias* Bellaghconmoger, 41a. pasture and 14a. bog and wood; the quarter of Lisclagh, *alias* Lismacmanus, *alias* Aghenegine, and parcel of the cartron called Aghaneshannagh, Aghenstucka, Agheneclorhefin, *alias* Aghnestribe, and Bumgenie, 76a.; Formoy-leoughhagh, 1 quarter, and a parcel of a certain cartron called Morene-formolagh, Faigmore, Fairghenskehin, and Faighenturley, 64a.; For-moileightragh, 1 quarter, and a parcel of a cartron called Cargyboy, Aghneleggy, Faigmore, Cowlefine, *alias* Loggan, and Murragh, 128a.; Carrowinlorry, 1 quarter, and a parcel or cartron of land called Aghemanragh, Aghenlingboy, Aghenahowla, and Aghowleggagh, 24a., adjacent to the quarter of Carrowinlorry; Lisawley, ½ quarter, and parcel of a cartron called Lisawley, Aughemore, Agheragh, and Caldorrigge, 34a. pasture and 7a. bog and moor, adjacent to the lands of Cashelbegg; all ancient glebe lands, rectories, and vicarages excepted; rent for the arable lands, £6 5s., Engl, and for the bog and wood, 10½d.; with power to alienate, as in preceding patents. To hold in free and common soccage, with all the tithes of corn, hay, flax, hemp, wool, and lambs.—11 May. 18th."

IX. 20.—" Grant under the same commission to James Ware, Knight, Auditor-General, Longford County.—All the termon, territory or precinct of land called Cloneogher, *alias* Clonoghery; the cartron of land called Coolnegor, Fyamore, Bunecloy, Ballyncor, Ballymore,

Toneyn, Aghanvilly, Aghawrahe, Garvagh, Bonowen, Leghetrien, Killen, *alias* Killyney, Aghewneure and Aghownecrevey, in the said termon or territory; the termon, territory or precinct of Clonbreny, with the several parcels of land called Clonbrony, Fyamore, Rowe, *alias* Rough, Leytrim, Cloncoosc, *alias* Concoose, Laghellwoughtragh, Laghel-leightragh, Cullefadda, *alias* Cuillaghfaddagh, Correlagh, Aughmore, Clonenmullen, Marreogh, Termenagh, Ballynreaghan, Clonegormagan, Tomenechoan, Cosculter, Lisnegatt and Direville, in the said termon or territory; the termon or corb-land of Ardagh, called Hoye's land, in the fields of Ardagh and Bohermor, 2 cartrons; the whole termon land of Clindarragh, 4 cartrons, and Clenlonan, parcel of the same, 180a. pasture and 70a. bog and wood; Killfenton, *alias* Killfentons, adjacent to the lands of Killosoneitragh and Killoneoghtragh, barony of Ardagh; rent for the pasture land, £2 19s. 9d. Irish, and for the bog and wood, 4s. 9d.; Cloghan, *alias* Cloghans, 1 cartron; Moinskellaghan, 1 cartron; Etwerby, 2 cartrons; Moneard, 1 cartron; Killinbea, 1 cartron; and Clonemuckerry, 1 cartron; with all their appurtenances, parcel of the late dissolved abbey or monastery of Monasterdirge, *alias* Monasterick, rent, £2 0s. 6d. Irish. To hold in free and common soccage, and to enjoy all waifs and strays, with free warren and all fines and emoluments.—6 May. 18th."

X. 21.—" Grant under the same commission to Thomas Beare.—Longford County. The 2 Cloghcornells, viz., Cloghercornellwoghtragh and Cloghercornellyeightragh, 272a.; the castle and lands of Creeve, Gounod, Aghenedin and Killinteige, 173a. arable and 139a. bog and wood, except 3a. pasture granted to the Lord Baron of Delvin; Ballinrud, 55a. pasture and 80a. bog and wood; rent for the pasture lands, £6 5s., and for the bog and wood, 9s. 1½d.; all ancient lands, rectories and vicarages excepted. To hold in free and common soccage, with all tithes, great and small, oblations and obventions, wrecks of the sea, and with power to make tenures.—10 May. 18th."

XIII. 31.—" Grant under commission to Brent Moore.—Longford County. The towns and lands of Clonkilly, 115a. arable and 90a. bog and wood; in Clonemore, Agheneskehene, 104a. pasture and 70a. moor and wood; Aghetacken, 66a.; Shervoge, 103a.; Rarrenure and Aghekeirin, 12a. pasture and 5a. bog and wood; Derryda Macmoriertagh, wood, 60a., barony of Moydow; rent for the pasture land, £5, English, and for the bog and wood, 9s. 4½d. To hold in free and common soccage.—28 June. 18th."

XIV. 33.—"Surrender to the Crown by Edmond Nugent Fitz-Piers, of the following lands.—Longford County. Carhı, 1 cart.; half of Corehelline, Kıllemodagh, 8a.; half of Cartrenreogh, barony of Granard.—1 June. 18th."

XV. 33.—"Grant under the same commission to Edmond Nugent Fitz-Piers.—Longford County. The castle, town and lands of Castlenbrock, 114a. pasture, 33a. bog and wood; Kıllinesoy, 57a. pasture, 12a. bog and wood; Senclone, part, 11a., barony of Granard; Camagh, 78a. pasture and 109a. bog and wood; Laughill, 165a. pasture and 234a. bog and wood; Caloge, 107a., Cloñemacknee and Clonewhelan, 78a. pasture, 185a. bog and wood; and Monedarragh, 71a., barony of Ardagh; rent for the pasture lands, £4 18s. 0½d., English, and for the bog and wood, 9s. 5½d. To Gerard Nugent—The castle, town and lands of Lissagheneden, Killeoge and Aghnegeeragh, 372a. pasture, 76a. bog and wood, excepting 40a. pasture and 20a. moor, near Ballinrye, lately assigned to Shane O'Ferrell; Leackan, 154a. pasture and 82a. bog and wood; Cranelaghes, 18a., barony of Ardagh; Ballinegossanagh, in Correboy, 19a.; Gurtincaslane, 19a, barony of Longford; rent for the pasture land, £6 7s. 11d., English, and for the bog and wood, 5s 9d. To Maurice Dıllon—The town and lands of Cornecarte, 65a. pasture and 9a. bog and wood; Mollemorne, 76a. pasture and 49a. bog and wood; Cartrenboy, 8a.; Aghowhınlarragh, 47a. pasture and 20a. bog and wood; Monefadda and Quillagh, 50a., barony of Rathclyn; rent for the pasture land, £3 1s. 3d., and for the bog and wood, 3s. 3d. To Connell MacIrrıell Ferrall—Tirelecken, 154a. pasture and 40a. bog and wood; Killgeffrey, 156a. pasture and 78a. bog and wood; Lissenoske, 31a., barony of Rathclyn; Barnenure, 87a. pasture and 55a. wood and moor,

in the territory of Moyh; Lynyneightragh and Boherboy, 79a. pasture
and 88a. wood and moor, barony of Moydow; a parcel of wood called
Grellaghgarragh, *alias* Grillaghgarrowe, *alias* Clonfeigh, Annaghmore
and Annaghlegg, 80a.; rent for the pasture land, £5 5s. 7½d., and the bog
and wood, 14s. 1½d.   To Edward MacBrien—The town and lands of
Aghedonnogho, near Aghafin, 69a.; Aghentarra and Garryandrowe,
37a., rent, £1 2s 1½d. To Thomas Kearnan—Rahcor and Aghenevelogue
alias Aghnevedag, 66a., Tegarwe, 43a., except 20a. of same adjoining
the church of Clonbrany, as glebe land; Aghenekelly, east part, 7a., in
the territory of Muntergarran, barony of Granard; rent, 20s. To James
Nugent—Ballagh, Dromenchreher, Coolrowan, and all parts of the
territory of Muntergerran, adjoining the lands of Clonyne, containing
120a. arable, and 36a. moor, bog and underwood; Kilmore east and
north, adjoining the waters of Loughgawny, with the fishing of the same,
barony of Granard; rent for the arable, £1 3s. 10d., English; for the
bog and wood, 11d.   To hold in free and common soccage; all ancient
glebes, vicarages and rectories excepted.—2 June.   18th."

XVIII. 41.—" Grant under the same commission to John Knocks.—
Longford County. The town and lands of Ballyduff, 600a., adjoining
the lands of Formoyle and Larte, barony of Granard, and all tithes
great and small; rent, £6 5s., Engl.   The above   lands   created
into the manor of Knock, with power to hold courts leet and baron,
and to have jurisdiction in *all* actions for debt under 40s., Ir.   To hold
in free and common soccage.—5th August.   18th."

P. 469, XXX. 3.—Commission directed to Sir Francis Aungier,
Knt., Master of the Rolls, Sir Christopher Sibthorpe, Knt , Justice of
the court of chief place; Sir Christopher Nugent, Knt., Henry Crofton,
Esq., High Sheriff of the County of Longford; Maurice Fitzgerald,
Robert Dillon, of Caneston; Edmund Nugent, *Edward Dowdall*, Andrew
Nugent, Thomas Nugent, of Coolamber; George Griffeth, and Henry
Piers, Esquires, as Commissioners of the new plantation of Longford,
for the purpose of deciding all questions, controversies and troubles
between the undertakers and natives in said county, that might arise

through the alteration of possession in settling their several proportions, and to see such former pretended inheritors as could *not* be made freeholders in the said plantation provided for, and placed as lessees and tenants under the undertakers and principal natives who have proportions of land ; also, to ascertain the mears and bounds of said lands, according to a Schedule hereto annexed.—10 April. 18th."

" SCHEDULE.

" 1. They are to take view of Schedule under the Survey's hands, containing the names of such pretended freeholders in the County of Longford as were seised of 100a. after the deduction of a fourth part, &c., and who, by his Majesty's instructions, could *not* be made freeholders.

" 2. To consider how they, or any of them, may, without inconvenience or just grievance, be placed as tenants under the principal natives, former patentees excepted, or undertakers of the said county, always foreseeing that there be a convenient demesne left to the said principal native or undertaker, lying near his house, to the number of 300a. at the least.

" 3 The estates to be made to the said lessees, to be made for 3 lives, 41 years, or under, as said Commissioners shall see cause.

" 4. The quantities to be appointed to each lessee to be had at the discretion of the Commissioners, having respect to their former holding, and to their present ability and likelihood to manure and stock the same ; and none to be respected therein, but such as they shall find to have been of honest behaviour, and for the most part householders.

" 5. The rent to be set down at the discretion of the Commissioners, having respect to the value of the land, near the rate which the land may be now set for, *bonâ fide*

" 6. If any difference arise in the country for the mears and bounds of any towns or villages, for or by reason of any claim of land under pretence of names inserted or *not* inserted in any patent, the Commissioners are to decide the same, wherein they are to observe that old mears are *not* to be questioned, but that each man's proportion is to stand according to the number of acres now assigned to him, and according as the same was lately measured together, as the mears thereof were shown to the measurers and by them trodden with the chain, according to his Majesty's direction in that behalf.

"7. If any difference shall arise for setting out the glebes now granted by his Majesty, when the measurers shall come down to lay them out, the Commissioners are to decide the same, always taking care that those lands be laid most conveniently to the several churches.

"8. The Commissioners are also to view and appoint the places where the several undertakers shall build, which are to be chosen either near the straites or otherwise, as shall be most fit for the settlement and security of the country.

"9. When the measurers shall have come down to set forth and measure the particular portions of towns or villages assigned to any undertakers or natives, for filling up his number of acres; if any difference in that case arise, the Commissioners are to order the same, according to the true intent of their several patents, and as shall be found most convenient for each party; and this be as well for arable lands, profits of rivers, as for bog and wood."

XXXVIII. 9.—"King's letter, directing that the 400a. in Longford and Ely O'Carroll, appointed to be granted to William and James Lermeuth, he conferred on James and Robert Forbes, brothers of Captain Arthur Forbes; subject to the condition of the plantation.—Westminster, 13th January. 17th."

P. 472, XLVI. 13.—"King's letter, directing the Lord Deputy to send to England, with the Survey of Longford, Ely O'Carroll and Leitrim, Wm. Parsons, Surveyor-General, whose judgment in those affairs and experience in the whole course of the plantations will enable him to answer any questions that may arise in the dispatch of the business of the plantations, as we have found by experience they are the only ordinary means to reduce the people to civility and religion;

RUINS OF THE ANCIENT CASTLE OF ELFEETE, ON THE BANKS OF THE SHANNON.

and ,in his absence to take care that he sustains no injury in his employments or perquisites of office.—Westminster, 26th Feb.　17th."

XLIX.—" Complaint presented by the Lord Delvin, Sir Christopher Plunkett, and Mr Dougan, Recorder of Dublin, setting forth to James Rex, among other things, the bad system prevalent throughout Leinster, of the Registry of Deaths, &c., &c. ; Spirit Licenses, Ploughing by the Tail, Registry of Horses, &c., &c." (p. 472).

LX. 21.—" King's letter to Sir Richard Nugent, Lord Delvin, doubting lest there might be omission or misrecital in former letters patent, and that in order that he may securely and quietly enjoy his possessions, to have a new grant of the late dissolved monastery or abbey of Inchmore, *alias* Inishmore, in the County of Longford, and the late dissolved priory and manor of Fower, in the County of Westmeath, and *all* his other lands and tenements, subject to such tenures, rents, and services as they appear of record formerly to have been subject to.— Westminster, 15 July.　18th."

" Grant under the commission for the plantation in Longford, etc., to James McConnell Farrall.—Longford County　The castle, town, and lands of Tenelick, with one water-mill and 145a. ; Lisgilbert, 90a. ; Macereogh, 60a. ; 2 Drombardoons, 268a. ; Cartronfyn, 67a. ; Kilcurre, 120a. pasture, 8a. wood and bog ; Kyllynegawkan, 208a. ; Pellicebegg, 86a. pasture, and 8a. bog and wood ; Rath, 98a ; Killmacshane, *alias* Ballyclynshemas, 77a. pasture, and 42a bog and wood ; Killynevoare, 27a. pasture, and 15a bog and wood ; Lismacmurgh, 22a. ; Knappoge and Tybber, 170a. pasture, and 68a. bog and wood, barony of Shrowle ; Ballykenny, 180a. pasture, and 60a. bog and wood ; Kilmore, 291a pasture, and 194a wood and bog ; and 1 water-mill on the lands of Tullagh, containing 70a. pasture, and 70a. bog and wood, adjacent to Ballykenny, barony of Longford, and a parcel of bog and wood called Derrychanbegg, Derrychanmore, and Derrychanbulskane, 55a.　To hold *in capite*, by military service ; with remainder to his heirs male, and in default thereof to Faghny McConnell Farrall, his brother, and his heirs male, and in default thereof to the right of the said James ; rent for the

G

2,035a. pasture, £2 3s. 11½d., and for the 466a. bog and wood, 14s. 8d., Engl. The above lands erected into the manor of Tenehck, with 500a. for demesne lands, power to hold courts leet and baron, to appoint seneschals and other officers, and to have jurisdiction in all actions for debt, covenant, and trespass for any sum under 40s., Ir.; to have free warren and park; to enjoy *all* waifs, strays, all wrecks of the sea, and all tithes, great and small; 1 yearly fair, to be held for ever at Drombarden, *alias* Taghseny, on 29 June, the feast of St. Peter the Apostle, with a court of pie-powder, and the usual tolls and customs; rent, 20s., Engl. To Faghny McConnell Farrall—Longford County. Coweishell, 140a. pasture, 210a. bog and wood; Drombane, 160a.; Killinlasseragh, Lissivare, and 1 water-mill, 170a. pasture, 203a. bog and wood; Dromlogher and Grillagh, 122a. pasture, and 49a. bog and wood; Cloncawell, 73a. pasture, and 101a. bog and wood; barony of Ardagh. To hold in free and common soccage for ever to him, and in default thereof to the heirs of his brother, James McConnell Farrall, and in default thereof to his right heirs; rent for the 655a. pasture, £6 18s. 6½d., and for the 563a. bog and wood, 17s. 7½d, Engl. The above lands erected into the manor of Killinlasseragh, with courts leet and baron, and power to appoint seneschals and other officers, with jurisdiction in all actions for debt, covenant, and trespass, for any sums under 40s., Ir.; to enjoy all waifs and strays, and to have all wrecks of the sea, and the tithes, great and small. To Gerald McKeady Farrall—Longford County. Corecloncallowe, Balletampane, *alias* Monetampane, Tennecossane, and Killingall, 124a. pasture, and 113a. bog and wood; Cartronkeele and Kaldrakevin, 84a. pasture, and 68a. bog and wood, barony of Moidowe; rent for the 208a. arable, £2 3s 4d., and for the 191a. bog and wood, 7s. 11¼d, Engl. To Edmund McHubbert Farrall—Longford County. Liscormick, 41a. pasture, and 14a. bog and wood; Calvamanus, 43a. pasture, barony of Shrowle; rent for the 122a. pasture, £1 6s. 5½d., and for the 48a. bog and wood, 2s., Engl. To Donell McWilliam Farrall—Derrymore, 64a.; Tril, 30a. wood and underwood; rent for the pasture lands, £1 10s. 4d., Engl, and for the 30a. underwood, 3d.

To Keadagh McConnell Farrall—Longford County. Camlisks, adjacent to the lands of Lacken and Mullinvroe, containing 113a.; rent, £1 6s 6½d. To Richard McBrian Farrall—Longford County. Dirrynegody, 61a., barony of Longford; rent, 6s., Engl. To William McOwny Farrall—Longford County. Killemehan and Derrinecross, 61a. pasture, and 394a. wood and bog, barony of Longford; rent for the 60a. pasture land, 12s. 6d., and for the 394a. wood and bog, 8s. 2d., Engl To Murrough McTirlagh Farrall—Liscarrileightra, 45a. pasture, and 5a. bog and wood; Lisscarrillowghtragh, 13a.; Ballymacwilliamowghtra, 47a., barony of Ardagh; rent for the 105a. pasture, £1 1s. 10½d., Engl., and for the 5a. bog and moor, 2½d. To hold in free and common soccage, with all the usual clauses as are inserted for the native proprietors; to enjoy all waifs and strays; to have free warren and all wrecks of the sea, with tithes, both great and small; all antient glebes, vicarages, and rectories excepted; not to *alien* or make leases to any person not of the English race or name —10th July. 18th."

XXVIII. 12.—"Grant from the King to Gerald Murtagh.— Longford County. The ruined fort of Ballybighand, the lands of Braccagh, Belaleigh, Knock, and Aghamore, 200a. pasture, and 30a. wood and moor; Clonbonmogh, Garry and Corry, 200a. pasture, and 10a. wood and moor; Leary, 224a. pasture, and 100a. bog and moor; excepting 60a. of Leary, assigned to Lisagh Oge O'Farrall; rent for the ruined fort, and 564a. pasture, £5 17s. 6d., Engl.; and for 140a. bog and wood, 5s. 10d. To hold a Tuesday market, and a fair on St. Peter and St. Paul's, at Belaleigh, for ever, with a court of pie-powder, and the usual tolls and customs; rent, £1, Ir. To Andrew Verdon— Longford County. Rathmore and Bealagare, part 100a., adjacent to the lands of Tangie, barony of Shrowle; rent, £1 0s. 10d., Engl. To Donald McJames Farrall—Longford County. Prucklesan, *alias* Phrulesan, 74a. pasture, and bog and wood; rent for the 74a. pasture, 15s. 5d, Engl.; and for the 18a. bog and wood, 9d.; all ancient glebes, rectories, and vicarages excepted. To hold in soccage for ever, in the

territory of Ely O'Carroll, with the usual covenants to native proprietors, not to set or let to the mere Irish, but to persons of the
English race or name.—18 Aug. 18th."

II. 2.—" Grant from the King to Oliver Fitzgerald, gent.—Longford County, in Rathcline barony. The town of Moylackan, containing a
water-mill, and 1,045a. arable and pasture, 177a bog and wood; except
all glebe lands, with their tithes. To hold for ever by military service;
rent for the arable and pasture, 23s. 0½d., Engl.; and for the bog and
wood, 7s. 0½d. To Garrott Fitzgerald, gent.—The town and lands of
Carrowle, 198a. arable and pasture, and 165a. bog and wood, 7s. 0½d.;
6a. arable and pasture in Cornedoogh, and Barneviaragh, adjoining
Carrowle; and the wood of Dirriechallin, in the Mointaghcallowe, 20a.
arable and pasture, and 40a. bog and wood, in said barony, lately in the
tenure of Connor McThomas O'Mulvihill, except all the other woods
and underwoods in the Mointaghcallow, and all glebe lands, with their
tithes. To hold for ever, as of the Castle of Dublin, in free and common
soccage; rent for the arable and pasture, 46s. 8d., Engl.; and for the
bog and wood, 8s 6½d. To Teige McConnocke, gent.—The town and
lands of Lislea, 105a. arable and pasture, also 58a. arable and pasture,
and 14a. bog and wood, in Corbally, adjoining Glanmore, and 50a.
arable and pasture, and 10a. bog and wood in Glanmore, adjoining the
lands of Corbally, in Moydow barony; the town and lands of Lisglassoge,
52a. arable and pasture, and 10a. bog and wood, in Shrowle barony;
except the glebe lands, with their tithes. To hold for ever, in
free and common soccage; rent for the arable and pasture, 12s. 6d.,
Engl.; and for the bog and wood, 5d. To William Oge O'Farroll,
gent.—The town and lands of Ballymicknemeaeltra, 60a. arable and
pasture, and 16a. bog and wood, in Shrowle barony, the wood of Clonagh-
beg, otherwise Clonberly, in the Mointaghcallowe, 12a. bog and wood;
except *all* other woods and underwoods in the Mointaghcallowe, and
the glebe lands, with their tithes. To hold, &c, as before; rent for
the arable and pasture, 12s. 6d, Engl.; and for the bog and wood, 14d.
To Connor Ferrall, gent.—Kynaghootra, 52a. arable and pasture,

and 87a. bog and wood; Lawghill, and Tullenedalle, 159a. arable
and pasture, 55s. 2½d., Engl., and for the bog and wood, 1s. 5d. To
Richard Fitzgerald, gent.—The town and lands of Cornedoogh and
Barneviaragh, in Rathclin barony, except 6a. adjoining the town of
Corrowe; 171a. arable and pasture, and 1a. bog and wood; the woods
of Corleagh and Dirrebroliske, 30a. bog and wood; except glebe lands,
with their tithes. To hold, &c., as before; rent for the arable and
pasture, 35s. 7½d., Eng., and for the bog and wood, 4s. 7½d. To Lissagh
Oge O'Farroll, gent.—60a. arable and pasture; 10a. arable and pasture,
and 10a. bog and wood, in Leherie, adjoining Corfin and Tulleveran,
in Rathclin barony; except the glebe lands, with arable and pasture,
and 98a. bog and wood, Creagh, 34a. arable and pasture, and 50a. bog
and wood; Cartron-Ivare, 66a. arable and pasture, and 15a. bog and
wood, in Rathlin barony; a parcel of wood and underwood, called
Edera, adjoining Lawghill, 30a.; except the glebe lands, with their
tithes. To hold, &c., as before; rent for the arable and pasture,
£3 4s. 9½d, Engl, and for the bog and wood, 8s. 8d. To Garrott
McShane Farroll, gent.—The town and lands of Cornemucklagh, 145a.
arable and pasture, and 61a. bog and wood; Kildordan, 71a. arable and
pasture, in Shrowle barony; except the glebe lands, with their tithes.
To hold, &c., as before; rent for the arable and pasture, 45s., Engl.,
and for the bog and wood, 2s. 6½d. To Lissagh M'Connock Farrall,
gent.—The town and lands of Listibbot, 28a. arable and pasture, and
40a. bog and wood; Killinteeteige, 68a. arable and pasture, and 26a.
bog and wood; except glebe lands, with their tithes. To hold, &c., as
before; rent for the arable and pasture, 20s., Engl., and for the bog
and wood, 2s. 9d.; saving of a right for 3 years to raise and draw away
timber, stones, and slates. The tenants of the grantees to erect their
houses in town-reeds, and not scattered, under a penalty of £5 per
annum for every house *not* so built; each grantee to sow 1a. of hemp
for every 100a.; to exact no uncertain rents or Irish exactions; *not* to
demise for a longer term than] 31 years to any mere Irish, or *not* of
English descent or name, on penalty of forfeiture; like penalty for

rebellious or treasonable practices, for taking the name of the Great
O'Farroll, or for demising any lands on the Irish tenure of gavelkind.—
10 July. 18th."

P. 490, XIII. 30.—"Grant from the King to Richard Browne and
Mary, his wife, lately wife of James McIrriell Farrall.—Longford
County. The towns and lands of Cargin, 48a. arable and pasture, and
25a. wood and bog; Lissekitt, 51a.; Clonskoteightra, 61a. arable and
pasture and 21a. wood and bog; Clonkeene, 49a. arable and pasture,
and 24a. wood and bog; Caldraghmore, 69a. arable and pasture,
and 39a. wood and bog; the castle and lands of Castlereogh, with
a water-mill, 203a. arable and pasture, and 125a. wood and bog;
Tonyn, 53a.; Clonevett, 38a. arable and pasture, and 25a. wood
and bog; Clonkirr, 201a. arable and pasture, 69a. wood and bog;
Lissegory, 52a.; Bruckin, 64a. arable and pasture, and 44a. wood
and bog; Cullagh, 50a. arable and pasture, and 72a. wood and
bog; 45a. in Multyny, adjoining Aghenaspick; Correlagan, *in capita*,
by military service; rent, £8, English. To Roger Farrall, son and
heir of James MacIrriel Farrall— The castle, town and lands of Mornyn,
with a water-mill; the town and lands of Bealagh, Mauragh,
Coryn and Clonefad, 268a. arable and pasture, and 131a. wood and bog;
Corrkreaghan, 132a.; Corhobereny, 69a.; Clonscotoughtra, 97a. arable
and pasture, and 40a wood and bog, all in Moydowe barony; Barry-
begg, 70a.; ⅔ of Doory, estimated to contain 62a. arable and pasture,
and 8a. wood and bog, adjoining the town and lands of Aghnoran, containing 88a. arable, 49a. arable and pasture, and 22a. wood and bog,
all in Moydowe barony; Clantymoylan, 63a. arable and pasture, and
208a. wood and bog, in Ardagh barony; except all ancient glebes belonging to rectories or vicarages; containing in all 1,096a. arable and pasture, and 689a. wood and bog. To hold during the life of said Mary;
remainder to Roger Farrall, son and heir of the aforesaid James
McIrriel Farrall, and the heirs male of said Roger; remainders to the
heirs male of Irriell, father of said James McIrriell; remainder to
the right heirs of said Roger for ever. To hold and pasture, and 6a.

wood and bog, in Shrowle barony; a parcel of wood and underwood called the Moher, 167a. in Moydowe barony; Cloghankeogh, Garrimore, Aghelost and Tornegeegh, 193a. arable and pasture; Camaghmore, Collokenurbill, Aghnegrannagh and Shanvallyloskey, 171a.; Camagh-begg and Aghanaspick, 75a. arable and pasture, *all* in said barony; Neddevarry, Boledrynagh and Carrowgurtin, 79a. arable and pasture; 64a. arable and pasture, and 29a. wood and moor in Aghoneagh, next adjoining Castlereogh and Mornyn; 9a. arable and pasture in the Ardes, Aghehowne and Kilmakonlane, next adjoining Cullegh; 34a. arable and pasture in Clonany, next adjoining Bruckin, 4a. arable and pasture in Knockantirlagh, next adjoining Lissegory; Corromore, 71a. arable and pasture, and 55a. wood and moor, in said barony; $\frac{4}{25}$ of Aghnegore, Garrynecrech, Bealadrihid, Munyhille, Shee, Tawnarrigge, Royn, Clonard, Cloncorkie, Meelegg, Ouappoge, Tristernan, Ballyntobber, Thogher and Curraghmore, being 82a arable and pasture, and 108a. wood and moor, in Longford barony; $\frac{1}{5}$ of the wear of Snavosule, on the Shenen; Eneyn, 40a. arable and pasture, and 46a. wood and moor; Litterkeeragh and Tonemachugh, 40a. arable and pasture, and 174a. wood and moor; Crodromyne, 4a. arable a pasture, all in said barony; Briskelbegg and Briskilmore, 60a. arable and pasture, and 260a. wood and moor; the parcels of wood and underwood called Donchill, Magherymeene, Magherygarrowe, and one of the three Clontees, next adjoining Derryoghill, being 30a. wood and moor, in Rathclin barony; all the ancient glebes pertaining to any rectory or vicarage within the premises excepted; the whole being 1,712a. arable and pasture, and 1,414a. wood and moor. To hold *in capite* by Knight's service, by the said Roger Farrall, and his heirs male; remainder to the heirs male of Irriell Farrall, grandfather of Roger; remainder to the right heirs of said Roger for ever; rent, £12, English The castle of Mornyn and all the rest of the premises to be the manor of Mornyn, with 1,000a. of demesne land; license to alienate the rest to any persons *not* being mere Irish in blood and name; to hold a court leet and view of frank-pledge twice in the year, also a court baron, with jurisdiction of debts under 40s.

Irish, with the fees and other perquisites thereof. In case Roger Farrall die before the age of 21 years without heirs male, the premises to go to his sister, Jane Farrall, and her assigns, for fifteen years after, with remainder to the heirs male of Roger, and afterwards to his right heirs, she and her assigns paying to the heirs of Roger during said period £20, English, annually, besides the £20 payable to the Crown thereout. To Terence Farrall—The town and lands of Corrycahill, 53a. arable and pasture; 100a. arable and pasture in Ederclone and Gortinroe, next adjoining Corrylongford, in Granard barony; all glebes, as in preceding, excepted. To hold for ever, as of the Castle of Dublin, in free and common soccage; rent, 31s. 10½d., English To Keadagh McConnell Farrall—The town and lands of Bealanamore and Caldraghobedagh, 79a. arable and pasture, and 91a. wood and moor, in Moydow barony; Clontehy, 18a. arable and pasture, and 221a. wood and moor; Clonelane, 40a. arable and pasture, and 170a. wood and moor, in Longford barony; all glebes, as before, excepted; all being 137a. arable and pasture, and 482a. wood and moor, 10s. 0½d. To Edmund Nugent Fitz-Edward, the town and lands of Tonyn, 97a. arable and pasture, in Granard barony; 130a. arable and pasture, in Killereher and Bealacryn, next adjoining Janaghmore, in Longford barony; 33a. arable and pasture, and 15a. wood and moor, in Janaghmore and Bundonagh, next adjoining Killereher; Corkillen, 49a. arable and pasture; a moiety of Shangar, 32a. arable and pasture, and 145a. wood and moor; a moiety of Donchill, 16a. arable and pasture; *all* glebes, as before, excepted. To hold, &c., as before; rent for the 357a. arable and pasture, £3 14s. 4½d., English, and for 160a. wood and bog, 3s. 4d. To John, otherwise Shane McHulbert O'Farrell, ½ of Clonrollo, 20a. arable and pasture, and 135a. wood and moor, in Longford barony; ⅔ of Shenballyteige, being 82a. arable and pasture; all glebes, as before, excepted. To hold, as before; rent for the 102a. arable and pasture, 21s. 3d., English, and for the 135a. wood and bog, 5s. 7½d. The grantees to allow the cutting down, raising and drawing away of timber, stone, slates and sand, during three years, for erecting buildings in Longford

County, or Ely O'Carroll, to exact no uncertain rents or Irish exactions; to cause their tenants to build in town-reeds and *not* dispersedly, on penalty of £5, English, for each offence ; to sow hemp at the rate of 1a. for every 100a. ; to forfeit any lands granted to mere Irish, and *not* of English surname ; *not* to assume the title of the Great O'Farrall or to let the lands according to the Irish custom of gavelkind, on pain of forfeiture.—8th Feb. 18th."

XIV. 34.—" Grant from the King to Kedagh McLisagh Farrall — Longford County The towns and lands of Clonfowre, viz., Kilnerana, Knocknedarragh, Trienboy, Carrownegappull, Carrowarale, Boynagh, Aghentobane, Carrowenchollen, Carrownaghyady, Corgarruff, Carrow-nesringie, Carrowneshane, and Shanballyhugh, parcel of Clonfore, 279a. arable and pasture, and 106a. wood and bog ; $\frac{11}{23}$ of Aghnegor, Garryne-crech, Bealadrehid, Munyhill, Shee, Tawnarigg, Royn, Clonard, Clan-korky, Meelegg, Knappoge, Trislernan, Ballintober, Clogher, and Curraghmore, towards the west and adjacent to Clonogher and the River Shenen ; 221a. arable and 158a. bog and wood, and $\frac{2}{3}$ of the weir of Shanveowle, on said river ; Clonsillen, 100a. wood, underwood, and bog, near Monytaghcallowe ; *all* other woods and underwoods in Moinytaghcallowe, and 126a. wood and bog ; Cloncalgo, 18a. arable and pasture and 105a. wood and bog ; Clongiherry, 18a. arable and pasture, and 107a. wood and bog —Longford County 22a. arable and pasture in Corry-Longford, next adjoining Ewkynyeghtragh ; all ancient glebes excepted. To hold, &c., as before ; rent for the 158a. arable and pasture, 32s. 11d., Engl., and for the 796a. wood and bog, 16s. 8d.. To Gillernow O'Kenny and Tirlagh M'Uhny Farrall—Dromodowtra and Gurtinboy, 102a. arable and pasture ; Carhowmeanagh, 23a. arable and pasture, and 30a. wood and bog, in Moydow barony ; all ancient glebes excepted. To hold, &c., as before ; rent for the 125a. arable and pasture, 26s. 0½d., Engl., and for the 34a. wood and bog, 17d. To Rory McCahell Farrall—Longford County. Leytrim, 95a. arable and pasture and 111a. wood and bog, in Longford barony ; all ancient glebes excepted. To hold, &c., as before ; rent for the 95a. arable and pasture,

19s. 10½d., Eng., and for the 111a. wood and bog, 4s. 6½d.   To Thomas
McTeige Farrall—Clonyn, 73a. arable and pasture, and 40a. wood and
bog; 78a. arable and pasture, and 20a. wood and bog in Tenemoldone,
next adjoining Clonyn, in Granard barony; all ancient glebes excepted.
To hold, &c , as before; rent for the 151a. arable and pasture, 31s. 6½d.,
Engl., and for the 60a. wood and bog, 2s. 6d.   To James McMelaghlin
Farrall—Carricke, 54a arable and pasture, and 176a. wood and bog;
Clonproghlissee, 82a. arable and pasture, and 85a. wood and bog, in
Longford barony, all ancient glebes excepted.   To hold &c., as before;
rent for the 136a. arable and pasture, 28s. 4d., Engl., and for the 261a.
wood and bog, 10s. 10½d.   To Peter or Piers McMelaghlin Farrall—
Clonart, 24a. arable and pasture, and 116a. wood and bog; Cloninn-
slughtamagha, 15a. arable and pasture, and 73a. wood and bog;
Bunenassa, Boheene, and Clonynbegg, 24a. arable and pasture, and
252a. wood and bog; Aghnagh, 16a. arable and pasture, and 180a. wood
and bog; Clonbarr, 10a. arable and pasture, and 49a. wood and bog, in
Longford barony; all ancient glebes excepted.   To hold, &c., as before;
rent for the 89a. arable and pasture, 18s. 6½d., Engl., and for the 670a.
wood and bog, 13s. 11½d.   To Magha M'Shane Farrall—Ballagh
Iknolane, 63a arable and pasture, 149a. wood and bog; Corgrany, 20a.
arable and pasture, and 220a. wood and bog, in Longford barony; all
ancient glebes excepted.   To hold, &c., as before; rent for the 83a.
arable and pasture, 17s 3½d , Engl , and for the 369a. wood and bog,
15s. 4½d.   To Robert Magenor—420a. arable and pasture, 108a. wood
and bog, in Leytrim, Lisnecorr, Lismacgillegad, Aghnekille, Coolerowan,
Aghekanan, Toome, Corbane, and other parts of the territory or precinct
of Mountergarran, in Granard barony, next adjoining the County of
Cavan, and as far as Loughgawny, with an island there called Inesh-
kerin; all ancient glebes excepted.   To hold, &c., as before the
420a. arable and pasture and 12a. wood and bog, in Lisryan, next
adjoining Kilfenton and Blewtoge, in Ardagh barony; 21a. arable and
pasture and 6a. wood and bog in Freaghan, next adjoining Ballygoola;
all ancient glebes excepted.   To hold, &c , as before; rent for the 120a.

arable and pasture, 25s , Engl., and for the 18a. wood and bog, 9d. The grantees to allow the assignees of the Lord Deputy to cut, raise, and draw away, during 3 years, timber, stone, sand, and slates, for buildings in Longford County or Ely O'Carroll country; to cause their tenants to build their houses in town-reeds for mutual defence, and *not* dispersedly, on a penalty of £5 for each house so built; to sow one acre with hemp for every hundred acres; *not* to let the lands on undetermined leases, nor to grant lands to the mere Irish, or to persons *not* of English blood or surname, for a longer term than three lives, or 40 years, on pain of forfeiture."

P. 492, XIX. 41.—" Grant from the King to James Yonge, Knt.— Longford County. The castle, town and lands of Barne, 102a arable, wood and pasture, and 14a. bog; Lissenure, 214a. arable, wood and pasture, and 74a. bog; Tomdoghan, Liscahelmore, and Lisoweene, 217a. arable, wood and pasture; Lissegreesie and Gneeve, 122a. arable, wood and pasture, and 268a. bog; Motvoad, 96a. arable, wood and pasture, and 43a. bog; Kilsallagh and Cleamuck, 190a. arable, wood and pasture, and 89a. bog; Aghadonoghowe, next adjoining Barne and Lissenure, 46a. arable, wood and pasture; 13a. arable, wood and pasture in Ballinrie, next adjoining Toandogham, all in or near Ardagh barony. To hold for ever, *in capite*, by military service; rent for the 1,000a. arable, wood and pasture, £12 10s., Engl.; and for the 488a. bog, 20s. 4d. The premises to be the manor of Barne, with 500a. of demesne land; license to set any part of the other lands to persons not being under-takers in Longford, or Ely O'Carroll, or mere Irish in blood and surname, with a penalty of forfeiture for so doing. To hold a court leet and view of frank-pledge at Barne, twice in the year; also a court baron, with jurisdiction to the amount of 40s., Ir., with the fines, forfeitures, and other perquisites thereof; right reserved to the Crown to cut, raise and draw timber, stone, sand and slates during three years, for erection of buildings in Longford and Ely O'Carroll, the tenants to build their houses in town-reeds, and not dispersedly, penalty of £5, Engl., for each offence; to sow under one acre of hemp annually for every 100 acres.—20 July. 18th."

XXII. 47.—" Grant from the King to Thomas Dallyell, gent.—
Longford County. The town and lands of Mollalogher, 119a. arable
and pasture, 228a. wood and bog ; Lisenorlane, 63a. arable and pasture,
and 34a. wood and bog ; Mullagh, 65a. arable and pasture, and 23a.
wood and bog ; Liscloghan, 34a. arable and pasture, and 24a. wood and
bog ; Aghereogh, 74a. arable and pasture, and 185a. wood and bog ;
45a. arable and pasture, and 40a. wood and bog in Tullagh, adjoining
Mullagh, all being in Longford barony ; ancient glebe lands excepted ;
rent for the 400a. arable and pasture, £5, Engl., and for the 534a. wood
and bog, 22s. 3d. To Claude Hamilton, gent.—400a. arable and
pasture, and 150a wood and bog, in Ennagh, adjoining Cavan County,
and Lough Gawney, in Granard barony ; ancient glebe lands excepted ;
rent for the arable and pasture, £5, Engl , and for the wood and bog,
6s. 3d. To hold for ever, as of the Castle of Dublin, in free and
common soccage, by fealty only ; the reservation of a right in the
Crown to cut timber and raise stone, sand and slates for three years,
for the erection of buildings in the Queen's County and Ely O'Carroll
country. The grantees to cause their tenants to build their houses in
town-reeds, and *not* dispersedly, on penalty of £5, Engl., for every
house otherwise built ; to sow hemp at the rate of one acre for every
hundred ; to have their principal mansion in their respective premises
on penalty of forfeiture ; not to alienate to the mere Irish, or to persons
not of English or British surname, and *not* to English undertakers
having lots in the county, unless by favour of the royal license.—30
Oct. 18th."

P. 498, LXXXIV. 33.—" Grant from the King to ·Patrick Hanna,
gent.—Longford County. The " octo decim octavam pt." of the town
and lands of Drominge, Garrycaw, Killmeene, Dorroge, Mullaghdrom,
Ballaghlaskagh, Bealacloghan, Corderybeg, Corderymore, and Boulskan,
being 162a. arable and pasture, and 110a. wood and bog ; 110a. arable
and pasture and 68a. wood and bog in Lisduffe, Cartronkeele, Towrallen,
and Cartrongarrow, adjoining Drominge, *all* in Moydow barony ; 28a.
arable and pasture in Lisraiellowtra, in the western part thereof, in

Ardagh barony; except 4a. wood in the lands from Drominge to Boulskan, both inclusive, adjoining the *togher* of Ardagh, set apart for the glebe of Ardagh church, and *all* other ancient glebes; rent for the 300a. arable and pasture, £3 15s., Engl., and for the 178a. of wood and bog, 7s. 5d. To Robert Hanna, $\frac{10}{13}$ of the above lands from Drominge to Boulskan, both inclusive, except the ancient glebes, being 200a. arable and pasture, rent, 50s. Engl., and 100a. wood and bog, rent, 4s 2d. To hold to Patrick and Robert Hanna for ever, as of the Castle of Dublin, in free and common soccage, by fealty only; to have *all* tithes, and to enjoy *all* waifs and strays, with free warren and chase Right reserved to the Crown to cut, raise, and draw timber, stone, sand, and slate, for three years; the tenants to build their houses in town-reeds, and *not* dispersedly, under a penalty of £5, Engl , for each transgression; to sow hemp at the rate of 1a. for every 100a. To hold for ever, as of the Castle of Dublin, in free and common soccage, by fealty only. Right reserved to the Crown to cut, raise, and draw timber, stone, sand, and slates for building for three years. Grantees to demise their lands on fixed rents only, and *not* to demand Irish exactions; to build their houses in town-reeds, and not dispersedly, under a penalty of £5, Engl., for each transgression; to sow hemp at the rate of 1a for every 100a. ; not to demise lands for a longer term than 3 lives or 40 years to mere Irish, or to persons *not* of English surname, on pain of forfeiture; the like penalty in case of rebellion, or for assuming the title of the Great O'Ferrall, or for granting lands in gavelkind.— 24 Nov. 18th."

XCl. 41.—"Grant from the King to Tho. Nugent, Esq.—Longford County. Coolamberbegg, 129a. arable and pasture, and 14a wood and bog; Cartron, Mallyah, and Monegehowlegan, 91a.; Correlie, 83a.; Freaghmeene, 82a. arable and pasture, and 32a. wood and bog, with a water-mill; Cloncahy, 65a. arable and pasture, and 246a. wood and bog; 24a. arable and pasture, and 7a wood and bog in Freighan, adjoining Freighanmeene; 44a arable and pasture, and 11a. wood and bog in Clonshenagh and Motewrally, adjoining Freighan and Freighanmena,

all in Ardagh barony ; a castle, 100a. arable and pasture, and 30a. wood
and bog, in Blightoge, adjoining Lisreane ; rent for the castle and 618a.
arable and pasture, £6 8s 9d , Engl , and for the 340a. wood and
bog, 14s. 2d., Engl. To Cahall Farrall—166a. arable and pasture,
and 21a. wood and bog, in Lisrian, adjoining Ballaghgoole ; Ballaghgoole, 114a. arable and pasture, in Ardagh barony ; rent for the
280a. arable and pasture, 58s. 4d. English, and for the 21a. wood and
bog, 10½d. English. To Oliver Nugent—162a. arable and pasture, and
41a. wood and bog in Bleoghtoge, adjoining Lisrean ; rent for the
arable and pasture, 33s. 9d. English, and for the 41a. wood and bog,
1s. 8½d. English.   To Connell McMurogh Farrall—Camagh, 108a.
arable and pasture, and 269a. wood and bog in Longford barony ;
rent for the arable and pasture, 22s. 6d. English, and for the
wood and bog, 5s. 7¼d. English. To Brian McTeige Farrall and
Donough McBrian Farrall—Carrhey, 155a. arable and pasture in Granard
barony ; rent, 32s. 3½d. English. To James McTirlagh Farrall and Connock McMorogh Farrall—120a. arable and pasture, and 61a. wood and
bog in Clonshennagh and Mottenevally, adjoining Freaghan ; rent for the
arable and pasture, 25s. English, and for the 61a wood and bog, 2s 6½d.
English.   To Tirlagh Farrall—162a arable and pasture, and 28a. wood
and bog in Freaghan, adjoining Clonshannagh in Ardagh barony ; rent
for the arable and pasture, 33s. 9d., English, and for the wood and bog,
14d., English.   To Brian McRory Farrall—One-fourth of Dowlerick,
30a. arable and pasture, and 30a. wood and bog ; Dirrekelan, 20a
arable and pasture, and 131a. wood and bog ; Cornehunshin, 20a. arable,
and 220a. wood and moor in Longford barony ; rent for the 70a.,
14s. 7d English, and for the 381a. wood and bog, 8s. 9½d. English ;
all ancient glebes, rectories and vicarages excepted.   To hold for ever,
as of the Castle of Dublin, in free and common soccage, by fealty only.
Right to reserve to the Crown to cut, raise, and draw away timber,
stone, sand and slates for building, during 3 years ; the grantees'
tenants to build their houses in town-reeds and not dispersedly, on
penalty of £5, English, for each trangression ; to sow hemp at the rate

of 1a. for every 100a. ; not to levy uncertain rents or Irish exactions, not to demise lands for more than a term of life, or 40 years, to the mere Irish, or to persons *not* of English descent or surname, on pain of forfeiture ; not to engage in rebellion ; not to assume the title of the Great O'Farrall, or to let their lands in gavelkind, on like penalty.—18 May. 18th."

XCV. 57 —" Grant from the King to Catherine Dalton of an annual rent-charge of £10, Engl., out of the following lands.—Longford County. The castle, town and lands of Mornyn, with a water-mill; Beallagh, Mauragh, Corry and Cloonfeed, 268a. arable and pasture, and 131a. wood and moor; Corrkreaghan, 132a. arable and pasture ; Corhobereny, 69a. arable and pasture ; Clonskotowghtra, 97a. arable and pasture, and 40a. wood and moor, all in Moydow barony; Barrybegge, 70a. arable and pasture, in Shrowle barony ; ⅔ of Doory, 62a. arable and pasture, and 80a. wood and moor, near Aghenoran; Aghenoran, 88a. arable and pasture, and 6a wood and moor ; the Moher, wood and underwood, 167a.; Cloghan-keogh, Garrimore, Aghelost and Tarnegeehe, 193a. arable and pasture ; Camaghmore, Collokenurwill, Aghnegrannagh, Shanvallylosky, 171a arable and pasture ; Camaghbegg and Aghanaspick, 75a. arable and pasture ; Neddevarry, Boledrynogh, and Carrowgurtin, 79a. arable and pasture ; 64a. arable and pasture, and 29a. wood and moor in Aghoneagh, adjoining Castlereogh, and Mornyn ; 9a. arable and pasture in Ardes, Aghmehowne, and Kilmakonlane, adjoining Cullegh; 30a arable and pasture in Clonany, adjoining Brackin ; 4a, arable and pasture in Knockantirlagh, adjoining Lissegorry ; Corromore, 71a arable and pasture, and 55a. wood and moor ; $\frac{4}{25}$ of Aghnegore, Garry-nekreegh, Bealadrihid, Monyhille, Shee, Tawnaccarrigg, Royn, Clonard, Clonkorkie, Meelegg, Cuappoge, Tristernan, Ballintobber, Clogher, and Curraghmore, being 82a. arable and pasture, and 108a. wood and moor, in Longford barony ; $\frac{1}{5}$ of the weir of Suaveowle on the Shennon ; Enyn, 40a. arable and pasture, and 46a. wood and moor; Litterkeragh, and Tonemachugh, 40a. arable and pasture, and 174a. wood and moor ; Crodomoyne, 4a. arable and pasture, all in Longford barony ; Briskillbegg, and Briscolmore, 60a. arable, and 260a. wood and moor; Donchill, Maherymeene, Maherygarrowe, and one of the 3 Clontees adjoining Derryoghill, being 30a wood and moor, in Rathclyn barony. To hold for life. To Honora Dillon—A rent-charge of £18, Engl., out of the above stated lands. To hold for life. To Jenn Farrall, daughter of James McIrnell Farrall—A rent-charge of £50, Engl, out of said grant to Kath Dalton. To hold for 10 years, if Roger Farrall, son and heir of James, or any issue male of Roger live so long. And if said Roger attain the age of 21 years and then die without issue male, the King grants a further rent-charge of £50 sterling out of the premises, for 4 years after Roger's death.—5th Feb 14th."—The end of the 18th Patent.

Pat. 19, Pt. I. (96), X. 15.—" Grant to Francis Aungier, Knt., of the title of Baron Aungier of Longford, and to his heirs male, in consideration of his justice and prudence as Master of the Rolls, and his services in the plantations of Ulster, Leitrim, and Longford, and in a great many parts of the province of Leinster.—29 June 19th."

P. 503, XIII. 24.—" Grant to Daniel Gookin.—Longford County. The lands of Coolermerigan, 26a.; Killenawse and Garrynegree, 48a; Rossemyne, Lisduffe, and Garriduff, 78a. pasture, and 29a. bog and wood; Lissemagunen, 96a.; Lissard and Corribolum, 101a.; Shiroe and Kilderin, 61a.; Bragwie, 90a. pasture, and 40a. bog and wood, adjacent to the lands of Lismagunen, in the territory of Ely O'Carroll; rent for 500a pasture, £6 5s., Engl, and for 69a. bog and wood, 2s. 10½d. To hold in free and common soccage, subject to the conditions of the plantation of Longford; with the addition of the *prime* bird out of every eyry of great hawks annually.—10 June. 19th."

P. 511, CV. 33.—" Grant to Daniel Gookin.—Longford County. The towns and lands of Coolemerigan, 26a.; Killenawse and Garry-negree, 48a.; Rossemyne, Lisduffe, and Garryduffe, 78a. pasture, and 29a. bog and wood; Lissemagunen, 96a.; Lissard and Corrybolum, 101a.; Shiroe and Kilderin, 61a.; Breaghwie, 90a. arable, and 40a. bog and wood; excepting *ill* rectories, vicarages, and ancient glebes.

The "Steeple Church," on Quakers' Island (See "Iniselothrann," in "Ecclesiastical History of the County.")

To hold for ever, subject to the conditions of the plantations in Ely O'Carroll's territory, the Queen's County, and Longford.—15 July. 19th."

CVI. 34.—"Deed, dated 16th July, 19th James I., whereby Daniel Gookin, in consideration of the sum of £350, Engl., granted, bargained, sold, and assigned to Francis Edgworth, *all* the lands and premises in Ely O'Carroll's country, in the County of Longford, in the preceding patent more particularly mentioned. To hold to the said Francis, his heirs and assigns, for ever, subject to the previous conditions and covenants in said patent mentioned. Livery and seisin delivered according to the tenor, form, and effect of the within deed, by Thomas Stafford, attorney for the said Daniel Gookin."

P. 512, CXXXVI. 50.—" Grant of livery and pardon of intrusion to Andrew Newgent, brother and heir of Robert Newgent, late of Dissert, in the County of Westmeath ; for a fine of £90, Ir.—28 Nov. 19th."

Dorso, P. 518, XXX. 7.—"King's letter to create Thomas Nugent a baronet, with remainder to his heirs male.—Westminster, 10th Dec. 19th."

P. 519, XLV. 24.—"King's letter for a grant, without fine or rent, to Sir George Calvert, Knt., or to such persons as he shall nominate and appoint, of certain lands within the plantation of the County of Longford, undisposed of to any undertakers, namely, Dromlish, Barraghbegg and Barraghmore, Derrowle, Greaghmore, Greagisboll, Meneoghill, Knockmaguiskin, Gorteneny, Garncochild, in Janabegg, and Corlea, Calfeed, Aghowadan, Carrowdonegan, Cowletegle, Caldraneged, Carrowhobbegan, Carrowbolgenagh, Carrickglingh, Liswilliam, Ballingurtin, Lismackegan, and Mullaghbreake, containing 2,314a. ; subject to the usual provisions in the grants to undertakers in the plantations of Leitrim and Longford, &c.—Westminster, 2 January. 19th."

L. 26.—" King's letter to the Lord Deputy, to admit, as undertakers for the plantation of Longford and Ely O'Carroll, such persons as

H

Walter Alexander, servant to the Prince of Wales, shall nominate, for the portions of land granted to William Dromond, 600a.; James and William Alexander, 1,000a., and·to James Philip, 300a., he having purchased the same for the benefit of his children, who are so young that they cannot perform the conditions of the plantation.—Westminster, 28th March. 19th.''

XIV. 54.—"Grant to Emanuel Downinge and Robert Dixon, reciting a direction, by privy signet, to pass letters patent to Theobald Bourke, Baron of Brittas, of lands and tenements of the annual value of £50; and that the latter, by deed dated 15th December, 19th year, assigned to Emanuel Downinge and Robert Dixon so much of the said lands as would amount to the annual value of £50 sterling, and all the interest and benefit of the said letters patent.—Longford County. The great pool, commonly called Loughry, in the Shannon, and the entire fishing and all the islands in the same; Minchinfarme, 2 messuages and 70a. in several parcels in the town and fields of Cromblin; *all* the lands lately parcel of the possessions of the monks of Gracedew, *alias Gratia Dei*, in the lands of Cromblin; 7a. of mountain in Hollywood, in the occupation of John Bath, late the estate of the Hospital of St. John of Jerusalem; the entire fishing in the river, water, bay, or creek of Bree, *alias* Brae, and in the high sea next the lands of Brae, with all liberties thereto appertaining.''

XLIV. 34.—"Grant to George Calvert, Knt, Chief Secretary of Ireland.—Longford County. The castle, town, and lands of Ulfeede, 295a. arable, and 272a. wood and bog, in the barony of Rathclyn; Aghowadan, 116a. arable; Carrowdonegan, 47a. arable; Cowletegle, 37a. arable; Coldraghnegee, 109a. arable; Carrowhobbegan, 99a. arable; Carrowbolganagh, 122a. arable; Carrickglingh, 211a. arable; Liswilliam, 25a. arable; Ballyngurtin, 136a. arable; Lismacegan, 64a. arable, and 10a. wood and moor; Mullaghbrack, 63a. arable, in the same barony; Dromlishe, 223a. arable, and 74a. bog and wood; Barrowbegg and Barraghmore, 104a. arable, and 248a. bog and wood; Dorrowle, 99a. arable, and 98a. wood and bog; Greaghmone, 109a.

arable, and 109a. wood and bog; Greaghisell, 24a. arable, and 41a. bog
and moor; Moneoghill, 49a. arable, and 99a. bog, Knockmaginskin,
41a. arable, and 83a. bog; Gortevonny, 90a. arable, and 35a. bog;
Garveoghill, 102a. arable, and 206a. bog; 159a. arable, and 130a. bog
and wood, in Shanaghbegg and Corlea, adjoining Moneoghill and
Garveoghill, excepting 20a. in Ulfeede, assigned for the glebe of the
Church of Cashell, barony of Longford. To hold *in capite*, by military
service; rent for the arable land, £28 16s., Engl.; and for the bog and
wood, 12s. 0½d. All the lands erected into the manor of Ulfeede;
with courts leet and baron, and jurisdiction under 40s.; subject to the
conditions of the plantation of the county.—18th Feb. 19th year."

P. 533, VIII. 17.—"Grant under the commission for the plantation
of Longford, and the territory of Ely O'Carroll, to Robert O'Farroll.—
Longford County. The castle, village and lands of Bawne, 88a.,
Cartronvally, 59a.; Breackagh, 80a. pasture, and 10a. bog; Aghene-
knappagh, 74a., Corredevine, 81a.; Townnacossane, Townelostrane,
Townetaskyn, and Townedrassoge, 70a.; Trilligtemple 56a.; Gurting-
law, *alias* Gurtineglum, 74a.; Glasclone, 39a. pasture, and 53a. bog and
wood; Trilligmore, *alias* Thrilligpatrick McDonnogh and Clonakre, 81a
pasture, and 96a. bog and wood; Tonebegan and a water-mill, 123a.
pasture, and 28a bog and wood; Graffoke and Liststan, 65a., barony
of Moydowe. The castle, town and lands of Lissardowle and Torefin,
75a. pasture, and 6a. wood and bog; Agharickard, 33a.; Aghaneevan,
80a. pasture, and 6a. bog and wood; Frehalmen, 84a. pasture, and 17a,
bog and wood; Cloncosury, 68a pasture, and 4a, bog and wood; Car-
troncappull, 61a. pasture, and 6a. bog and wood, Ballymacwilliam-
yeightragh, 80a.; Coolcagh, *alias* Vallereagh, 80a. pasture, and 89a. bog
and wood, barony of Ardagh; the wood and land in Mointaghcallow,
called Cloncrew, 24a. To hold *in capite*, by military service; rent for
the mill, and 1,451 pasture, £15 2s. 3½d, Engl; and for the 339a. bog
and wood, 14s. 1½d. The premises created the manor of Bawne, with
courts leet and view of frank-pledge, and courts baron; power to
appoint seneschals and other officers, with jurisdiction in all actions

for debt and covenant where the damages do *not* exceed 40s., Ir.; with power to make tenures; to enjoy all waifs and strays; to have free warren and park. To Robert Cadell—Longford County. Lehard and Monny (except 4a. adjoining the lands of Corleagh, assigned to Gerald Murtagh), containing 117a., and 39a. bog and wood, barony of Ardagh, Cartronreagh, 35a. pasture, and 8a. bog and wood, adjoining Crane-laghes; Millegan, 16a. pasture, and 142a. bog and wood; rent for the 168a. pasture, 20s., Ir. To John McJames boy Farrall—Longford County. Bealaglassan and Lissegowher, 36a.; Toorenegore, 37a. pasture, and 16a. bog and wood; Agherannagh, 53a. pasture, and 46a. bog and wood; Tunnercduffe, Coreneheffin and Correchsirke, 60a. pasture, and 18a. bog and wood; Cornehowne, *alias* Aghownehowne, 33a., barony of Shrowle; rent for the 209a. pasture, £2 5s. 7½d., and for the 80a. bog and wood, 3s. 4d. To Gerrott McHubert Ferrall—Longford County. Trillickbegg, 45a. pasture, and 70a. bog and wood Clonkyne, 66a. arable, and 26a. bog and wood, barony of Moydow; rent for the 111a. pasture, £1 0s. 1½d., and for the 96a. bog and wood, 4s. To Hugh McFirlagh Farrall—Longford County. Lissardlissenore, Aghenoddy, Rynnenye, Aghecrenin, *alias* Aghanacreehee, and Correveline, *alias* Corvelneline, 160a., barony of Ardagh; rent, £1 13s. 4d. To Bryan McEdmond Farrall—Longford County. Craighduffe and Cartronwogan, 141a. pasture, and 123a. bog and wood; Cartronkeele, Lisduffe, Toorallen and Cartrongarrow, 170a. pasture, and 100a. bog and wood, barony of Moydow; rent for the 311a. pasture, £2 4s. 9½d., and for the 223a. bog and wood, 9s. 3½d To Faghny McRory Farrall--Longford County. Ravaldren, 107a. pasture, and 32a. bog and wood, barony of Ardagh; rent for the 107a. pasture, £1 2s. 3½d., and for the 32a. bog and wood, 1s. 4d. To Brian McMelaghlin Farrall—Longford County. Lissenegard, Cowle-cray, Currin, *alias* Srahnecarrow, and Shenballyntegell, 120a. adjoining the lands of Brackagh, and the River Shannon; Clonfoune, *alias* Clontefounes, containing 30a. in Mointaghcallow; rent for the 120a. pasture, £1 5s., and for the 30a. wood and underwood, 1s. 3d. To

Jacob McHubert Farrall—Longford County. Gortnornyn, 148a., barony of Longford; rent, £1 12s. 11d. To Connell McMurrough O'Ferroll—Longford County. The castle and lands of Bealaclare, and a water-mill, 82a. pasture, and 61a. bog and wood; Dromodeightra, 60a. pasture, and 244a. bog and wood; Agatramore and Aghatrabegg, 50a., and a parcel of underwood called the 2 Clontyes, adjoining Derradda, containing 33a., barony of Moydow, excepting all wood and underwood in Mointaghcallow; rent for the 192a. pasture, £2, and for the 335a. bog and wood, 7s. To Richard McJames Farrall—Longford County. Lenynowtra, 205a.; Cargin, 31a. pasture, and 12a. bog and wood, and a certain part of underwood called Derrygart, containing 16a. in Mointaghcallow, barony of Moydow; rent for the 236a. pasture, £2 9s. 2d., and for the 28a. bog and wood, 1s. 2d. To Gerald McRory Farrall—Longford County. The castle and lands of Barry and Bunn-valla, *alias* Cartrondrome, and a water-mill, 45a. pasture, and 30a. bog and wood; Aghafyn, 28a.; Barnegoole, *alias* Lisneroige, 80a. pasture, and 41a. bog and wood; Toyme, 113a. pasture, and 95a. bog and wood; Corbane and Aghenemauragh, 113a.; Agherannagh, 84a. pasture, and 36a. bog and wood; Cleduffe, *alias* Cartroncleycheny, Tenecrosse, Teneclabbechan and Loynedihie, and a fishing wear on the river Enny, 62a. pasture, and 42a. bog and wood; Killnecarrow, 30a. bog and wood, in Mointaghcallow; rent for the castle and 523a. pasture, £5 9s. 4½d., and for the 274a bog and wood, 11s. 5d.; all ancient glebes, vicarages and rectories excepted out of the above grants. To hold in free and common soccage, as of the Castle of Dublin; to have free warren, with all escheats and fines, and all tithes, great and small; not to assume the stile or title of the Great O'Farrall, or to receive or pay any rent, tax-ation or service, or to divide their lands, or hereditaments according to the Irish custom of gavelkind. The above grants to be subject to the conditions of the plantation of Longford, according to the King's letter, dated 30th Sept., 17th.—3 Jan. 19th."

IX. 29.—"Grant under the commission for the plantation of Long-ford, to Thomas Nugent.—Longford County. The town and lands of Corroboymore, Correyboybegg, Aghenteskin, Carrickmacinleney, Fyermore, Aghencownalle, *alias* Aghenitanvally, Lissenuske, Killoge, Keallragh, Clennenegenny, Lenemore, and Corlukillog, 643a. pasture, and 46a. bog and wood, excepting thereout the lands of Ballene-goshenagh, 96a., and Ballygarnett, 296a. pasture, and 43a. bog and wood; Cornemow, 50a. pasture, and 6a. bog and wood, barony of Longford; the castle and lands of Lissenoannagh, 113a pasture, and 24a. bog and wood, barony of Granard; Clonedarramner and Annaghguillen, 32a. pasture, and 298a. bog and wood; Clonfelym, Clonynbegg, Diry-ushy, and Derrycullin, 30a. pasture, and 137a. bog and wood, barony of Longford.   To hold *in capite*, by military service; rent for the 1,164a. pasture, £12 2s. 6d., Engl., and for the 554a. bog and wood, 11s. 6½d. Those lands created the manor of Correboymore, with court leet and view of frank-pledge and court baron; with power to appoint seneschals and other officers, with jurisdiction in all actions for covenant and trespass where the damages do *not* exceed 40a., Ir.; with power to make tenures; to have free warren; to enjoy all escheats.   To Phelim Quym —Longford County.   Lissedrinagh and Lisscrossan, 100a., barony of Ardagh; rent, £1 0s. 10d.   To Richard Delamere—Longford County. Colraghquillan, 34a. pasture, and 38a. bog and wood; Corclaragh, 93a. pasture, and 151a. bog and wood; Camliskes, adjoining Balinesegart, 40a.; rent for the 167a. pasture, £1 14s. 9½d., and for the 189a. bog and moor, 4s.   To Cormick McBryen and Murrogh McIrriell Farrall—Longford County.   Agnegore, Garrynekreeth, Bealadrehid, Munyhille, Shee, Tatbuanarrig, Royn, Clonard, Clonkorkie, Meeleg, Cnappoge, Tristernan, Ballintobber, Clogher, and Curraghmore, 80a. pasture, and 108a. bog and wood, barony of Longford, adjoining Aynenore; rent for the 80a. pasture, 16s. 8d., and for the 108a. bog and wood, 4s. 6d.   To Edmund Nugent FitzChristopher—Longford County.   Shanmullagh, 60a. pasture, and 539a. bog and wood, barony of Longford; rent for the 60a. pasture, 12s. 6d., and for the 539a. bog and wood, 16s. 10½d. To John Quin—Longford County.   Half of the lands of Correchorke, Tumreduffe, Correnaghfyn, and Aghnerannagh, 60a. pasture, and 9a.

bog and wood, barony of Shrowle; rent for the 60a. pasture, 12s. 6d.,
and for the 9a. bog and wood, 4½d. To Brian Quinn—Longford
County. Tenelagh, 70a. pasture, and 33a. bog and wood; Tireneene,
45a. pasture, and 15a. bog and wood, barony of Shrowle; rent for the
115a. pasture, £1 3s. 11½d., and for the 48a. bog and wood, 1s. To
Edmond McMurrogh Farrall—Longford County. Kilfentons, 60a.
pasture, and 26a. bog and wood, barony of Ardagh; rent for the 60a.
pasture, 11s. 6d., and for the 25a. bog and wood, 13d. To Theobald
Delamare—Longford County. Ryngawny, 159a. pasture, and 57a. bog
and wood, barony of Ardagh; Calraghquillan, 31a. pasture, and 37a.
bog and wood; a parcel of wood, called Esker, adjoining Drombada-
more, 20a. pasture, and 155a. bog and wood; rent for the 210a
pasture, £2 3s. 9d., and for the 249a. bog and wood, 5s. 2½d. To
Lissagh Duffe Farrall—Creene, 118a., barony of Longford; 10a. bog
and wood in Dromeerely; the castle and lands of Newton, 241a.
pasture, and 37a. bog and wood; Glannaghowghtragh, 59a.; Aghen-
teese and Ballehoulegan, 136a., and a water-mill; Mullynoragh, 128a.
pasture, and 10a. bog and wood; rent for the castle and 682a. pasture,
£7 2s. 1d., and for the 57a. bog and wood, 2s. 4½d. The above lands
created the manor of Newtown, with power to hold courts leet, view of
frank-pledge, and courts baron; power to appoint seneschals and other
officers, with jurisdiction in *all* actions for debt and covenant where
the damages do *not* exceed 40s., Ir.; with power to make tenures, to
have *all* waifs and strays, escheats and deodands. To Brian Duffe
McConnell—Longford County. Agheleasse and Burrin, and other
parts of the territory called Muntergarren, adjoining the land lately
assigned to William Dermott on the one part, and the above lands on
the other part, and from thence to the lake called Laughgawny, barony
of Granard; rent for the 100a. pasture, £1 5s., and for the 33a. bog
and wood, 1s. 4½d. To hold in free and common soccage, as of the
Castle of Dublin; to have all tithes, great and small; *all* ancient glebes,
vicarages, and rectories excepted; not to assume the name, style, or
title of the Great O'Farrell, or to give or pay any rent, taxes, or

services, or to divide their lands according to the Irish custom of gavelkind. The above *grant* subject to the conditions of the plantation of Longford, like the last grant.—14 June. 19th."

XVI. 2 —"Grant to William Hamden, under the commission for the plantation of Ely O'Carroll's country.—Longford County. Clough-Thomas-Brown, 86a. arable, and 35a. bog and wood; Monisillagh, 64a.; Corgina, 68a. pasture, and 11a. bog and wood; Cartrinbrack, *alias* Cartronveagh, 66a.; Lismacmorrogh, 116a.; rent for the 400a. pasture, £5, Engl., and for the 45a. bog and wood, 1s. 11d. To Henry Piers—Longford County. Glanmore, 150a. pasture, and 31a. bog and wood; Corbally, 50a. pasture, 31a. wood, and 12a. bog; rent for the 200a. arable, £2 10s., and for the 43a. bog and wood, 1s. 9½d. To Walter Hodges—Longford County. Knockivagan, the Ardes, Kilmac-kanlan and Aghenehowne, 80a. arable, and 80a. bog and wood; Coolene-hinsie, 80a. arable, and 242a. bog and wood; Aghowla, 140a., barony of Moidowe; rent for the 300a. arable, £3 15s., and for the 320a. bog and wood, 13s. 5d. To Andrew Newgent and Richard Delamare—Longford County. The castle and lands of Mastrim and Bungare, 94a., always excepting 20a. pasture adjoining the Church of Mastrim as a glebe; Aghenriaghan, 76a. arable and 7a. bog and wood; Aghefinmore, 149a.; Aghencarea and Garryandrew, 63a.; the freedom and common-age of turbary in the lands of Lisnekeeragh, barony of Ardagh; rent for the 372a. arable, £3 17s. 6d., and for the 7a. bog and wood, 3½d. To hold in fee and common soccage; all ancient glebes, rectories and vicarages excepted; power to make tenures; to enjoy free warren and chase, and to have all tithes, great and small, subject to the conditions of the plantation of Longford.—20th August. 18th."

XVIII. 8.—"Grant to William McFergus Farrall, under the commission for the plantation of the County of Longford.—Longford County. The castle, town and lands of Ballintobber, and the lands of Agheglass, 43a. pasture; Aghagortie, 77a.; Carrickedmond, 97a.; Knapoge, 103a. pasture, and 33a. bog and wood; Ballybeg and Leggan, 145a. pasture, and 95a. bog and wood; *Keele*, 45a. pasture, and 167a. bog and wood;

Knockneskeagh, Coolenagh and Tonemrinagh, 146a. arable, 6a. pasture, and 6a. bog and wood, barony of Moydowe; Lagan, 27a. pasture and 4a. bog and wood; Scriboge, Aghenedin, *alias* Senaghmore, Lisclogher-nagh, Lisclevan, and Segmagh, part of Scriboge, 93a. pasture and 37a. bog and wood; Carne, Aghedarragh, Lisard, Aghemahin and Quinlagh, 147a. pasture, and 30a. bog and wood; Carrickullen, Carrickboy, Toorenemona, Ardvarne and Aghenemauragh, 106a.; Derrygerin and Clonfimvoye, 30a. bog and wood, barony of Shrowle. To hold *in capite*, by military service; rent for the castle and arable lands, £10 16s. 5½d Ir., and for the 400a. bog and wood, 12s. 6d. The above lands created the manor of Ballintober, with power to create tenures, and to empark 500a. for demesne land; to hold courts leet and view of frank-pledge and courts-baron; to appoint seneschals and other officers, with juris-diction in *all* actions for debt, covenant and trespass, where the damages do *not* exceed 40s. Engl.; to enjoy all waifs, strays and deodands; to have free warren and chase, with *all* tithes, both great and small. To Lisagh McJames Farrall—Longford County. Killshrooly, 52a. arable and 118a. bog and wood; Lislea, 37a. pasture and 5a. bog and wood; Dromderge, 150a. pasture and 223a. bog and wood; Kilcloagh, 14a. pasture and 130a. bog and wood; Corlenan, 92a. arable and 272a. bog and wood; Curredine, 21a.; Baghelboy and Carrowentoyne, 52a. pasture and 18a. bog and wood; Agheshanka, 101a. pasture and 112a. bog and wood, barony of Granard; rent for the 518a. pasture, £4 7s. 1d.; for the 772a. bog and wood, £1 4s. 1½d.; for the 101a. pasture in Agheshanka, £1 1s. 1d., and for the 112a. bog and wood, 3s. 6d. To Brian Boy McHubbert Farrall—Longford County. The house in which he resides, and all the buildings belonging thereto, and ⅕ part of the lands of Aghenore, Garrynekreeth, Bealadrehid, Manyhille, Shee, Tawnanarregg, Royn, Clonard, Clonkorkie, Meelegg, Knappoge, Tris-ternan, Ballyntobber, Clogher and Curraghmore, convenient and adjacent to the house in which said Brian resides, containing 100a. pasture, and 48a. bog and wood, barony of Longford; rent for the house and 100a. arable, £1 0s. 10d., and for the 48a. bog and wood, 2s. 5d. To

Christopher Browne—Longford County. Agheboy, 60a. pasture and 25a. bog and wood, barony of Granard; Bracklagh, 80a.; a moiety of Shangare, 33a. pasture and 108a. bog and wood, barony of Longford; rent for the 101a. pasture, £1 1s. 0½d., and for the 173a. bog and wood, 7s. 2½d.   To Teige McCormicke—Longford County. The 2 Farnaghts, 69a. pasture and 70a. bog and wood; Lismacever, 69a., always excepting 20a. pasture out of the 2 Farnaghts, adjoining the Church of Ballymaccormicke, as glebe land for said church, barony of Ardagh; rent for the 108a. pasture, £1 4s. 7d., and for the 70a. bog and wood, 2s. 11d.   To Shane McHugh Farrall—Longford County. Dromure, 24a. arable and 24a. bog and wood ; Inaghmore and Bundonagh, 55a. pasture and 15a. bog and wood, barony of Longford ; rent for the 79a. arable, 16s. 5½d., and for the 39a. bog and wood, 1s. 7½d.   To Lisagh McGillernew Farrall—Longford County. Fivorkill, 474a. pasture and 325a. bog and wood ; Lisnegan and Casraghbegg, 115a ; Kealdramore, 104a.; Aghenloghan, 23a., and a certain parcel of wood and underwood called Derrymigran, Derrymanny and Derrynduffe, 40a., barony of Rathclin ; rent for the 716a. pasture, £7 9s. 2d., and for the 366a. bog and wood, 7s. 5¼d.   The above lands created the manor of Fivorkill, with power to create tenures ; to hold courts leet and view of frank-pledge and courts baron ; to appoint seneschals and other officers, with jurisdiction in all actions for debt, covenant and trespass, where the damages do not exceed 40s. Ir. To Edmund Kearnan—Longford County. Ennagh, adjacent to the County of Cavan and the water of Loughgawny, containing 48a. pasture and 12a. bog and wood; two islands in Loughgawny, called Inshestavoge and Inshconnill, 12a. and 149a. pasture, and 48a. bog and wood in the town and lands of Aghnekilly and Aghacanon, and *all* parts of the territory or precinct of land called Muntergeran, adjoining the lands now assigned to Richard Nugent, *on the one side*, and William O'Dermott's on the other side, along to Loughgawny, barony of Granard ; rent for the 219a. pasture, £2 5s. 7½d., and for the 60a. bog and wood, 2s. 6d.   To hold in free and common soccage all ancient glebes, rectories and vicarages excepted; to enjoy *all* waifs, strays and *deodands*; to have free warren, subject to the conditions as undertakers of the plantation of Longford.—9 July. 19th."

P. 538, XX. 20.—"Grant to Edward Dowdall under the commission for the plantation of the County of Longford.—Rynroe, 164a. pasture, and 96a. bog and wood; Killasonnowtra, 239a. pasture, and 102a. bog and wood; Ardcullen, 193a. pasture, and 110a. bog and wood, barony of Granard; Ballow, 132a. pasture, and 22a. bog and wood, barony of Ardagh. To hold in free and common soccage for ever; rent for the 780a. pasture, £7 9s. 7d., Engl., and for the 330a. bog and wood, 13s. 9d. The above lands created the manor of Ardcullen, with power to make tenures, to hold courts leet and view of frank-pledge and courts baron; to appoint seneschals and other officers, with jurisdiction in *all* actions for debt, covenant and trespass to the extent of 30s., Engl.; to enjoy *all* waifs and strays; to have free warren and chase, with power to empark a moiety of the above lands. To William McDonnell—Longford County. Clownefynne, 179a. pasture, and 100a. bog and wood, barony of Granard; rent for the 179a. pasture land, £1 17s. 3½d, and for the 100a. bog and wood, 4s. 2d. To Edmund Dillon—Longford County. Ardughill and Cartronkeel, 95a. pasture and 23a. bog and wood; Gurtinclarin, Aghevicgillemore, Cowlelina, Aghewmonekayne, Aghowgooddan, Lissbrenny, *alias* Lissevrenny, Gustingare, Lissindorragh and Graffely, 188a. pasture, and 212a. bog and wood; Garryuchurry, Cartrontullagh, Cartronestraide, Cartronkealdragh and Bealanore, 76a. pasture, and 30a. bog and wood; Ballyboy, Cartroneghnegnene, Cartronlachill, Cartronshanvally, Lackagh and Cartronaghuncha, 124a., barony of Rathclyn; and also a certain wood and underwood called Dirryloghbannow, 10a., part of Mointaghcallow; rent for the 483a. arable, £5 7s., and for the 275a. bog and wood, 11s. 5½d. To Nicholas Archibald—Longford County. Formolughe, 100a. pasture, and 333a. bog and wood; Dromard, 80a. pasture, and 200a. bog and wood; Corgrane and Ballenlogh, 126a. pasture, and 43a. bog and wood, barony of Longford; Garvagh, 28a. pasture, and 20a. bog and wood; Balline-

geeragh, *alias* Ballaghnekeeragh and Moinduff, 90a. pasture, and 39a.
bog and wood ; Ewkyneightra, *alias* Ewkinbane, 67a., barony of
Granard ; rent for the 490a. pasture, £5 2s. 3½d. ; and for the 635a.
bog and wood, 10s.   To Fergus Farrall—Longford County. The castle
and lands of Tully, 83a. pasture, and 46a. bog and wood ; Ballynemony,
alias Mony, 46a. ; Leyn, 34a. pasture, and 7a. wood ; Tooreknappagh,
35a. ; Lisraghtegan, 82a. ; Cartronkardagh, 45a. bog and wood ;
Asnaghes, 25a. pasture, and 29a bog and wood ; Aghetoome, 50a. ;
Toonebardon, 373a. pasture, and 259a. bog and wood ; Mickershawe,
199a. pasture, and 54a. bog and wood ; Coolecorre, 146a. pasture, and
17a. bog and wood ; Shenclone, 93a. pasture, and 30a. bog and wood,
Annaghkilleene, 100a. pasture, and 127a. bog and wood, barony of
Granard ; rent for the 1,401a. pasture, £14 11s. 10½d., and for the 569a.
bog and wood, £1 3s. 8½d. To hold *in capite*, by military service. The
lands created the manor of Tully, with power to make tenures ; to hold
courts leet and view of frank-pledge and courts-baron ; to appoint
seneschals and other officers, with jurisdiction in *all* actions for debt,
covenant, and trespass, where the damages do *not* exceed 30s., Engl. ;
to enjoy *all* waifs and strays ; to have free warren and chase.   To
Edmund McRichard Farrall—Longford County.   Barnerekelly, 40a. ;
a moiety of Dougall, 16a. ; ⁴⁄₇ parts of Annow, 10a. pasture, and 100a.
bog and wood, barony of Longford ; Lisnekeeragh, 70a. pasture, and
5a. bog and wood ; Killfentons, 20a. pasture, and 4a. bog and wood ;
Lissenune, 8a., barony of Ardagh ; Clownfynn, 52a. pasture, and 72a.
bog and wood, barony of Granard ; rent for the 260a. pasture, £2 5s.,
and for the 181a. bog and wood, 7s. 6½d. To William O'Dermott—
Longford County.   Clonagh, Killmore, Terenes, *all* other parts of the
territory of Mountergerran, containing 480a. pasture, and 143a. bog
and wood ; adjoining the lands of Richard Nugent, Sir Christopher
Nugent, Knt., William Parsons, Edward Dowdall, Henry Crofton,
Robert Dillon, and Thomas Nugent ; barony of Granard ; rent for the
480a. pasture, £5, and for the 143a. bog and wood, 5s. 11½d. To hold
in free and common soccage ; all ancient glebes, vicarages, and rectories

excepted out of the above grants. Those grants are subject to the conditions as undertakers of the plantation of Longford.—24 June. 18th."

Patent Roll, 20 Jas. I., Pt. 1.—V. 9.—"Plantation of Longford.— Ol. Grandison.—Whereas the King's most excellent Majesty, out of his royal favour to the undertakers in the territory of Ely O'Carroll and County of Longford, hath, by his Highness's letters, dated at Westminster the 28th of March, in the year of our Lord God 1621, given direction to us, the Lord Deputy and his Highness's Privy Council in this kingdom, that the fines and rent for the said territory and county being answered to his Majesty, the conditions and other particulars concerning the undertakers there should be framed like to those of the plantation in the County of Leitrim, notwithstanding any former instructions to the contrary, as by the said letters further appeareth. And whereas some of the said undertakers, which had passed their patents upon the former instructions, and were to have the benefit of his Majesty's said letters, have been humble suitors to us, that they might not be put to the charges of taking out of new several letters patent, but that some provisional act of state might be made for their relief and ease, and yet his Majesty secured that they shall perform the articles and conditions appointed for the County of Leitrim; which request we think very reasonable, in regard the said undertakers have been put to great charges in taking forth several letters patent, according to the former instructions for Ely O'Carroll and the said County of Longford; and that it would be very burthensome unto them to obtain new letters patent of their several portions; and for that his Highness hath signified, by his said letters, that his Majesty is ready to afford them any favour which may stand with the good of his Highness's service; and therefore, for the ease of the said undertakers, and for their encouragement to perform the conditions and articles of the plantation, according to his Highness's said letters, we do, by this our act of state, declare, order, and decree that the said undertakers, their heirs and assigns respectively, shall not, from henceforth, in any-

thing, fines and rents only excepted, which are to be answered according
to his Majesty's directions for the said plantation of Ely O'Carroll and
Longford, be charged, restricted, or bound, by virtue or colour of any
former letters patent, or instructions in that behalf, to observe, keep, or
perform any articles, covenants, and conditions for or concerning the
said plantation, other than such articles, covenants, and conditions as
the undertakers which have like portions in the County of Leitrim,
respectively, are tied and bound, and ought to perform and observe,
anything in the said former letters patent, or former instructions, or
any other thing, cause, or matter to the contrary, in any sort, notwithstanding; provided always, that the last-mentioned articles, covenants,
and conditions be well and duly observed by the said undertakers of
Ely O'Carroll and the County of Longford, their heirs and assigns,
respectively, or that in default thereof he or they *which* shall *not*
observe and perform the same, shall incur and be subject to the same
forfeitures and penalties which, by the intent of the articles, covenants,
and conditions, and letters patent for the undertakers in the County of
Leitrim, are to be incurred and sustained by the undertakers of like
proportions in that county, for or by reason of any breach of the same
covenants, conditions, and articles, and letters patent, respectively,
anything in this act of state to the contrary notwithstanding. And
to the intent that his Majesty's officers, and others whom it may
concern, may take due notice hereof, we *do* hereby further order that
this present act of state shall be enrolled in his Majesty's
Courts of Chancery and Exchequer. Given at his Majesty's Castle
of Dublin, the 6th day of April, 1622 Ad. Loftus, Chanc.; Hen.
Valentia, Toby Caulfield, Ed. Blayney, Dvd. Norton, W. Parsons,
J. Kinge."

VIII. 12 — " Grant to Arthur, James and Robert Forbes, natives of
Scotland, to be free denizens, and to have all the benefits, franchises
and privileges of the Kingdom of Ireland, with a grant to Arthur
Forbes.—Longford County. The town and lands of Clongisse, 120a.
pasture, and 298a. bog and wood; Ballinibrien, Quinesin, Lisse and

Correnallin, 393a. pasture, and 299a. bog and wood; Tooreboy, Lissnegard, Carre and Dromneshee, 42a. pasture, and 31a. bog and wood; and also 65a. pasture and 40a. bog and wood in the lands of Lishbrack and Corvelane, excepting 20a. pasture adjacent to the Church of Clongisse, barony of Longford; rent for the 600a. pasture, £7 10s., Engl.; and for the 600a. bog and wood, 13s. 11d. James Forbes—Longford County. The town and lands of Sorne, 126a. pasture, and 380a. bog and wood; Derrylahan, 74a. pasture, and 37a. bog and wood, barony of Longford; rent for the 200a. pasture, £2 10s., Engl., and for the 417a. bog and wood, 8s. 8½d. Robert Forbes—Longford County. The town and lands of Dromeelie, 83a.; Corgarrow, 29a. pasture, and 22a. bog and wood; Ewkyneowtra, 44a. pasture, and 118a. bog; more in the same, 13a., and also 31a. pasture and 17a. bog and wood in the lands of Breaghwy, adjoining Ewkyneowtra, barony of Granard; rent for the 200a. pasture, £2 10s., Engl., and for the 147a. bog and wood, 3s 3½d. All the lands in the County of Longford created the manor of *Castleforbesse*, with court leets and view of frank-pledge and courts baron; power to create seneschals and other officers, with jurisdiction in all actions for debt, covenant and trespass where the damages do *not* exceed 40s., Ir.; to enjoy *all* waifs and strays; to have free warren and chase, with all tithes, great and small; excepting all ancient glebes, rectories and vicarages. To hold a Thursday market at Clongisse, and one fair on the feast of St. Bartholomew the Apostle, (24) August, and the day after, for ever, with a court of pie-powder and the usual tolls and customs; rent, 10s., Engl. To hold in free and common soccage; subject to the conditions, provisoes, limitations and agreements, as undertakers of the plantation of Longford and Leitrim.—1st April. 20th "

P. 546, XXXVII. 9.—" Commission to Lord Aungier, *Master of the Rolls*, authorizing him to minister the oath of supremacy to the Lords Commissioners.—2nd May. 20th."

P. 548, LXXXII. 44.—" Grant creating Oliver Tuite, of Sonnagh, a baronet, with remainder to his heirs male.—16th June. 20th."

IV. 8.—" Grant to James Gibb, under the commission for the plantation of Longford County.—Kilreher and Ballacryn, 104a.; $\frac{1}{12}$ part of the lands of Cornemo, 10a.; 136a. pasture and 136a. bog and wood in the lands of Dromenewre; the lands of Lissevaddy, containing 70a., and 35a. pasture, and 40a. bog and wood in the lands of Clonany; Lismore, 161a, in the barony of Longford; Barlane and Cordooe, 121a. pasture and 35a. bog and wood; Cappagh, in Kiltebegg 149a. pasture and 66a. bog and wood; Lisneenrragh and Allmagh, 139a ; Clownecrosse, 75a. pasture and 40a. bog and wood, barony of Ardagh; rent for the 1,000a. pasture, £12 10s., and for the 317a. bog and wood, 9s. 11d. Those lands created the manor of Lissevaddy, with power to make tenures ; to have free warren, with all waifs and strays, and tithes, great and small; to hold courts leet and baron, with view of frank-pledge; to appoint seneschals and other officers, with jurisdiction in all actions for debt where the damages do not amount to 40s. Ir. To hold *in capite*. To Henry Acheson—Longford County. Gurtincaslane, 109a.; Forehoe *alias* Fogher, 125a. pasture and 151a. bog and wood; Greagfin, 18a. pasture and 55a. bog and wood; Dromhowghloe, 124a. pasture and 215a bog and wood; Cornedan, 86a. pasture and 84a. bog and wood; Dromnenceely, Killencore and Dromhtter, 56a. pasture and 17a. bog and wood ; a moiety of Clontumchor, 22a. pasture and 91a. bog and wood; $\frac{6}{12}$ parts of Cornemoe, 61a. pasture and 80a. bog and wood; Gurtinhowle, 19a. pasture and 79a. bog and wood; always excepting 20a. pasture of the lands of Dromhowghloe, adjoining the Church of Kills, assigned as glebe-land, barony of Longford; rent for the 600a. pasture, £7 10s. Engl, and for the 700a. bog and wood, £1 1s 10½d. Those lands created the manor of Forehoe, *alias* Fogher; with power to make tenures to the extent of 200a.; to hold courts leet and baron ; to appoint seneschals and other officers, with jurisdiction in *all* actions for debt where the damages do *not* amount to 40s. Ir.; to enjoy free warren and chase, with all waifs and strays, and tithes, great and small. To Walter Alexander—Longford County. The castle of Ballynlagh, *alias* Ballinlogh, and the lands of Ballynlagh and Lissafatt,

THE VILLAGE OF NEWTOWNFORBES.

102a. pasture and 47a. bog and wood; Ballincunelle, 60a. pasture and 10a. bog and wood; Aghegneagh, 328a. pasture and 24a. bog and wood; $\frac{1}{13}$ part of the lands of Aghekilmore, 10a. pasture and 6a bog and wood, barony of Granard; rent for the castle and 500a. pasture, £6 5s. Engl., and for the 87a. bog and wood, 3s. 7½d. To Sir Archibald Acheson, Knt —Longford County. Aghekillmore, 17 parts, into 18 parts divided, 170a. pasture and 112a. bog and wood; Malle, 30a. pasture and 441a. bog and wood; Sonnagh, 123a. pasture and 295a. bog and wood; Aghecordrinian, 10a. pasture and 307a. bog and wood , Geilsagh, 3 parts, into 4 parts divided, 159a. pasture and 97a. bog and wood, barony of Granard; rent for the 500a. pasture, £6 5s., and for 1,332a. bog and wood, £2 15s. 7½d. To William Carr—Longford County. Torregowen and Calraghalbany, 72a.; Aghamoreba, Curraghleeteige and Morh, 83a. pasture and 6a. bog and wood , Cartrondoragh alias Lisnedoragh, and Knockboy, 272a. pasture and 78a. bog and wood; Monyfadda and Quillagh, 50a., in the barony of Rathcline; Lisduffe, 43a., in the barony of Shrule; excepting always 20a. pasture of the lands of Cartrondoragh, alias Lisnedoragh and Knockboy, adjoining the church of Killdacomoge, assigned as glebe land for the church; rent for the 500a. pasture, £6 5s., Engl., and for the 84a. bog and wood, 3s. 6d. To James Achmowty—Longford County . Geilsagh, 1 part, into 4 parts divided, 65a. pasture, and 62a. bog and wood; Cordrinane and Agherine, 30a. pasture, and 208a. bog and wood, barony of Granard; and 205a. pasture and 79a. bog and wood in the lands of Lisleagh; rent for the 300a. pasture, £3 15s., Engl., and for the 349a. bog and wood, 10s. 11d. To hold, as of the Castle of Dublin, in free and common soccage; subject to the conditions, provisoes, and agreements, as undertakers for the plantation of Longford.—30 March. 20th."

X. 11.—"Presentation of the Rev. William Gregory to the perpetual vicarages of the churches of the respective parishes of Cashell and Rathcleane, Ardagh Diocese, now vacant and in the King's gift, for this turn only.—11 April. 22nd."

I

P. 584, CIV. 41.—" Letter of the Lords of the Council, directing that the number of provinces, and the extent of each province, shall remain as they are at present constituted, and that the 3 counties of Westmeath, Eastmeath, and *Longford*, which petitioned to be separated from Leinster, do continue a part of the same, and that province to consist of the following counties : Dublin, Meath, Westmeath, *Longford*, Louth, Kildare, Carlow, Wicklow, King's County, Queen's County, Kilkenny, Wexford, the County and City of Dublin, County of the City of Kilkenny, and the Town of Drogheda.—Whitehall, 23rd Jan., 1623." —End of the Patent Rolls (22 in number) of James I.

The foregoing extracts will be found a valuable guide to tracing the old families of the county further on. At present I am concerned mainly in tracing the history of the county, which will show the principal great political events that occurred at this remote age.

For eighteen long years after the above document was issued, the people of Longford groaned under their miseries. In those remote days the democratic spirit of the present age was unknown. The too easily gulled Irish had not learned the great lesson, that to demand, and not to beg redress, was the way to get it. Doubtless, it may be fairly argued that it is easy enough for those who have lived to see the fruits of this century's political advancement to talk, whereas in those days the answer to such demands would be the bullet, the pitch-cap, and the triangle. Nevertheless, there is little to be proud of in the following very humble petition sent in 1641 to the Lord Deputy.

The following is the full text of the petition :

"Nov. 10, 1641.

" Our very good Lord,

" Our alliance unto your lordship's ancestors and yourself, and the tryal of your and their performance of trust unto their friends in their greatest adversity, encourageth us and engageth your honour to our fruition of your future favours The fixion of our confidence in you before any other of the peers and privy councellors of the kingdom doubleth this obligation. Your Lordship may, therefore, be pleased to acquaint the Lords, Justices, and Councel (to be imparted unto his Sacred Majesty) with our grievances, and the causes thereof, the reading of which we most humbly pray, and the manner of it.

" First, the Papists in the neighbouring counties are severely punished, and their miseries might serve as beacons unto us to look unto our own, when our neighbours' houses are on fire; and we and other Papists are, and ever will be, as loyal subjects as any in the King's dominions; for manifestation whereof we send herein inclosed an oath solemnly taken by us, which, as it received indelible impression in our hearts, shall be sign'd with our hand, and seal'd with our blood.

" Secondly, there is an incapacity in the Papists, of honour and the immunities of true subjects, the royal marks of distributive justice, and a disfavour in the commutative, which rais'd strangers and foreigners, whose valour and vertue was invincible, when the old families of the English, and the major part of us, the meer Irish, did swim in blood to serve the Crown of England; and when offices should call men of worth, men without worth and merit obtain them.

" Thirdly, the statute of the 2 Eliz. of force in this kingdom against us, and they of our religion, doth not a little disanimate us and the rest.

" Fourthly, the avoidance of grants of our lands and liberties by quirks and quiddities of the law, without reflecting upon the King's royal and real intention for confirming our estates, his broad seal being the pawn betwixt his Majesty and his people.

" Fifthly, the restraint of purchase in the meer Irish of lands in the escheated counties, and the taint and blemish of them and their posterities, doth more discontent them than that plantation rule; for they are brought to that exigent of povertie in these late times, that they must be sellers, and *not* buyers of land.

" And we conceive and humbly offer to your Lordship's consideration *(Principiis obsta)*, that in the beginning of this commotion, your Lordship, as it is hereditary for you, will be a physitian to cure this disease in us, and by our examples it will doubtless beget the like auspicious success in all other parts of the kingdom; for we are of opinion it is one sickness and one pharmach will suffice, *sublatâ causâ tollitur effectus*; and it will be recorded that you will do service unto God, King, and country; and for salving every the aforesaid soars your Lordship is to be an humble suitor in our behalf, and of the rest of the Papists, that out of the abundance of his Majestie's clemency, there may be an act of oblivion and general pardon, without restitution or account of goods taken in the time of this commotion; a liberty of our religion; a repeal of all statutes formerly made to the contrary, and not by proclamation, but parliamentary way; a charter free denizen in ample manner for meer Irish; all which in succeeding ages will prove an union in all his Majestie's dominions instead of division, a comfort in desolation, and a happiness in perpetuity for an imminent calamitie; and this being granted, there will be all things, *Quæ sunt Cæsaris* and *Quæ sunt Dei Deo*; and it was by the poet written (though he be prophane in other matters, yet in this) prophetically, *Divisium Imperium cum Jove Cæsar habet*; all which for this present we leave to your honourable care; and we will, as we ever did, and do remain,

"Your very humble and assured, and ever to be commanded,

"HUGH MAC GILLERNOW FARRALL.
"JAMES FARRALL.
"BRYAN FARRALL.
"KEADAGH FARRALL.
"EDMUND MAC CONNOR FARRALL.
"CAHEL MAC BRYNE FARRALL.
"EDMOND MAC CAEL FARRALL.
"JOHN FARRALL, in Carbury.
"GARNET FARRALL.
"LISAGH MAC CONEL FARRALL.
"BRYAN MAC WILLIAM FARRALL.
"JOHN MAC EDMUND FARRALL.
"JOHN FARRALL.

" ROGER MAC BRYNE FARRALL.

" JOHN FARRALL.

" BARNABY FARRALL.

" JAMES MAC TEIG FARRALL, his mark.

" MORGAN MAC CARBRY FARRALL.

" DONNAGH MAC CARBRY FARRALL.

" RICHARD MAC CONEL FARRALL.

" WILLIAM MAC JAMES FARRALL.

" FAGHNA MAC RORY FARRALL.

" CORMACK MAC RORY FARRALL.

" CONOCK MAC BRYNE FARRALL.

" KEADAGH MAC LISAGH FARRALL.

" CONNOR OGE MAC CONNOR FARRALL."

In John O'Curry's " Review of the Civil Wars in Ireland," vol. I., p. 194, he speaks of this document as follows :—

" On the 10th of November, 1641, the O'Farralls of the neighbouring County of Longford sent up also to the Lords Justices a remonstrance of their grievances, which was of much the same tenor with that from Cavan, entreating redress in a Parliamentary way " " These gentlemen," says Mr. Carte,* " had deserved well of the Crown, and were on that account particularly provided by King James, in his instructions for the planting of that country. But the commissioners appointed for the distribution of the lands, more greedy of their own private profit than tender for the King's honour or the rights of the subject, took little care to observe these instructions; and the O'Farrells were generally great sufferers by the plantations."

"Several persons," continues Curry, "were turned out of large estates of profitable land, and had only a small pittance, less than a fourth part, assigned them for it in barren ground. Twenty-four proprietors, most of them O'Farrells, were dispossessed of their all, and nothing allotted

---

* In a manuscript of Bishop Stearne, we find that in the small County of Longford, twenty-five of one sept were all deprived of their estates, without the least compensation, or any means of subsistence assigned to them.

them for compensation. They had complained in vain of this undeserved usage many years; and having now an opportunity afforded them of redress, by the insurrection of their neighbours, had readily embraced it and followed their example (for it does not appear that any of them were antecedently concerned in the conspiracy), as they likewise did in laying before the Lords Justices a remonstrance of their grievances and a petition for redress, which, like that from Cavan, came to nothing."

In 1641 broke out the celebrated war of the Confederated Catholics, in which the O'Farrells seem to have taken more or less of a prominent part. During the war Col. Preston, who commanded the Leinster division of the army, besieged and captured the Castle of Longford and Castle-Forbes, in which Lady Forbes and a body of her planted tenantry held out for a considerable time. The gallant Preston treated the lady most chivalrously on her surrender; but the Castle of Longford which was held by a renegade O'Farrell, who bartered his faith and fatherland for English gold and confiscated acres, was mercilessly sacked and the garrison slaughtered. Amongst those of the name of O'Farrell who distinguished themselves at this period was Col. Richard O'Farrell, who had come from Flanders in 1643; "he and Henry O'Neill, Owen Roe's son, landed at Wexford, with a few officers and arms for one troop of horse. He was the trusted friend of Owen Roe O'Neill."

The author of the "Aphorismal Discovery" always speaks in the highest terms of O'Ferrall's bravery and skill. In a battle fought in Meath, he was defeated near Trim by Lord Inchiquin. Subsequently, when Cromwell appeared in Ireland, the annalist says :—

P. 130.—" So eager was he [Owen Roe O'Neill] to show his good will and his entire forgetfulness of past injuries, that even before the treaty between him and Ormonde was signed, he sent 3,000 men under Lieutenant-General O'Ferrall to his [Ormonde's] assistance."

P. 220.—" He was appointed military governor of the city of Waterford, January 24th, 1650, on account of the implicit confidence placed in him (Ferrall) by the Papal Nuncio, Rinuccini."

He gallantly replied to Cromwell's summons to surrender the town of Waterford.

"On arriving before the city, Cromwell had sent a trumpeter to summon the garrison to yield upon quarter. Ferrall would give way to none to answer other than himself; he requested the trumpeter to return to his master with this result, that 'he was Lieutenant-General Ferrall, governor of that place [Waterford], and would not yield the town.'"—"Aphor. Discovery," vol. ii., p. 57.

This boldness on the part of Ferrall, and sudden appearance with reinforcements, made Cromwell change his plans.

From the same volume we learn that "Ferrall attempted to surprise Passage, but is obliged to retreat, being hotly pursued by the enemy." In the same page it is recorded that he was "chosen Lieutenant-General of the Ulster army, during the battle of Scariffhollis, June 21st, 1649."

June 22nd, 1649, being defeated in this battle, he (Ferrall) and a few more who survived sought safety in flight, and hid themselves in the mountains and woods to avoid the certain death that awaited them, if they were taken. In this fight three priests and friars were killed, and 3,000 were slain on the Irish side.

From "A Contemporary History of Ireland, from 1641 to 1652," published by Mr. Gilbert, it appears in Section 27, p. 19, that during those days "the O'Fferralls cleered the Countie of Longford from garrisons and enemies, as far as the Countie of Westmeath : there was none to be gained there," &c.

In the same work it is recorded that—

"Bryan Oge O'Duyne, a rank Puritan, a brother-in-law of Sir John Pigott (the hated ancestor of the Pigott dynasty in Ireland), and chiefe motor of his obstinacie, was saved by the generous Colonel O'Fferall."

In the same work it is also recorded that at the battle of Letterkenny, "of the verie Ferralls there were killed eighteen captains."

This Lieutenant-General O'Farrell commanded a special regiment which was raised in and around his native county. Of this regiment the following details are found in a muster-roll of the Catholic army, taken at Waterford, 24th January, 1649 :—

"Major Farrall's company does consist of 7 officers and 38 men.

"Captaine Bryan O'Rourke's, of 9 officers and 49 men.

"Captaine Nangle's company, of 3 officers and 14 men.

"Captaine Fergus O'Ferrall's company, including servants, etc., etc., doe amount in all vnto 46.

"Captaine Michael O'Ferrall's company, including servants, etc., etc., doe amount in all vnto 43.

"Captaine Richard O'Farrall's company, including servants, etc., etc., doe amount in all vnto 29.

"Captaine Walter Phillips' company, including servants, etc., etc., doe amount in all vnto 58.

"Captaine Connell O'Farrall's company, including servants, etc., etc , doe amount in all vnto 27.

"Captaine Gerrald O'Farrall's company, including servants, etc., etc., doe amount in all vnto 22.

"Captaine Hanly's company, including servants, etc., etc., doe amount in all vnto 38.

"Captaine Charles Reynold's company, including servants, etc., etc., doe amount in all vnto 59.

"Absent at Ballyhack, by certificate, from the lieutenant-generall, from all the regiments, 12.

"Staff officers, 6.

"Lieutenant-Generall Richard O'Ferrall's regiment, including servants, corporalls, drumes, and common soldiers, doe amount in all vnto 430.

"In the Roconnell skirmish, in 1642, the Irish lost in this vnhappie skirmish the honor of the place, theire armes and amunition, 25 colours, many gentlemen killed, among whom was one named Conacke McRosse Fferrall."

RUINS OF THE ABBEY OF REGULAR CANONS,

Founded by St. Columbkillo on Inchmore, in Lough Gowna, before his Departure for Iona.

. The foregoing few extracts may counterbalance in the reader's mind the dismal effect of reading the previous whine from the late owners of the county in 1641.

We now pass on to the advent of Oliver Cromwell on the scene of Irish affairs.

Oliver Cromwell landed in Ireland in 1649, almost at the close of the war of the Confederated Catholics, which had been waged unceasingly in different parts of the country for seven years. Haverty says of this visit:—"Oliver Cromwell, the extraordinary man who was then beginning to sway the destinies of England, had, by a unanimous vote of the Parliament, been made lieutenant-general of the forces in Ireland so far back as March 28th, 1649. But the troubles with the 'levellers' and others had so far retarded the setting out of his expedition for this country. At length he sailed from Milford Haven on the 13th of August, and landed at Dublin on the 14th, having altered his original plan, which was to land in Munster. He brought with him 9,000 foot, 4,000 horse, several pieces of artillery, an abundant supply of all kinds of military stores, and £20,000 in money. His son-in-law, Commissary-General Ireton, followed as second in command. The Parliamentary force in Dublin now exceeded 16,000 men, and on August 30th Cromwell took the field with a well-provisioned army of 10,000 picked men, and marched to lay siege to Drogheda, then deemed next in importance to Dublin as a military post."

Then follows a description of the reduction of Ireland by Cromwell and his Scripture-canting barbarians, which, from the very horrors depicted in it, as well as the fact that, in all probability, every reader of history knows more or less about it, is here omitted A second quotation from Haverty will bring the matter about to be here inserted more properly and more thoroughly before the reader :—"A.D. 1652.—The ruin that now overspread the face of Ireland must have been dark and sorrowful enough, but the measure of her woes was yet to be filled up. War, and famine, and pestilence, had done their share, but the rapine and vengeance, which assumed the name of law, had yet to complete the work of desolation. Cromwell and his Council had, indeed, seriously contemplated the utter extermination of the Irish race ; but the fiendish project appeared still too difficult, and even to them too revolting. And, accordingly, by the Act passed for the settlement of Ireland by the Parliament of England, August 12th, 1652, it was decreed that full pardon should be granted to all husbandmen and others of the inferior sort not possessed of lands or goods exceeding the value of £10, whilst persons of property were to be otherwise disposed of, according to a certain classification. All the great landed proprietors and all the Catholic clergy were EXCEPTED from pardon of life or estate ; others, who merely held commissions as officers in the army, were to be banished and forfeit their estates, except the equivalent to one-third, which would be assigned for the support of their wives and children. Those who, although not opposed to the Parliament, might be found worthy of mercy, and who were not included under any of the preceding heads, also forfeited two-thirds of their estates, but were to receive an equivalent to the remaining third wherever the Parliament chose to allot it to them ; and, finally, all who were perfectly innocent, that is, who had no share whatever in the war, but yet were not in the actual service of the Parliament, or had not manifested their constant 'good affection' to it, forfeited one-third of their estates, and were to receive an equivalent to the remainder elsewhere. Thus, all the Catholic gentry were indiscriminately deprived of their estates ; and such as might be declared by Cromwell's Commissioners innocent of the rebellion, and were to receive back any portion of them, should transplant themselves and their families beyond the Shannon, where allotments of the wasted tracts of Connaught and Clare would be given to them. The other three provinces were reserved for the Protestants, and any of the transplanted Catholics who might be found in them after the 1st May, 1654, without a passport, might, whether man, woman, or child, be killed without trial or order of magistracy by anyone who met or knew them ! Moreover, those who, by 'the Act of Grace,' were given allotments in Clare or Connaught, were obliged to give releases from their former titles in consideration of what was now assigned to them, in order to bar them ever again seeking their former inheritance; and they were sent into wild and uncultivated districts, without cattle to stock the land, or implements to till, or houses to shelter them, so that many of the Irish gentlemen and their families perished of cold and hunger. They were not suffered to reside within two miles of the Shannon, or four miles of the sea, or in any garrison or market town whatever."

The excessive barbarity of the Puritans to the Irish in this matter was bad enough, but the utter carelessness of what became of the Irish when they went across the Shannon was even worse. It was in the midst of winter, and, as Haverty says, "Many of the Irish gentlemen, and their weak, young families, perished of cold and hunger." But what recked the iron-hearted monster who directed the murderous proceeding? Very little wonder is it, indeed, that the Irish people would shudder at the "curse of Cromwell," for, indeed, they were cursed by him in those days.

Under this state of things the following landed gentlemen of the County of Longford and their families were dispossessed of their estates, which were either sold to Cromwellian troopers or other adventurers— the hereditary owners having to transplant themselves and their families beyond the Shannon immediately :—

COUNTY OF LONGFORD, 1653.

Fergus Farrell, Ardanragh; Feaghny Farrell, Coolcroy; John Farrell, Tyrlicken; Francis Farrell, Mornyne; Thomas Dowling, Abbeyshrule; James Farrell, Tynelick; Edmond Farrell, Lisryian; Edmond Dalton, Loughrill; Thomas Fitzgerald, Newcastle; John Murtagh, Crinaghmore; Hubert Dillon, Cartronboy; James Dillon, Ballymulvey; William MacJames Farrell, Moherboy; Ellinor Farrell, Ballmore; William Geoghagan, Robbinstown; John Nugent, Ballinlogh; Faghny Farrell, Newtown; Lysagh Farrell, Listibbot; Bryen

Farrell, Flaslongford; Garret Fitzgerald, Cornadonchy; Hubert Farrell, Ballynahay; Faghny Ffarrell, Crygh.

In 1657, Cromwell assumed the title of Protector and a sovereignty over the three kingdoms, which so disgusted his co-regicides that they withdrew from his army, and left him to enjoy his glory alone; and the same year he ordered one Christopher Gough to make out a list of the "forfeiting" Papist proprietors in each county in Ireland. This list embraces the names of all those whose estates had been confiscated, but from which they had not been driven, but were allowed to remain in a state of dependency; and in many cases, as if by the intervention of a kind Providence, the officers of the Commonwealth, as well as those who were to receive the lands, either failed to claim them or were persuaded by some momentary consideration not to disturb the old proprietors, and merely held the deeds which subsequently made them landlords; otherwise there had been no native Irish left in Longford County.

County of Longford, 1657.

A List of the Papist Proprietors named in the County of Longford, as they are returned in the several surveys of the said county.

Barony of Longford.

There were 37 confiscations in this barony alone:—

Sir Richard Browne, Ballinamore; Connor O'Casie, William Cliffe, Teig O'Casie, Cormock O'Casie, Hugh Duffe, Doolerocke; Laurence Dowdall, Aghnemodda; Laurence Dowdall, Cronrish; Bryan Ffarrell, Ballygorrow (Garve); Bryan M'Manus Farrell, Conn Oge Ffarrell, Ardronin; Daniel Farrell, Corglass; Francis Ffarrell, Mornin; Faghny Ffarrell, Newtown; Edmond Flynn, Uriell Farrell, Garrett Farrell, Esker; James Farrell, Killashee; Morrogh Farrell, Rhyne; Rory Farrell, Cornacally; Thomas Ffarrell, Ballycarr; Anthony Ffarrell, Cornefinthane; Conge Ffarrell, Edmond M'Donnell Farrell, James Ffarrell, Tinelicke; Hugh Ffarrell, Drimure; Hubert Ffarrell, Gortmorin; Lysagh Farrell, Clonbalt; Moha MacShane Farrell, Bellagh; Robert Farrell, Camagh; Oliver Fitzgerald, Portinare; Bryan Farrell, Bannery; Edward Nugent, Lisaghnedin; Owen Reynolds, Kiltervagh.

Barony of Moydow.

There were 21 confiscations here :—

William Ffarrell, Ballintobber; William Ffarrell, Curry; Conagh M'Teigh Ffarrell, Lislea; Faghny Farrell, Cloonrine; Edmond Ffarrell, Gillaghmine; John M'Kedagh Ffarrell, Ballycore; Hubert Ffarrell, Clonee; James M'Garret Ffarrell, Ballymahon; Roger MacBryan Ffarrell, Lisduffe; Daniel MacShane Ffarrell, Bunerboy; John M'Bryen Ffarrell, Bunerboy; Kedagh M'Garrold Ffarrell, Ballintampan; Teig Kenny, Gortenboy; Roger M'Bryan Ffarrell, Creyduff; James M'Kedagh Ffarrell, Ballyneclude; Fergus M'Shane Ffarrell, Bunerboy; Hugh M'Gerald Ffarrell, Carrow; Morrogh M'Terlagh Farrell, Carhuemanagh (Caramanna); Francis Farrell, Moynin; Richard Farrell, Bawn.

Barony of Ardagh.

There were 37 confiscations in this barony :—

Geoffrey Cormack, Farnagh; Garret Dellamore, Streete; Richard Delamore, Ballinfid; Sir John Dungan (Dunigan), Castletown; Connor Farrell, Ballow; James Farrell, Tinerare; Comrogh Ffarrell, Kilfinton; Donnogh Ffarrell, Ballow; Hubert Ffarrell, Ballow; Connogh Ffarrell, Motenwally; William Ffarrell, Lisrian; Edmond Farrell, Kilfinton; Hugh Ffarrell, Rinminy; Hugh Ffarrell, Ffrighan; Richard Ffarrell, Ballinree; James Ffarrell, Clonfinagh; Connell Ffarrell, Camlisk; Donnogh Ffarrell, Kilkrihy; Charles Ffarrell, Cartronragh; Edward Ffarrell, Garryandrew; Garret Ffarrell, Killmasleragh; William Ffarrell, Liscarrell Eghter; Luke Hiraghty, Kilfinton; Patrick Hiraghty, Kilfinton; Owen M'Kiernan, Kilfinton; Lord Netterville, of Ballygart; James Nugent, Coolamber, Westmeath; Edward Nugent, Lisaghnedin; Bartholomew Nangle, Longford; Edward Nugent, Mostrim (Edgeworthstown); John Nugent, Druming; John Newgent,

Culwin, County Westmeath; Christopher Nugent, Moynnstowne, County Westmeath; James Quinn, Lisdrinagh; Sir Oliver Tuite, Sonnagh, County Westmeath; Patrick Ffox, Rathreagh.

Barony of Rathcline.

Thirty confiscations; no addresses given:—

Nicholas Barnwell, Mary Clarke, Edmond Dalton, James Dillon, Edmond Dillon, Hubert Dillon, Garret Dillon, Hubert Dillon, Garret Dillon, James Dillon, Sir James Dutton, Thomas Dutton, Bryan Ffarrell, Edmond Ffarrell, Ffaghny Ffarrell, James Ffarrell, Ffrancis Ffarrell, Hubert Farrell, James Ffarrell, John Ffarrell, Richard Ffarrell, William Ffarrell, Oliver Fitzgerald, Gerald Fitzgerald, Thomas Fitzgerald, John Ffox, Oliver Fitzgerald, Donnough Keoghan, William Ffarrell, The Lord of Roscommon.

Barony of Shrule.

Twenty confiscations; no addresses given:—

Nicholas Barnewell, James Dillon, Edmond Ffarrell, Ffergus Ffarrell, Francis Ffarrell, Garrett Ffarrell, Thomas Fitzgerald, James Ffarrell, John Ffarrell, Lisagh Ffarrell, Richard Ffarrell, Teig Ffarrell, Thomas Fitzgerald, Charles Fox, John Murtagh, John Murlogh, James Quinn, and Sir John Seaton.

Barony of Granard.

Nicholas Archbold, Moyne; Henry Connell, Cloyshoge; William Dermot, Clonagh; Connill Ffarrell, Kilosona; James Ffarrell, Kilosona; Edmond M'Hugh Farrell, Coolearty; Fergus M'Bryan Farrell, Tully; Donald M'William Farrell, Clonfin; Edmond M'Hubert Farrell, Monascriba; Bryan Farrell, Carragh; James M'Cahell Farrell, Killasonnagh; Patrick M'Bryan Farrell, Rinroe; Bryan Farrell, Tomewarden; Charles Farrell, Canan; Daniel Farrell, Kilfrielly; Connoch Farrell M'Rosse, Clonlawchill, Edmond Ffarrell Duffe, Gurtinechuill; Hugh Ffarrell, Kilnemodagh; James Farrell M'Fergus, Tully; Nicholas Jones, Leitrim; Thomas Kiernan, Rathcarr; Bryan Kiernan, Justhavogue; Bryan Keernan, Aghakine; Nicholas Nugent, Aghanigarran;

Andrew Nugent, Donore, Westmeath ; John Nugent, Ballinclogh ; Christopher Nugent, Drumenewher ; Richard Nugent, Aghnagarrowne ; Oliver Ffarrell, Corbehy.

As history tells us, Cromwell died on September 4th, 1658, and his son Richard, who had been made Protector, retired from that post in 1659, whereupon General Monk marched from Scotland to London with his army, and there had Charles II. proclaimed King, and on May 1st, 1660, royalty was restored in England.

By order of the Governors of Ireland, a census of this country was taken in the year 1659, when the population of the County Longford was found to be laid out as follows :—

In the barony of Ardagh there were 19 English, 971 Irish, and a total of 990 people. The resident gentlemen were :—Richard Archbold, Glynn ; Darby Toole, Lisdrinagh ; Captain J. Edgeworth, Cranalagh. And the names of the principal Irish families were .—Cline, Cargy, Cormack, and MacCormack, Cowley, M'Connell, Farrell, Kiernan, Kenny, M'Loughlin, Leavy, Murtagh, Mulligan, Moore and Reilly.

In the barony of Longford there were 396 Irish and 67 English. The gentlemen residing in the barony were :— Sir Arthur Forbes, Castle-Forbes ; Alexander Aghmooty, Ballybrian ; William Pillsworth Minard ; Lieutenant Thomas Babington, Longford ; and Hannibal Seaton, of Moneylagan. The principal Irish families were :—MacDonnell, 10 people ; Farrells, 17 ; O'Hagans, 6 ; MacElvay, 5 ; Knowlan, 5 ; Quinn, 4 ; and MacKay, 4. The total population of Longford barony in those days was 463 people, all told ; of these, 52 formed the population of Longford borough.

In the barony of Rathcline there were 849 Irish and 83 English, making a grand total of 932. The principal Irish families were .—The MacBryans, O'Connors, O'Cronines, Cormicks, and MacCormacks, Dowlans, Kellys, Keegans, O'Dowleys, Mulvihills, Gills, Murrays, Hopkinses, Murtaghs, and Skellys. And the gentry of the barony were :—Adam Molyneux and Nicholas Dowdall, of Ballimulloe (not now existing, I think); Thomas Robinson and Griffith Jones, of Clagh; Edward Clarke, of Claris; and Robert Mills, of Fermoyle.

In the barony of Shrule there were 694 Irish and 42 English, making a total of 736. The principal Irish families were the Bardens, MacCormicks, Cahills, Corrigans, MacDowels, Daleys, Farrells, Kaines, M'Jeffreys, Keenans, Keegans, Kennys, Quinns, and Mulledys. The local gentry were :—Mathew Wilder, of Cliduff; Richard Certaine, of Cloghanbiddy; Tibbott Dillon, of Clonkeen; and Hubert Farrell and Simon Sandys, of Crevaghmore.

In Moydow barony there were 182 Irish and 4 English. The principal Irish families were :—The Caseys, 12 people ; Cormicks and MacCormicks, 19; Donlans, 7 ; Dooners, 5 ; Duffs, 6 ; Farrells, 23 ; Kennys, 16; Morrows, 7; Powers, 6; Keegans, 7; and M'Evoys, 5. The local gentry were:—Thomas Newcomen, of Ballinamore ; and Walter Tuite, of Castlereagh.

In the great barony of Granard there were only 1,416 Irish and 66 English, making a total of 1,482 people. The principal Irish families were :—The Biglanes, 7; Bradys, 23; MacBryans, 5; M'Cabes, 7; M'Connells, 6; Cahills, 6; Connellans, 5; Dermotts and MacDermotts, 11 ; Donobos, 18; MacDonnells, 8; Duffys, 10; Farrells, 25; Gaffneys, 10 ; Maguires, 8; MacHughs, 6; O'Haras, 5; Kiernans, 34 ; Kellys, 6; Mulligans, 16; Mahons, 5; Mastersons, 9; Nugents, 8; Reillys, 67; Smiths, 5; and Sheridans, 7. The principal resident gentlemen were:— Thomas Flood, Newtown; Richard Kennedy, Glenaughill; William Longford, Cloncoss; and Andrew Adaire, of the Corporation of St. Johnstown (now Ballinalee).

This would go to show that the whole County of Longford only contained, in the year 1659, a population of 5,392, of which 281 were of English, and 5,111 of Irish birth or descent.

On March 19th, 1661, Charles II. appointed a Court of Claims, to reinstate those persons in their estates who had been dispossessed of them by the Cromwellians. This appointment was made in pursuance of a declaration by Charles II. on November 30th, 1660, in which it

The River Inny, with Ruins of Abbeyshrule Monastery in the Distance.

was ordered that every soldier and adventurer who had become possessed of lands in Ireland prior to or during the late rebellion, and who had since aided his restoration, would enjoy (and his heirs) for ever the lands so obtained; and every innocent Papist who had neither aided the Nuncio, Rinuccini, prior to 1647, or Cromwell after that period, was also ordered to be restored to his estate, and a crown rent was then fixed on all the lands in Leinster, Munster, Connaught and Ulster, at the rate of 3d., 2¼d., 1½d. and 1d. respectively, per acre. The following persons in the County of Longford who had been deprived of their estates, were admitted by this declaration to their enjoyment again :—

Connell Farrell,* Camlisk; Lewis O'Farrol, Lieut-Col. Terence Ferall, John MacRory Farrell, Faghny Ferrall, Gerald Ferrall, Richard Farrell, John Farrell, Charles Ferrall, Sir Richard Barnewell, Francis Lord Aungier (Lord Longford).

No further effort was, however, made to restore all the confiscated property which belonged to the native chieftains; and true to the treacherous record of the Stuart family, Charles II. left his wretched subjects in Ireland to pine under the weight of their miseries.

In 1685, James II., the weak and vacillating monarch who lost his kingdom so easily, ascended the throne. From him the Catholics and the Irish expected relief ; nor would they have been disappointed were it not for the weak character of the King, and the powerful factions which barred the way to reform. Very little could be done, and at length, in 1688, the Protestants of England resolved to throw off their allegiance to James, and to set up a Protestant King in his stead. The big lords and fat squires, whose ancestors had robbed the monks and plundered the abbey lands of England, were afraid that if Catholicity were restored they would have to disgorge some of their ill-gotten possessions, and they were all so terrified at the bare idea of the return of Papacy, and the granting of the commonest principles of justice to their fellow-citizens, who demanded liberty of conscience and a free exercise

---

* His descendants are still holding some of the land to which he was restored in 1660.

L

of their religion, that they resolved to hurl from his throne the man who dared to go to a Mass or keep a Popish chaplain   Whilst James's conduct as a soldier and a statesman is decidedly the reverse of praiseworthy, certainly his heroism and fortitude in defence of what he prized most on earth—his religion—and his charity towards the ungrateful children who ruled on his downfall, compels even adverse critics to give their meed of praise; and if any one thing more than another contributed speedily to ruin him, it was the fact that his fervour in the Catholic cause " o'erleaped " itself, and precipitated the decision of the Protestants.   This was to invite to their assistance, as the saviour of Protestantism, the renowned " glorious, pious, and immortal " William of Orange.   William was just then after saving his own country from the attacks of the French, having vowed, it is said, that he would die in her " last ditch " to uphold Luther and the Bible.   To him was married Mary, daughter of James—even a more furious bigot than her amiable spouse—and they landed in England on November 5th, 1688. The unfortunate James, having been deserted by all his troops and highest officers, was taken prisoner in his own kingdom at Torbay, from whence he escaped to France on December 23rd, 1688.   Here he was received and sheltered by the French King, and, having been given a supply of men, arms, and money, he landed in Ireland on March 11th, 1689, to endeavour to recover at least that part of his kingdom.   The Irish Catholics at once flocked to his aid, and forgetting, as they are wont to do, the awful injustices heaped on them by his father and grandfather, professed their loyalty and devotion to him.   James marched straight to Dublin on landing, and on May 20th called a Parliament there, which is known as King James's Parliament.   This assembly, in which the County of Longford was represented by Roger Farrell and Robert Farrell, and the borough of Lanesborough by Oliver Fitzgerald and Roger Farrell, sat for six weeks, during which they passed Acts repealing all that had been done by Cromwell's Parliament and Charles II.'s Parliament, turning the Protestants out of all their lands got by confiscation, and reinstating the Catholic proprietors.

⋅ But in July 1690, James II. was defeated, as we all know, by his own cowardice at the battle of the Boyne, and the Protestants of Ireland, as well as England, succeeded in setting up a King to their liking. During the rebellion, the County Longford was invaded by a large party of Catholics, who besieged Lord Granard's castle, burned Newtownforbes and Killashee, and looted several country seats. The same year it was made a frontier English post, and large military forces were massed at Lanesborough, Rooskey, and Newtownforbes, in order to prevent the passage of the Shannon; and so, in Longford as elsewhere, ended the total subjugation of the Irish chieftains; the break-up of their clan system by Queen Elizabeth, the plantation of their country by James I. and Charles I.; the murder and massacre of thousands of their numbers by Cromwell; and, finally, the extinction of the last vestige of Irish liberty at the Boyne, on July 1st, 1690.

For the continuation of our county history we cannot look for better material than to turn to the journals of the Irish Houses of Parliament, which contain records of county events of considerable importance.

EXTRACTS FROM THE JOURNALS OF THE IRISH HOUSE OF COMMONS.

Date—5th Oct., 1692; 24th Dec., 1713.

Extracts of Petitions.

No. 4 —" Oct. 17th, 1692.—Petition of Mr Fergus Farrell, of Lanesborough, to be discharged negatived; charged in his place in the House with bearing arms under the late King James II. A letter from him produced, to which he refuses to own his handwriting; the same proved, and resolution adopted that he has been an active instrument against the Protestant and English succession and interest in Ireland; expelled the House—discharged, Oct. 31."

No. 78.—" David Cairnes, Esq., a Member, and others, the Protestant creditors of one Jas. Hewetson, of Springtown, pray for a bill to enable him to satisfy his debts.—Presented, Oct. 7th, 1695, and granted."

No. 140.—" Sir Robt. Newcomen, Bart., and others, of Counties Longford and Roscommon, pray for a bill to charge estates of Irish Papists for the cost of building a bridge across the River Shannon, at Lanesborough.—Petition presented, Oct 30, 1703; leave granted."

No. 295.—" Christopher Hewetson, a Member, wrote explaining that Sir George Lane, Knt., passed a certificate and letters patent of the manor of Rathline and Lisduffe, in the County of Longford, under *colour* of being a forfeited estate, and obtained a clause in the Act of Settlement for confirmation thereof, and, as a bill is now preparing for settling the possessions of those who derive under the Acts of Settlement and Explanation, praying that he may have a clause in the said bill to enable him to recover his said right.—Presented, 1695, Sept. 26. Referred to Committee appointed to prepare said heads (72). Leave to withdraw petition, and amend same, Dec. 3 " (129).

No. 346.—" Edward Davis, Esq., setting forth that Robert Sands, Esq., Collector in the County of Longford, distrained Irish lands for the three years' rent due to his Majesty from Easter, 1692, to Easter, 1695, contrary to the vote of this house, and forced payment, although the lands were waste at that time.—Presented, 1697, Sept. 24 (p. 208). Referred to a committee. Committee instructed. Petition sustained."

Longford Borough.

No. 3133.—" Roger Hall, Esq., stating he was unanimously elected for said borough, and an indenture of the election under the seal of the Corporation of said borough was duly executed; that the writ and return were lost, but that the counterpart of said indenture remains in the hands of the Sovereign of said Corporation, and praying relief.— Presented, 1757, Nov. 15 (34). Referred to Committee of Privileges and Elections. Order for hearing petition discharged, writ and return being found. Nov. 24."—(41), Vol. VI.

Longford County.

No. 3134.—" Sir James Nugent, Bart., complaining of an undue election and return of the Hon. Robert Pakenham for the County of Longford.—Presented, 1769, Nov. 8. Referred to Committee of Privileges and Elections. Poll-book and registry-book to be lodged with Clerk of the House, Nov. 10 (305). Late Sheriff and Clerk of the Peace to attend with the aforesaid books. Two returns presented. To lie on table. Sheriff examined relative to poll-book. Committee instructed to hear petition, Nov. 27. Dec. 23, Order, referring petition to committee, discharged."—Vol. VIII.

No. 3135.—"Sir James Nugent, Bart., complaining of an undue election and return for the County of Longford.—Presented, 1771, March 14. Committee instructed to hear petition, March 16. Petition withdrawn, May 8."

No. 329.—"Lord Baron Longford, for assistance to purchase a proportionable quantity of wheat to be stored in a granary, built by him for the use of the public.—Presented, 1763, Nov. 17. Referred to a committee. To meet forthwith.—Granted, Dec. 5."

No. 245.—"Sir Robert Newcomen, Bart., and others, of the Counties of Roscommon and Longford, for heads of a bill for charging estates of Irish Papists for rebuilding the Bridge of Lanesborough over the River Shannon.—Presented, 1703, Oct. 30.—Leave granted."

No. 3,739.—"James, Lord Viscount Lanesborough, for satisfaction for a scandalous case, written by Christopher Hewetson, a Member, which reflects on the honour of the petitioner's father and himself.—Presented, 1695, Dec. 2. Referred to a Committee for Laws. Case to be amended."

No. 3,098.—"Henry Fox and William Burgh, complaining of an undue election and double return for the Borough of Lanesborough.—Presented, 1715, Nov. 18. Referred to Committee of Privileges and Elections. Petition withdrawn, Nov. 29."

No. 3,101.—"Wentworth Harman and Robert Bray, Esq., complaining of an undue election and double return for said borough.—Presented, 1727, Dec. 8. Referred to Committee of Privileges and Elections. Instruction 'to committee · That the said Thomas Newcomen, who acted as Sovereign at the said election, is to lay before the House *all* books in his custody belonging to said borough (481). Also, all books in possession of William Burgh, who likewise acted as Sovereign at said election. Report, that *merit* of election were only in part heard, Jan. 24 (505). Instruction to proceed. Resolutions, that the petitioners be *not* admitted to go into the disqualifications of the Sovereigns for the Borough of Lanesborough before the year 1716, Feb. 2 (514). That petitioners be admitted to disqualify any burgess that voted for a magistrate at Lanesborough in the year 1716, so as they do *not* call in question the legality of any Sovereign before whom such burgess was elected and sworn. Thomas Marley, Esq., duly elected. Wentworth Harman, Esq., *not* duly returned. Robert Bray, Esq., *not* duly returned. Thomas Marley, Esq., duly elected. Thomas Burgh, Esq., duly returned.

We cannot do better at this stage than glance over the names of the men who represented the various boroughs and the county at large in " the old house." From a study of the names, it will be perceived that many of them were men who made their mark in the history of the country.

House of Commons, 1616—1660.

The names of Connell O'Farrell and John O'Farrell are recorded as having been the representatives of the County Longford from 1616 to 1660.

1661—1692.

Longford.—Henry Sankey, Adam Molyneux.

Ballinalee.—Henry Pierce, Baronet ; John Edgeworth.

Lanesborough.—Maurice Barklay, Edward Crofton.

There were no representatives for the County at large, nor for the Borough of Granard, in this Parliament.

1692—1713.

County.—Sir Robert Newcomen, Robert Choppin.

Longford.—Frederick Cuffe, John Nicolls.

• Granard.—Colonel Robert Smith, Sir Walter Plunkett.

Lanesborough.—Fergus Farrell (subsequently expelled for being a Papist), Humphrey Jervis, Thomas Handcock, elected to replace the Papist, Fergus Farrell.

Ballinalee.—Alexander Frazer, John Edgeworth.

August 27th, 1695

A Parliament sat on this date, when the representatives were :—

The County.—Sir R. Newcomen, Bart.; William Harman.

Longford Borough.—Colonel W. Wollesley, Captain J. Nicholls (died), Ambrose Aungier (elected instead).

Granard.—Walter Plunkett, John Percival.

Lanesborough.—Thomas Handcock, Richard Gardiner.

Ballinalee.—John Edgeworth, Captain J. Aghmooty.

10th February, 1704.

The County.—Sir Richard Newcomen, Anthony Sheppard.

Longford Borough.—Richard Levinge, Francis Edgeworth.

Granard.—John Percival, Wentworth Harman.

Lanesborough.—Nicholas Sankey, Henry Fox.

Ballinalee.—John Aughmooty, Ambrose Edgeworth.

5th May, 1709.

Same representatives, except the Borough of Longford, for which George Gore was elected in place of Francis Edgeworth, deceased.

19th May, 1710.—Same representatives.
9th July, 1711.— Do.   do.

1715—1730.

Parliament was dissolved, and a new Parliament summoned, which continued to sit, with a few changes, until 1730 ·—

County Longford.—Sir Thomas Newcomen, Anthony Sheppard.

Borough of Longford.—George Gore, Attorney-General; James MacCartney, jun.

Granard.—John Parnell, afterwards Sir John Parnell, and ancestor of the present illustrious Charles Stewart Parnell, M.P., leader of the Irish people; Jacob Peppard.

Lanesborough.—Henry Fox, William Burgh, Wentworth Harman, Robert Bray, William Burgh, and Robert Bray, elected to sit for other places.

Ballinalee.—Henry Edgeworth, Robert Edgeworth.

1717.—Same.
1719.—Same.

1723.

Longford Borough.—John Ffolliot, in place of George Gore, made Earl of Lanesborough.

Granard.—Charles Coote, in place of John Parnell.

1725.—Robert Jocelyn, in place of Jacob Peppard, deceased.

November 14th, 1727.

County Longford —Same representatives.
Longford Borough.—Michael Cuffe, Anthony Sheppard, sen.
Granard.—James MacCartney, John Ffolliot.
Lanesborough.—Thomas Marlay, Thomas Burgh.
Ballinalee.—Henry Edgeworth, Thomas Newcomen.

September 23rd, 1729.—Same representatives.

1731.

Lanesborough.—Anthony Marlay, in place of Thomas Marlay.

7th *October,* 1735.—Same representatives.
4th *October,* 1737.—Same representatives.

View of the Town of Granard from the Foot of the Moat.

9th October, 1739.

County Longford.—Arthur Newcomen, Arthur Gore.

Longford Borough.—Michael Cuffe, Richard Edgeworth.

Rest same.

> *6th October*, 1741.—Same representatives
> *4th October*, 1743.— Do.   do.

6th October, 1747.

Longford Borough.—Thomas Pakenham, elected in place of Michael Cuffe.

Other representatives same.

1753.

Ballinalee.—Hon. John Forbes, elected in place of Henry Edgeworth.

Other representatives same.

1757.

County Longford.—Henry Gore, in the room of Arthur Gore; sworn April 29th, 1757.

Longford Borough.—Roger Hall, sworn on the 24th November.

22nd October, 1761.

County Longford.—Robert Harman, John Gore.

Granard.—Edmund Malone, Robert Sibthorpe.

Lanesborough.—William Howard, John Hely Hutchinson, Henry Gore, elected in place of Hely Hutchinson, who, having been selected also for Cork, chose to sit for that borough.

Longford.—Thomas Newcomen, Joseph Hervey.

Ballinalee —Hon. J. Forbes (elected to sit for Mullingar), Charles Newcomen, Captain John Forbes.

22nd October, 1765.

County Longford.—Hon. Edward Michael Packenham, Ralph Fetherstone, Wentworth Parsons, elected in the room of Hon. E. M. Packenham, created Viscount Longford.

M

8th October, 1771.

County Longford.—Henry Gore, elected in place of Ralph Fetherstone.

Granard.—Jervaise Bushe, Richard Malone.

Lanesborough.—Mathew Carberry, E. Bellingham Swan.

Longford.—David LaTouche, Warden Flood.

Ballinalee.—Charles Newcomen, Ralph Fetherstone.

12th October, 1773.

Ballinalee.—Robert Jepson.

10th October, 1775.

County Longford.—Laurence Harman Harman.

18th June, 1776.

Granard.—Thomas Maunsell, John Kilpatrick.

Lanesborough —Robert Dillon.

Longford.— John Immodine.

Ballinalee.—Hon. J. Vaughan.

10th February, 1780.

Granard.—William Long Kinsman, in place of J. Kilpatrick.

Ballinalee.—Sackville Hamilton, in place of Sir Ralph Fetherstone.

14th October, 1783.

County Longford.—Laurence Harman Harman, Henry Gore.

Granard.—George Jephson, G. W. Molyneux.

Lanesborough.—David LaTouche, Robert Dillon, Cornelius Bolton.

Longford.—Hon. Thomas Packenham, Henry Stewart (elected to sit for Antrim), Hercules Rowley.

Ballinalee.—Sir Thomas Fetherstone, Nicholas Colthurst.

20th January, 1785.—Same.

19th January, 1792.

County Longford.—Laurence Harman Harman, Sir W. Gleadowe Newcomen.

Granard.—J. Ormsby Vandaleur, Thomas Packenham Vandaleur.

Lanesborough.—Gervaise Bushe, Stephen Moore.

Longford.—Hon. Thomas Taylor, Henry Stewart.

Ballinalee.—George Cavendish, John Taylor.

22nd January, 1795

County Longford.—Caleb Barnes Harman, in place of Laurence Harman Harman,

Lanesborough —William Smith.

Longford.—Thomas Pepper

21st August, 1797.

County Longford.—Sir Thomas Fetherstone, Sir W. Gleadowe Newcomen.

Granard.—G. Fulke Lyttleton, Ross Mahon.

Lanesborough.—Edmund Stanley, Richard Martin

Longford.—Hon. Thomas Packenham, Henry Stewart.

Ballinalee.—Richard Lovell Edgeworth, Hon. William Moore.

In the Irish House of Lords there were four peers who sat in virtue of patents of nobility for places in the County Longford. These were the Earls of Longford, Granard, Lanesborough and Annaly. As the private history of each of these families will appear further on, I do not deem it essential to the present subject to give extracts relating to their various acts in the gilded chamber of College-green. A few extracts will show as much of these as will be now necessary.

"In 1761, Lord Longford obtained leave of the House to petition the House of Lords for a public Granary at Longford"

"On the 16th February, 1789, the Earl of Longford was a dissentient on the motion, 'that in addressing the Prince of Wales, the Lords and Commons discharged an indispensable duty.'"

"In 1800 the Lord Granard, several times during the passing of the Act of Union of Great Britain and Ireland, vigorously protested against same, and was a dissentient at every stage up to the third reading of the Bill "

"On Monday, 27th January, 1766, the Right Hon John Gore, Attorney-General, was created first Lord Annaly, of Tenelick, County Longford. He was elected Speaker of the House of Lords in 1767, which position he held until his death in 1780. He was a vigorous opponent of the Volunteer movement."

Whilst many of the late events which are recorded in the foregoing extracts were occurring, the discontent of the Catholic inhabitants of Ireland was finding vent in the formation of that powerful secret society, the " United Irishmen ;" and before the century had closed, the time arrived when the last stand-up fight for Irish liberty took place. This was in 1798, when there broke out the desultory war, which our rulers are pleased to call a rebellion, and during which, on several occasions, the English felt a taste of that Irish chivalry which they had begun to despise. Strange as it may seem, it is nevertheless true, that it was in Longford County the great drama of the rebellion of 1798 was concluded.

The French Directory, at the solicitation of Wolfe Tone, who acted on behalf of the Irish Directory of the United Irishmen, determined to send an expedition of troops to Ireland, to assist the latter in their attempt to shake off the yoke of British thraldom. The United Irishmen rose in rebellion, as agreed among themselves ; but their rising was not simultaneous, neither was it organized ; and, to add to their misfortunes, the French expedition did not sail at the time the Dublin Directory expected. Consequently, the rising was crushed and past when the French commander, Humbert, sailed from Brest with his troops. Nevertheless, he landed in Killala early in August, captured Castlebar, and marched for Dublin The southern pass to the capital was closed at Athlone, and Humbert thought that by taking the northern route he would baffle pursuit, and bring a host with him who would strike terror to the hearts of the British. In both these expectations he was disappointed. The tyranny and oppression of the British soldiers and officers at the outset of the rebellion had crushed the spirit of the Irish peasantry, whose lives were daily sacrificed, homes burned, and crops destroyed, by the yeomen and soldiery; and so it was but the young and hardy men of each county who joined him. On the other hand, General Lake hung on his rear with a large force of troops, and Lord Cornwallis marched from Dublin with all the available troops in Leinster, to intercept Humbert in his route, so that when both armies effected a junction they were fully eighteen to one, Humbert's force not amounting to more than 2,000 men.

Humbert had marched from Coloopey to Boyle, thence to the north of Carrick-on-Shannon, where he crossed that river and halted at a small village called Cloone, in the County of Leitrim. Here, it is said, an English spy, called Neary, who had originally been a servant to a Mr. West, of Cloone, in the darkness of the night stole the chains of the French cannon; and, when about to move in the morning, there could be only some ropes got with which to bring along a few cannon, the major portion having to be left behind. It is but a very few days ago since I was told that the chains of Humbert's cannon are yet in the village of Cloone, in the possession of the Protestant gentleman there, to whose grandfather Neary had sold them. There are many thrilling tales told of this battle, and the names of a number of brave men who heroically distinguished themselves on the battle-field are held in profound veneration to this very day among the people of the County Longford. Such a one is Gunner M'Gee, whose services to the cause of Ireland at Ballinamuck were of the highest order. He was a soldier in the English artillery, and was present at the "Races of Castlebar" Here the inward promptings of a brave and noble heart inspired him to desert from the British ranks to those of his countrymen, and he became in the "rebel" (?) lines a tremendous aid to his brethren in many ways. At the battle of Ballinamuck he had charge of a cannon, which he used to such good purpose and aimed with such precision, that he twice confused the British ranks. At length his ammunition ran short, and he had not missiles to place in his gun In this extremity a number of the camp pots and kettles were smashed to pieces, and with these it was loaded. The British were advancing in heavy order, a massive column having just been ordered up to carry the day. But M'Gee, taking careful aim, fired his cannon with such precision that a lane of dead and dying was cut through the advancing host. This, however, was his last shot, for the British just then succeeded in capturing the other guns the French had, and they captured poor M'Gee, too, and strangled him as he bravely stood by the side of his faithful gun. It is related that there were two cousins of his at the gun at the last discharge, whose action was the bravest performed that day. When Magee was ready to fire, having just completed the loading, one of the stocks of a wheel broke, and the gun could not be fired, until these two cousins, stepping forward, propped it up with their backs whilst M'Gee applied the match. The discharge broke their spines, and their miserable state was soon put an end to when the gun was captured.

The following letters, written by British officers, who commanded at this battle, speak volumes for the humanity of the victors :—

" Ballina, October 3, 1798.

" My very dear Friend,—I was in Dublin the evening the express brought intelligence that the French had landed. I went the same day to Naas ; it was eleven o'clock at night when I arrived. You will admit that I had a great escape The army had marched ; I followed and overtook them at Frankfort. We marched from thence to Athlone, where we joined the Commander-in-Chief's grand army, destined for Castlebar. We then marched forward and encamped at a little village called Baltimore (Ballymore). The next evening we lay at Knock, on the side of a mountain. From that we proceeded to Tuam, and there encamped ; we were then ordered to join General Taylor's brigade on their march from Sligo ; our regiment (the Armagh) and the Reay Fencibles left Tuam Camp (consisting of 14,000 soldiers), and marched through Castlebar for Ballaghadereen, where we lay that night. Here it was that I met my brother with the Light Brigade from Blairs; you may conceive what I felt on the occasion. About two in the morning we marched from Swinford for Castlebar, but the French had given us the slip and went for Sligo; we encamped at Tubbercurry. The French and Limerick militia had a skirmish at Coolooney; many were killed on both sides; we lost two pieces of cannon. Same evening we lay at Drumahair. Our advanced guard pressed so hard after the French, that they left seven pieces of cannon and a great quantity of ammunition on the road; the road was dreary and waste, owing to their depredations, the houses being all plundered. Next day we marched upwards of twenty miles, and encamped near Leitrim. They attempted to break one of the bridges down, but the Hessians charged and killed many of them, which forced them to retire; the road was strewed with dead bodies. Near Cloon they drew up in line of battle, but on our advance they retreated towards Granard. At Ballinamuck they drew up again, and extended their line across a bog to prevent the cavalry from charging them, and planted their cannon on a hill to the left of the road, as it led through the bog; and in this order they awaited our approach. The Light Brigade attacked them first; our Light Company, after a few fires, leaped into their trenches, and a dreadful carnage ensued. The French cried for mercy. We ran for four miles before we could get into action, the men forgot all their troubles and fought like furies. We pursued the rebels through the bog; the country for miles was covered with their slain. We remained for a few days burying the dead; hung General Blake and nine of the Longford Militia. We brought 113 prisoners to Carrick-on-Shannon; *nineteen of them we executed in one day, and left the remainder with another regiment to follow our example,* and then marched to Boyle.—Yours," &c.

"Killeshandra, Sept, 1798.

My dear Brother,—God only knows my grief of mind for your present situation   You being still alive is a strong argument that the hearts of all men are in the hands of the Most High. Some days before the battle of Ballinamuck we were much alarmed here, although we little thought the French were so near us. The day previous to the battle our yeomen—horse and foot, Carrickgallon and Oakhill men, 106 in number—went to Ballinamuck, on an information that a vast number of rebels were there the day before; yet, after traversing the mountains, not a man could be seen; they returned by Ballinalee and Bunlahey. That evening, expresses from Ballinamuck informed us that the French were there. The yeomen of that place fled to Ballyconnel and Belturbet. The main body of the French lay in Cloon that night. A Lieutenant West had his horse shot under him while reconnoitring the enemy. The wounded beast carried his master two miles, when he fell; the helmet was also shot off the lieutenant's head. The French general and most of the officers agreed to take some rest at Cloon, giving orders that they should not be suffered to sleep more than two hours; the guard let them sleep four hours, by which time the English army came much nearer than the French expected. This was the place General Lake's vanguard skirmished with their rearguard, and from thence to Ballinamuck, four miles from Ballinalee, and four from Cloon. The French being closely pursued, prepared for an unavoidable battle. They formed on a hill to very great advantage, having a bog on their left, and a bog and lake on their right. Five flank companies, viz., the Dublin, Armagh, Monaghan, Tipperary, and Kerry, requested General Lake to let them mount behind the Hessians, Carabineers, and Roxburgh, &c., so ardent were they to overtake the enemy. This request was granted, and they soon came up with the foe. Seeing the enemy so advantageously posted, wisdom was needful on the part of our general. A column of our troops faced to the left, and marched behind an eminence; to this our artillery marched in front. The enemy had their cannon covered with pikemen, who were about to take our cannon under cover of our own smoke. General Lake, aware of their design, ordered the artillery to retreat to another hill, and finding his men so brave, he ordered his men to charge the French through the smoke. This they did, and, with a terrible war-shout, so overwhelmed the French

The Battlefield of Ballinamuck,

that they threw up their arms with caps on them, yielding themselves prisoners. Here I should observe that the whole of the French army was not engaged; four hundred and more remained concealed behind the entrenchments, and resolved by treachery to surprise our men. When attacking the rebels the point was to get them from this hold; a volley or two being fired, our men feigned to retreat. The end was answered; the French rushed out, and our soldiers as suddenly met them. Here the contest was desperate. In a little time the French fell down, offering up their arms, and as our men advanced to receive them, they treacherously arose and fired on our unguarded men, and then fell again on their knees. The enraged troops rushed in and killed numbers of them before they could be prevented. Thus they overpowered, disarmed, and made prisoners all the French, before the grand army arrived. The rebels, expecting no quarter, did all possible harm, fired many cannon-shot, but to no effect; they fled into a bog, *the whole of which was surrounded by horse and foot, who never ceased while a rebel was alive*—after which the Marquis marched off with his prisoners. They lay dead about 500. I went next day, with many others, to see them. How awful to see that heathy mountain covered with dead bodies, resembling at a distance flocks of sheep, for numbers were naked and swelled with the weather! We found fifteen of the Longford Militia among the slain. Our loss were twelve—two of which were Hessians, whom the yeomen took for French, and fired on."

Copy of a letter from Lieutenant-General Lake to Captain Taylor, Private Secretary to His Excellency the Lord Lieutenant, dated, " Camp, near Ballinamuck, September 8th, 1798 "

" Sir,—I have the honour to acquaint you, for the information of His Excellency the Lord Lieutenant, that finding upon my arrival at Ballaghy the French army had passed that place from Castlebar, I immediately followed them to watch their motions—Lieutenant-Colonel Crawford, who commanded my advanced corps, composed of detach-

N

ments of Hempesch's (?) and the 1st Fencible Cavalry, vigilance and activity, being so close upon their rear, that they could not escape from me, although they drove the country and carried with them all their horses.   After four days and nights' most severe marching, my column, consisting of the Carabineers, detachments of the 23rd Light Dragoons, the 1st Fencible Dragoons, and the Roxburg Fencible Dragoons, under the command of Colonel Sir Thomas Chapman, Lieutenant-Colonel Maxwell, Earl of Roden, and Captain Kerr; the 3rd Battalion Light Infantry, the Omagh, and part of the Kerry Regiment, the Reay, North-ampton and Prince of Wales' Fencible Regiments of Infantry, under the command of Lieutenant-Colonel Innes, of the 6th Regiment, Lord Viscount Gosford, Earl of Glandore, Major Ross, Lieutenant-Colonel Macartney, arrived at Cloon about seven this morning, where, having received directions to follow the enemy in the same line, whilst his Excellency moved by the lower road to intercept them, I advanced, having previously detached the Monaghan Light Company, mounted behind dragoons to harass their rear.   Lieutenant-Colonel Crawford, on coming up with the French rear-guard, summoned them to sur-render; but, as they did not attend to his command, he attacked them, upon which upwards of 200 French Infantry threw down their arms, under the idea that the rest of the corps would do the same thing. Captain Pakenham, Lieutenant-General of Ordnance, and Major-General Cladock arrived, upon which I ordered up the Third Battalion of Light Infantry, under the command of Lieutenant-Colonel Innes, and com-menced upon the enemy's position.   The action lasted upwards of half-an-hour, when, the remainder of the column making its appearance, the French surrendered at discretion.   The conduct of the cavalry was, on all occasions, highly conspicuous.   The Third Light Battalion, and part of the Armagh Militia (the only infantry that were engaged), behaved most gallantly, and deserve my warmest praise.   Lieutenant-Colonel Innes's spirit and judgment contributed much to our success.   To Briga-dier-General Taylor I have to return my most sincere thanks for his great exertions and assistance on this day; also to Lord Roden, Sir

Thomas Chapman, Major Kerr, and Captain Ferguson, whose example contributed much to animate the troops. I ought not to omit Lieutenant-Colonel Maxwell, Major Pakenham, and Captain Kerr, whose conduct was equally meritorious, and I feel infinitely thankful to all the commanding officers of corps, who, during so fatiguing a march, encouraged their men to bear it with unremitting perseverance. I cannot conclude my letter without expressing how much our success is to be attributed to the spirit and activity of Lieutenant-Colonel Crawford. I beg leave to recommend him as a most deserving officer.—I have the honour to be, &c.,

" G. Lake,

" Lieutenant-General."

Copy of the Lord Lieutenant's letter to the Duke of Portland, relative to the defeat of the French.

" St. Johnstown (Ballinalee),

" County Longford,

" 9th September, 1798.

" My Lord,—When I wrote to your Grace on the 5th, I had every reason to believe, from the enemy's movement to Drumahaire, that it was their intention to march to the North, and it was natural to suppose that they might hope that a French force would get into some of the bogs in that part of the country, without a succour of which kind every point of discretion for their march seemed equally desperate. I received, however, very early in the morning of the 7th, accounts from General Lake that they had turned to the right at Drumkeerin, and that he had reason to believe that it was their intention to go to Boyle or Carrick-on-Shannon, in consequence of which I hastened the march of the troops under my immediate command, in order to arrive before the enemy at Carrick, and directed Major-General Moore, who was at Tubbercurry, to be prepared, in the event of the enemy's movements to Boyle. On my arrival at Carrick, I found that the enemy had

passed the Shannon at Ballintra, where they attempted to destroy the
bridge , but General Blake followed them so closely that they were not
able to effect it.   Under these circumstances, I felt freely confident
that one more march would bring this disagreeable warfare to a conclusion; and having obtained satisfactory information that the enemy
had halted for that night at Cloone, I marched, with the troops at
Carrick, at ten o'clock on the 7th, to Mohill, and directed General Lake
to proceed at the same time to Cloone, which is about three miles from
Mohill—by which movement I should be able to join with General
Lake in the attack of the enemy, if they should remain at Cloone, or to
intercept their retreat if they should, as it was most probable, retire on
the approach of our army.   On my arrival at Mohill, soon after day-
break, I found that the enemy had begun to move towards Granard.
I, therefore, proceeded with all possible expedition to this place, through
which, I was assured, on account of a broken bridge, that the enemy
must pass on their way to Granard, and directed General Lake to
attack the enemy's rear, and impede their march as much as possible
without bringing the whole of his corps into action.   Lieutenant-General
Lake performed this service with his usual attention and ability; and
the enclosed letter, which I have just received from him, will explain
the circumstances which produced an immediate surrender of the
enemy's army.—I have the honour, &c.,

                    (Signed),   " CORNWALLIS."

A great many rebels were hanged after the battle.   Amongst them
was a man named Andrew Farrell, who, although some influence was
brought to bear on the authorities to save his life, was hanged out of a
spoke-wheel car.   When life was extinct, the body, and also the bodies
of several other men, were brought into a barn and stretched on a table
on some straw..   After a time, a Catholic soldier of the Longford
Militia, who knew Farrell, came into the barn, and seeing him, said:
" Poor Farrell, I'm sorry to see you there;" whereupon a yeoman
drew his clenched hand and smote Farrell's lifeless face, breaking his

nose, and forcing blood to the roof of the barn, whilst the Catholic soldier could do nothing to prevent this outrageous act lest he would bring himself into trouble. Farrell's friends afterwards attempted to bury the body in Longford graveyard, but the authorities prevented them; and they had to inter it at Newtownforbes.

Many tragic stories are told of this period of Longford history, which shall be done full justice to further on.

The Irish rebellion was crushed with a bloody hand; and amongst the counties whose people suffered for their share in it, few suffered more than Longford. The brutal treatment which they met with had the effect of driving them to the committal of many desperate deeds—deeds which to-day would cause a cry of indignation to arise all over the island, but which were then justified by the dragooning the people received. After the rebellion, for more than a period of twenty years, no Papist's life was safe in Longford County. There arose a class of men, the leaders of the yeomanry, who "spotted" Croppies for execution day by day as regularly as if the life they took was that of a dog or wolf It was during those days that the horrors of the Cromwellian era were revived in Ireland; that floggings and hangings were as certain to follow an assizes as the sun rose in the heavens at day-dawn. Above all others who distinguished themselves in ferocity towards the Papists were the " denouncing parsons " of that age. These men went about amongst the people on their religious calling, and woe to the Croppy who treated any of them with disrespect—a short shrift and a long rope was his reward. Was it any wonder, that under this state of things, a secret society would spring up which wreaked its vengeance on yeomen, denouncers, and exterminating landlords, as opportunity occurred. In those days the Irish tenant-farmers were the veriest slaves to their landlords. Dare one of them vote at an election contrary to the wishes of his lordship's bum-bailiffs, and his tenure of house and lands was short indeed thereafter. On the other hand, the National cause had an equally imperative claim on him, and between the both his lot was far from being a happy one. It was surprising how in those days people managed to get along ; and yet there were fought then fights for faith and fatherland, compared to which the fights of to-day are but toy-playing.   At length the oppressed Papists took heart of grace, and a leader being found in the person of Daniel O'Connell, they rallied to a man around him, and in 1829 the Catholic Relief Bill gave them a hold in their country which they had not possessed from the middle of the sixteenth century.   Is it necessary to say more ?   The history of Ireland's advancement since then is well known to every school-boy.   In the varying phases of success and defeat, prosperity and distress, Longford has, I am glad to say, borne an honourable part.   There are inside its borders men of as sterling qualities of head and heart for the welfare of their country as in any county in Ireland, whilst the vast mass of its 60,000 people are in active sympathy and support of the cause which has for its watchword at home and abroad,

GOD SAVE IRELAND.

APPENDIX—PART I.

ECCLESIASTICAL HISTORY OF THE COUNTY LONGFORD

THE County of Longford is within the episcopal jurisdiction of the diocese of Ardagh, which also extends into parts of the Counties of Westmeath, Roscommon, Leitrim, and Sligo. The ancient name of this diocese was Conmaicne Ardagha Hy Bruin, a title meaning that the diocese was in the territory of Conmac, whose name has been referred to in the preceding pages. The diocese was founded by St. Patrick, in 454. St. Patrick appointed St. Mel, his nephew, who died in 488, as first bishop. It is told traditionally that St. Mel was a very humble man who chose, by his humility and patience, to convert the people of the diocese of which he was first pastor to the true Gospel; and his staff, which he carried about with him in his missions, is preserved among the many old articles of antiquity belonging to the county. St. Mel worked as a labourer in the fields during the day, and prayed, like his uncle, St. Patrick, during the night; and at his death he was interred in his own church, in the town of Ardagh The remains of this church prove it to be, if of any height, a most formidable erection. It is enclosed in the churchyard of Ardagh, immediately behind the Protestant Church, and the ruins are somewhat considerable, measuring fully thirty feet long by twenty feet broad. It is composed of several immensely large blocks of rock, each fitting one on top of the other, as though chiselled by the stonecutter, although at this time stonecutters were not procurable. Some of these blocks of stones are fully ten feet long, and could not weigh less than some tons. One stone, which hangs on a natural pivot over the entrance, is likely from its apparently dangerous position, and the rocking which ensues on the slightest touch, to cause the visitor some uneasiness as to how to enter the building; and yet old men will tell him that that very stone has hung in that very position during their own and their sires' recollections, and has never stirred either in storm or sunshine. The entrance-door to this most venerable ruin is low, and the few windows extant are of the lancet description common to such buildings in old times, when the art of glazing was unknown; and yet, this is the old Cathedral of Ardagh, and underneath are interred the remains of the first bishop of its diocese, and several saints of Holy Church.

History does not contain any reference to the monastery erected in Ardagh, except that, in 488, St. Melchuo, a friar of the monastery of Lerha, and a brother to St. Mel, became abbot and bishop of the diocese.

We find in Colgan's "*Acta Sanctorum*" it is said :—"St. Patrick left Mel in Ardachadh to the east, and his sister in Drumcheo, to the west of the mountain called Brigh Leith (now Slieve Golry), which lies between both places." She was, according to Colgan, St. Brigid, the present patroness of Ardagh, but is not to be confounded with the celebrated patroness of Kildare. It was of her that the false story was told, which will be found related in another portion of this book.

As regards the erection of the cathedral, a legend (not a very probable one though) is handed down amongst the peasantry about St. Patrick. It is told that he arrived in Ardagh during the night, and, being guided by the apostolic spirit, commenced immediately to erect a building suitable to the worship of God. During this erection it is believed that he was assisted by preternatural power to fit the immense blocks of stones before-mentioned into the walls; but, having fallen short of material wherewith to complete his work, he searched about until he found some loose stones lying beside a dwelling which he proceeded to remove. During the course of removal the inhabitant of the dwelling, who happened to be a very cross old woman, wakened, and immediately putting out her head, demanded, in the name of the d——, what was there? St. Patrick answered that it was a servant of the Lord God, and bade her hold her evil tongue; then, deeming his work desecrated, he abandoned it. This legend, however, seems improbable,

RUINS OF ST. PATRICK'S ANCIENT CHURCH AT ARDAGH, BUILT IN 454, A.D.

considering that St. Mel was appointed by him as bishop about this time, and that the cathedral was used for religious purposes for hundreds of years afterwards.

The abbey, or monastery, over which St. Mel was first placed, was called an Abbey of Regular Canons, which existed for at least a period of five hundred years, during which time its abbots were generally Bishops of Ardagh. The dress of the monks of this order was a long black cassock, with a white rochet, or surplice, over which was a long black cloak and hood. Archbishop Usher says that St. Mel was a scholar of rare eminence, and that he wrote a learned treatise on the virtues and miracles of the patron of Ireland. Except, however, for the note made of the accession of St. Melchuo to this see in 488, no further mention is made of this abbey, or diocese, until 741, when it is recorded that St. Beochuill, Abbot and Bishop of Ardagh, died in his monastery and was interred there. It is also probable that St. Melchuo, who was St. Patrick's old master, was interred here, so that in the venerable ruins above described no less than three saints rest. It is right, therefore, that Ardagh would receive due credit for its remarkable sanctity in these early ages of Christianity, and that it should give name to the diocese Very little further mention is made of the Bishops of Ardagh until 1157, according to Keating, and 1152, according to Haverty, in which year was held the celebrated Synod of Kells, in which the Papal authority was represented by a legate for Ireland, and in which were appointed four archbishops for Armagh, Cashel, Tuam and Dublin, and the limits of every diocese in Ireland fixed. In this most celebrated council, over which the Bishop of Kilmore and Cardinal John Papiron presided as Pope's legates, the diocese of Ardagh was represented by Macraith O'Morain, bishop; and the diocese of which he was chief pastor was then placed, and has since remained, under the archiepiscopal jurisdiction of Armagh. In 1255 Brendan Magodaig, Bishop of Ardagh, was interred in the Abbey of Deirg, at the churchyard now called Abbey Dearg; and no further mention is made of Ardagh until 1492, when William O'Farrell was made bishop, and held, at the same

o

time, the important position of Chieftain of Annaly, and, in the discharge of his functions as the latter crossed the Shannon in the year 1504, for the purpose of assisting The Geraldine to wage war on the Burkes of Clanrickard. Had this warlike prelate lived in the days of the Irish Confederacy, he would, in all probability, have been a second Heber Mahon, or as the Bishop of Artois, in France, who, when taken prisoner in battle, appealed to the Pope to save him, and concerning whom, on hearing of his appeal, King Richard I. sent his coat of mail to the Pope, with the words : "See whether this be thy son's coat or not." I cannot explain how this clerical chieftain of Annaly was found in the English camp, except that, as MacWilliam Burke, surnamed the Red Earl, was a man of violent and ferocious temper, and clearly endeavoured to set himself up for King of Ireland, whereas he himself was of Anglo-Saxon extraction, O'Farrell deemed it his duty to assist in his subjugation; or, on the other hand, as his territory did not lie far from Burke's, the latter may have, as frequently happened in those days, devastated Annaly, and hence its chieftain wanted to return the compliment. The following passage from Haverty's History of Ireland may give the most satisfactory explanation to the reader :—

"A.D. 1504.—For some time an inveterate warfare had been carried on between MacWilliam Burke of Clanrickard, called Ulick III., and Melaghlin O'Kelly, the Irish Chief of Hy-Many. Burke was the aggressor and the more powerful, and this year he captured and demolished three of O'Kelly's castles in Galway, so that the Irish Chief, on the brink of ruin, had recourse to the lord lieutenant, Earl Kildare, for assistance. The latter mustered a strong army and crossed the Shannon. He was joined by Hugh Roe O'Donnell and his son, O'Connor Roe, MacDermott of Moylurg, Magennis, MacMahon and O'Hanlon; O'Rielly; the Bishop of Ardagh (who was then the Chief of the O'Farrells of Annaly); O'Connor Faley, the O'Kellys, and by all the forces of the north, except the O'Neills of Leath Cinna. In this battle Burke was defeated, with a loss of 2,000 men, and O'Kelly was restored to his possessions. The battle was fought at Knocktow, in Galway, on August 19th, 1504."

I append as fully as I can a list of the Bishops of Ardagh, from which it appears that at least half-a-dozen O'Farrells ruled the See of St. Mel almost in succession. Of these men, two, as has been said, were both Chieftains of Annaly and Bishops of Ardagh, and such of them as were not of blue blood were monks of some Order.

COMPLETE LIST OF THE BISHOPS OF ARDAGH, FROM THE EARLIEST DATE TO THE PRESENT DAY.

Name			Consecrated	Died
St. Mel (St. Patrick's Sister's Son) ...			—	457
St. Melchuo (St Patrick's old Pagan Master)		—		488
St. Beochuill ...	...	...	—	741
Cerli ...	..	...	..	—	1048
Macraidh O'Morainn	..	...	1150	1161
Christian O'Eatach	..	..	1172	1179
O'Firlenan	...	...	—	1187
O'Heslenan	..	..	...	—	1189
Adam O'Murray ...	..	...	—	1217
Robert ..	...	...	1217	1224
Simon M'Grath ..	.	..	1224	1230
Joseph Magodaig	...	...	1230	1231
Jocelyn O'Fairmaig	...	...	1233	1237
Brendan Magodaig	...	...	1238	1251
Miles Dunstable	..	.	1256	1288
Mathew O'Heathey	...	...	1290	1322
Robert, a Monk .	...	...	1322	—

Transferred to Clonfert.

John Magoie ...	...	...	1324	1343
Owen O'Farrell	...	..	1347	1367
William M'Casey	...	...	1367	1373

Name	Consecrated	Died
Charles O'Farrell	1373	1378
John O'Freyne	1378	1394
Gilbert O'Brady	1396	1400
Adam Lyons	1400	1416
Cornelius O'Farrell	1418	1424
Richard O'Farrell, a Cistercian Monk	1424	1443
MacShamridan (modernized Sheridan)	1445	1458
Cormac, a Monk	1460	1470
John, a Monk	1470	1479
William O'Farrell, Chieftain of Annaly	1479	1516
Thomas O'Comgall	1517	1518
Roderick O'Malone	1518	1540
Richard O'Farrell	1542	1553
Patrick M'Mahon	1553	1570
Richard Brady (transferred to Kilmore)	1573	1580
Edmond Maguire (transferred to Armagh)	1580	1588
Edmond M'Gauran (transferred to Armagh)	1588	—

Interregnum of sixty years, during which no bishop's name is recorded.

Patrick Plunkett	1647	—

Exiled the same year; after seven years' exile was made Bishop of Meath.

Oliver Casey	1647	—

Transferred to Dromore, 1670.

MARTYRDOM OF LONGFORD CLERGY.

It was at this time that the full fury of religious persecution burst on Longford, resulting in the capturing and murdering of every regular clergyman the bigoted and fanatical Puritans could lay hold of. We shall therefore interrupt our episcopal list, in order to insert a particular account of the cruel death of two Dominican clergy seized in the Dominican Convent at Longford:—

, The Rev. Fathers Laurence O'Farrell and Bernard O'Farrell, O.P., appear to have been brothers, and were of the ancient family of O'Farrell. Of Father Laurence, Dominick de Rosario remarks, that he was educated at Lisbon, and was subsequently Prior of their college there. De Burgo says that Father Bernard was Predicator Generalis of the Order. De Burgo and Fontana give the following account of their martyrdom :—

"They were seized at early morn, whilst praying in the church of their native convent, Longford, which had been abandoned by the brethren on account of the violence of the persecution. Father Bernard was at once overwhelmed by the persecutors with more than four-and-twenty deadly wounds, whereof he expired; yet lingered long enough to receive the last Sacraments from another of our Fathers before he died; and this he himself had foretold. Brother Laurence they dragged, wounded, before the governor, and on discovering that for the faith, and in obedience to the authority of the Nuncio, he had joined the Catholic army, he was condemned to death. He was to have been executed on the following day, and joyfully awaited his fate, but by the intercession of some friends it was deferred for three days. This was most grievous to Laurence, who blamed his intercessors, and spent the whole three days in prayers and tears, beseeching God *not* to suffer him to lose the palm of martyrdom. At length he obtained his desire, and from the top of the ladder he addressed an eloquent exhortation to the Catholics; then placing the rosary round his neck, and holding a crucifix in his right hand, and bidding the people farewell, he blessed them, and meekly folding his hands under the scapular, submitted himself to the executioner. When the executioner, after placing the cord round his throat, pushed him off the ladder, whilst hanging, he drew both his hands from under his scapular, and raised the cross on high in both as the emblem of his triumph. The heretical governor was so much struck, that he allowed his body to be given to the Catholics and solemnly interred by them, and gave a safe conduct for the clergy to attend, fearing lest otherwise there might be tumults."

Another Father Laurence O'Farrell, O.P., is mentioned who also was an *alumnus* of the Convent of Longford, and studied at Prague, in Bohemia, but read his philosophy in Rome, with the Irish Dominicans, in the Convent of SS. Sixtus and Clement, and theology with the English Dominicans, in the House of SS John and Paul. He thence proceeded to England, and, whilst discharging the duties of an apostolic missionary, was seized and confined in a most strict prison in London, where he suffered much for more than a year. At length, by the favour of God, he was set free, and proceeded to Belgium, where he patiently bore a long illness. He returned to England, and was again imprisoned, but was sent as a German into Portugal with the Archduke Charles, afterwards Emperor of the Germans. From thence he took an opportunity of going to Spain, where he piously died, serving as a chaplain to Berwick's regiment, in 1708. A beautiful account of his death is given in the Rinuccini MSS.

The Rev. Anthony O'Farrell, O.S.F., was taken, whilst preaching, by the Cromwellians, at Tulsk, in Roscommon, in the castle of Sir Ulysses de Burgo, and immediately hung, A.D. 1652.—Bruodin.

The Rev. Christopher O'Farrell died in prison, about 1664, for the defence of the authority of the Pope. Whilst in prison he was obliged to lie on the bare earth, the luxury of a bed being denied him.

From 1670 to 1710 an interregnum of forty years occurred, during which there was no bishop, owing to the severity of the penal laws and the general confusion in the affairs of the kingdom. It is recorded that Father Cornelius Gaffney, who had represented the diocese of Ardagh in the Catholic Confederation Council, ruled the diocese for some years; but the date of his death is not given.

Name			Consecrated	Died
Ambrose O'Connor	...	...	1710	1738
Anthony Blake ...	...	...	1738	1758
Dr. O'Mulligan ...	..	.	1758	1770
Dr. Brady ...		.	1770	1787
John Cruise ...	.	.	1788	1807

Name			Consecrated	Died
John M'Gauran ...	..	..	1815	1829
William O'Higgins	...	...	1829	1853
John Kilduff ...	...	...	1853	1867
Neal M'Cabe ...	...	...	1868	1870
George Conroy ...	...	...	1871	1878
Bartholomew Woodlock ...	...		1879, still living	

Between the years 741 and 1048, no name of any bishop can be found; but whether this arises from the loss of manuscripts bearing on the subject, or the neglect of contemporary chroniclers to record them, is a mere conjecture. About this time, however, occurred the Danish invasion of Ireland, which lasted for a period almost corresponding to the interregnum referred to; and it may be that during the confusion consequent on the many dire calamities which then befell the Irish people, their churches were overthrown and their bishops killed or exiled; or worse still, perhaps they were not appointed at all. History tells that those were days of great disturbance and disorder; and that no king, prince, or chieftain was sure of his life or property for a longer period than his sword was able to defend it. If such a state of things existed among the warlike elements of the nation, it is not unreasonable to expect that worse would exist in the ecclesiastical world, where peace was men's vocation.

Father Cornelius Gaffney was Vicar-General of the diocese during a great part of the time of the Cromwellian and Restoration persecutions, and is said to have been an eloquent preacher and a learned theologian. He was, on account of these great gifts, chosen at an early age to represent the diocese of Ardagh at the Confederation of Catholics, held in Kilkenny from 1640 to 1649, and in this capacity was elected a member of the Council of the Confederation, which was the virtual Parliament of Ireland for a period of ten years. It was during the continuance of this glorious assembly that Owen Roe O'Neill won the battle of Benburb, much to the mortification of Monroe—the boasted Scottish general. But it is sad—very sad, indeed—to speak of those days, for it recalls too vividly to the mind of a reader of history the inglorious termination of the Confederation and the loss of the Irish cause; whilst soon after came Cromwell and the horrors of his era, and Ireland was left a desert waste—murder, massacre, and transplantation having left the country, from the Shannon to the Boyne, a "field of human bones," as Lord Deputy Sidney, an English soldier, once phrased it.

With the era of the Volunteers came to the See of Ardagh a venerated and holy bishop, named Dr. Cruise, who ruled the diocese for a period of 19 years—during which it taxed a Roman Catholic bishop's endurance to the utmost to hold his own against the host of parsons and tithe-proctors who covered the country. Dr. Cruise was a native of the town of Longford, and his relatives had a shop in Bridge-street. The last of them died about thirty years ago. His remains were interred in Ballymahon. He was succeeded by a Dr. M'Gauran, or M'Govern, who is remembered by inhabitants of the neighbourhood to have been a fine big man, with a noble and majestic cast of countenance, and a gait which would do credit to a king. He died shortly after the Emancipation Act. To him succeeded a bishop whose life belongs rather to the political than the ecclesiastical history of Longford. This was William O'Higgins. This Bishop of Ardagh was descended in the paternal line from the Higginses of Mayo, whence his father migrated to Longford at an early age. He was related to a late bishop of Achonry, the learned Dr. M'Nicholas, and his mother, Elizabeth Tyrrell, was a near relative of the ancient family of O'Connell, of Cranary, in the County of Longford. His maternal family were remarkable for talent, particularly in poetry; and the songs of Peter Roe O'Connell may still be heard sung in the pathetic Gaelic by the milkmaid, as she passes the ruins of the old house at Cranary. The poet, George Nugent Reynolds, was a grandson of his, and worthily maintained the glories of the family. Peter and Harry O'Connell, also grandsons to Peter Roe, were killed at Granard in 1798, as they were leading on the insurgents; and local traditions teem with anecdotes of their bravery.

THE ANCIENT CHURCH OF CLUAN-DA-RATH.

William O'Higgins was born in 1794, and having been taught Irish and English by his mother, he was placed under the tuition of an itinerant classical teacher, concerning whose pedantic eloquence and high-flown Latin the bishop used often to tell funny anecdotes, for, as was then the custom, the tutor usually wore a red bag wig, which was never in its own place, and was always causing the wearer a world of trouble. When but nineteen years of age, he left Longford and adjourned to Paris, to pursue his classical studies in a Parisian seminary, and on the peace of 1815, he, in company with several other students, waited on the Duke of Wellington, and obtained from him the re-opening of the Irish College in Paris, as well as the restoration to it of many of its ancient bourses; and he entered its walls, not as a student, but as a professor.

Under date 1815, the following entries appear in an old diary kept by Dr. O'Higgins at Paris.—

"1815, March 20th.—Napoleon sailed from the island of Elba and landed in France on the same day. Then, marching on without any resistance, arrived in Paris on 20th, about half-past nine o'clock at night, where he was received by the people, particularly the soldiers, with loud acclamations.

"March 22nd.—Have gotten a plain view of him and his minister, Bertrand, from a window of the palace opposite the Luxembourg gardens.

"March 29th.—Got a full and plain view of Napoleon from the above-mentioned place, where he was waited on by a great multitude, all crying, ' Vive l'Empereur.'

"June 7th.—On the same day got a full view of Napoleon, his two brothers, Joseph and Lucian, all three dressed in their imperial robes; his uncle, Cardinal Fesch, and Cardinal Cambaceres, brother to the aforesaid Cardinal, and many more nobles—all of whom rode in coaches, drawn by six bay horses, from the royal palace to the Legislative Court, and that wherein the Emperor road was drawn by eight milk-white horses. His coach was most magnificent to be beheld, on the top

P

of which was a crown of gold about five feet round, on the top of which crown was an eagle of middle size made of solid gold. The body was deeply gilded. The body (of the coach) was deeply gilded, and all other parts of it, together with the harness, was proportionately grand. The number of the coaches consisted of twenty, none of which was much inferior to that of the Emperor in grandeur.

"June 16th.—Commenced the famous battle of Mount St. Jean, where the English and Prussians, with united forces, fought against Napoleon.

"June 19th.—On the 19th it terminated in favour of the English, who may be justly said to have gained the field as much by the bravery of the soldiers as the remarkable generalship of their noble commander, Wellington.

"July 8th.—I have seen the Prussians entering Paris. Have gotten a full view as they entered, and also along the quays and other parts of the city where they were stationed. Have also seen some of the English, viz.:—O'Neill, from Carrick-on-Shannon, in Ireland, and O'Farrell, from Dublin, who fought at Mount St. Jean and gave me the above account of it. On the same day, about five o'clock, I have seen His Majesty Louis XVIII. entering Paris, attended by several thousands of French gentlemen, who volunteered to protect him during his late absence from Paris. He was eagerly received by the people, who repeatedly, with all their might, cried ' *Vive le roi.*'

"20th.—Have seen in the 5th division of the English camp Malachi M'Garry, from Drumlish, who fought in the battle of Mount St. Jean, and gave me a particular account of it; also saw Peter Creegan, of Drumlish; Owen O'Reilly, of Monaduff; and O'Reilly, of the Rocks of Bohey, who were in the same camp after standing the battle.

"December 14th.—Mr. M'Cann, of Longford, received a letter from his brother, informing him of the death of Rev. Michael O'Farrell, who was (as is supposed) either killed by his own horse at Rooskey, or died of an apoplectic fit."

The above extracts will show that his lordship saw some of the principal events with his own eyes which took place in fickle Paris during the stormy days of 1815. The last extract is given simply to record an event which has previously been unknown. These extracts show the grasp of mind possessed by his lordship, and his extraordinary descriptive powers of such things; for these limited descriptions of so important events are more eloquent, in the opinion of the writer, than volumes from a critic.

William O'Higgins was, by a special licence, ordained priest on September 20th, 1817, after a remarkably brilliant student's career, in which he several times distinguished himself in his examinations before the highest dignitaries of the French Church; and, in the course of receiving his orders, he went through the ceremonies in company with several hundred ecclesiastics, many of whom afterwards became distinguished men. The Theses he sustained, also, during the course of his public examinations were remarkable for their vigour, terseness and clearness, for which at the time he was publicly congratulated.

After his ordination, he wrote a letter to the then Bishop of Ardagh, Right Rev. Dr. M'Govern, asking his permission to go out to Australia as vicar-general to its new bishop; but this request was, for good reasons of its own, refused by Dr. M'Govern. After spending eight years in constant hard work at Paris, his health began to decline. He set out for Rome, passing through Vienna, where he stayed a short time *en route;* and having reached Rome, where his health returned to him, he continued his studies there for a period of five years, spent alternately as a student to some and a teacher to others, and subsequently he could boast of having taught no less than twenty-five who became afterwards bishops. Having taken out his degree of D.D. in 1825, after a brilliant examination which lasted eight days, he returned to Ireland early in 1826, and succeeded in winning the important post of Professor of Dogmatic Theology in Maynooth College; and scarcely had he been a month in the office, when he appeared before the King's Commissioners to give evidence on the working of the Maynooth College

system.   His replies to all the questions then put to him, were the most
accurate and profound uttered in modern days.

On November 30th, 1829, he was consecrated Bishop of Ardagh,
and soon after his accession to the episcopate he commenced the erection of that noble cathedral which was completed by his successors, and
which will for ever claim, as it is justly entitled to claim, to be the
grandest and most stupendous erection of any similar building in Ireland.   In the councils of the Irish Hierarchy, Dr. O'Higgins held an
important place ; and such was the confidence that his brother prelates
had in his diplomacy and learning, that whenever an Irish question was
to be represented at a foreign court, he was always selected as their
envoy.   In this capacity he more than once travelled to Brussels and to
Rome on the question of Irish education.

As an Irish patriot, Dr. O'Higgins stood far in advance of the other
prelates of his day.   He was an ardent Repealer from the start of that
great agitation, which reached its climax in 1843, and was most intimate with the great Liberator, Daniel O'Connell.

Sir Charles Gavan Duffy says, in one of the notes to his "Young
Ireland," that the Bishop of Ardagh would have been a dashing
soldier had fortune so circumstanced him, and contrasts him with the
great Irish prelate who, in 1641, upheld the drooping hearts of the
Confederated Catholics by his voice, his pen, and his arm—Heber
MacMahon.

A monster demonstration in support of the popular demand for a
Repeal of the Union was held at Mullingar on the 14th of May, 1843,
which was one of the greatest gatherings addressed by O'Connell.   At
this meeting two bishops addressed the people—Dr. Cantwell, of Meath,
and Dr. O'Higgins, of Ardagh.   The address of the Bishop of Ardagh
was as fiercely patriotic in tone as the sword speech of Meagher.

A French writer, in the idiom of his language, says : " Monsieur
O'Connell had difficulty to restrain his enthusiasm whilst the glowing
words of the prelate electrified his audience."   The following is a rude
translation of Bishop O'Higgins' words on that great occasion:—"Gentle-

men," said he, " the merits of the noble body of dignitaries of which I
have the honour of being the most humble and most unworthy representative, have been already so well explained by the Liberator of Ireland, and by many other speakers, that I find myself released from
making reference to it. I will strive to tell you the way in which the
hierarchy regards this question of Repeal of the Union. I can affirm
in the most positive manner that every Roman Catholic bishop in Ireland, without exception, is a zealous advocate of this Repeal. I know
well enough that you have room to believe already that your bishops
are with you. Well, I come to announce it formally to you. All the
Roman Catholic bishops have pronounced in favour of your agitation ;
and from one end of Ireland to another we are all advocates of Repeal.

"I should, perhaps, guard myself in these observations ; but I do
not wish to sit down without explaining the means of which the bishops
could dispose, and which they would certainly use, if the ministry which
presides over the destinies of our country would dare to take against us
measures of harshness. As for me, I defy all the ministers of England
to stop the agitation in my diocese.

"My friends, if they want to filch from us the light of day, if they
want to hinder us from meeting in an open field, we will retire to our
churches and our chapels, and there we will preach no other doctrine
than that of Repeal. We will thus make Repealers in spite of England.
If they besiege our churches, if they sow spies amongst our brethren,
we will prepare the people for the result ; and if they make us ascend
the scaffold in dying for the cause of our country, we will bequeath our
wrongs to our successors. Let the ministry try it if they dare. But,
Irishmen, these fellows are too cautious ; they are too well determined
to continue their insidious schemes to furnish to us an occasion of dying
for our country. They will not do it ; and hence I have reason to say
that the bishops and the people of Ireland hold in their hands, despite
all the obstinacy of English ministers, the necessary power to counter-
act their designs, and to make triumphant Repeal of the Union in spite
of their resistance. Gentlemen, I am only an humble man—I am

nothing. Not only do I belong to the people, but more—I am proud to proclaim it—I belong to the most persecuted class of the people. I say it with pride, I owe nothing to any aristocrat on earth, except profound contempt, which I profess for every vicious aristocrat who forgets his mission and abuses his power.

" Gentlemen, several members of the episcopal body have not been able to be present here. Some have been detained by infirmities, others by indispensable duties—some of them are stretched on their bed of sickness; but 1 believe I can speak officially, and say without exaggeration, that not only are the bishops advocates of Repeal, but more, that they ardently join in all the sentiments I have expressed. I thank you, in their name and my own, for the flattering words spoken in praise of the episcopate, and in their name, also, I assure you that you can count on us as long as Ireland has a grievance."

For this splendidly patriotic speech at Mullingar, the English Press and the Anti-Irish Irish Press rabidly attacked him, and continued for months to shriek to the Government for his arrest or prosecution; but he had too fiercely thrown down the gauntlet for the British ministers to take it up, and so they contented themselves with setting one of the meanest and most pitiful members of the " vicious aristocracy " to revile his lordship before the British Senate on his obscurity; but O'Connell flew to the bishop's defence, and so mercilessly lashed the mean creature, that he slunk for ever from public gaze. The immortal Liberator on that occasion also delivered an address on the merits of the Bishop of Ardagh, which as a piece of oratory ranks first amongst his performances.

Shortly afterwards the great Repeal Meeting of Longford was held in the main street of the town, when Dr. O'Higgins, addressing the people on the subject of his recent deliverance at Mullingar, said he would ever remain true to the opinions he there expressed. He said :—

" A member of the House of Lords has spoken of my obscurity ; but I will teach him that in this obscurity I have enough of light to perceive the darkness in which are plunged those who attack me. Yes, I repeat what I said at Mullingar—whenever I shall see the possibility of rescuing one Irishman from his misfortunes, I shall ever be found in the breach.   This is why I demand Repeal of the Union. "

On many similar occasions Dr O'Higgins announced his firm determination on the question of Repeal, and there is every right to believe that had O'Connell recourse to arms to enforce his just demand, the Bishop of Ardagh would not be the least among his lieutenants; but everyone knows how the Repeal Agitation failed, and how the large-hearted leader died of a broken heart at Genoa, on his way to Rome. Dr. O'Higgins was then a prey to those fits of illness which from this date incessantly attacked him until his death.   The death of O'Connell completely disarmed him of all his hopes for Erin's freedom, and it was a common subject of discussion that after '48 the Bishop of Ardagh never appeared on a political platform.   He devoted the remainder of his life to the completion of his cathedral, and to the raising of what might be called a national testimonial to erect a fitting temple to God in the centre of Ireland; and at length, on the 3rd of January, 1853, he passed peacefully away, leaving behind him the memory of a saintly bishop, a patriotic Irishman, and an honest man—"the noblest work of God."   He was then in the sixty-third year of his age and the twenty-fourth of his episcopate, and was interred in the chapel of Ballymahon, whence, on the completion of the Cathedral of Longford, he was removed for burial in the vaults (as it was said) by his own last wish, in 1868.

The Right Rev. John Kilduff succeeded.   He had been a Vincentian friar, and was selected, it was believed, through the influence of the chapter of his Order in Rome.   Early in the year 1848 he was consecrated coadjutor to Right Rev. Dr. O'Higgins, whom he succeeded. Dr. Kilduff was the son of humble parents, his father being steward to Lord Kilmaine at Athlone.   He brought to the diocese a mind trained to discipline and regularity which speedily effected a change for the better in several departments of Church affairs in Ardagh.   Although he was as firm and strong-minded a man as ever lived, there was none so simple or so kindly disposed. His mother resided with him, and to her word he, her spiritual lord, was much more obedient and humble than his youngest curate. His charity to the poor will never be forgotten in Longford. He never could have sixpence without giving it to the first good beggar that beset him. To enumerate his many good qualities, or to convey an idea of the good he did in Longford, I cannot. The best proof of his worth was evidenced when a sudden fever took him too soon away. Then the people, one and all, rich and poor, followed his remains to the grave in tears, just the same as if their own fathers had been taken from them ; and to this day the people of Longford will talk as lovingly and tenderly of his memory as if it had been but yesterday, and not in 1867, he departed. Very little can be said of his successor, Dr. M'Cabe. He, too, was a member of the Order of Vincentians, but his term lasted so short, that his spiritual children preserve but a faint recollection of him. He attended the celebrated Ecumenical Council held at the Vatican in 1869-70, and died on his way home, at Marseilles, in France, where his remains are interred.

Right Rev. George Conroy succeeded. He was a celebrated man of letters and theologian, and, for his ability as a diplomatist, was sent out as papal legate, to settle a dispute between two archbishops in Canada in 1877. The mission was a complete success ; but its envoy died at Newfoundland on his return journey, August 4th, 1878. His remains were brought home, and are interred in the Nuns' Cemetery in Longford.

Right Rev. Bartholomew Woodlock, D.D., Rector of the Catholic University in succession to the late Cardinal Newman, succeeded, being consecrated at Rome by the Pope, on Whit-Sunday, 1879. Dr. Woodlock is not the first bishop of his name, there having been a Dr. Wodeloke, Bishop of Winchester, during the Crusades. The present Bishop of Ardagh is now advanced in years, yet he leads a most mortified and abstemious life. For a long time after his advent to the diocese he was unknown to most of his flock, so retiring was his disposition ; and even now, after ten years, he is best known to them by the extreme

MAIN HALL, CLOISTERS AND BELFRY OF THE CISTERCIAN ABBEY AT ABBEYSHRULE.

RUINS OF THE ABBEY OF LERHA.

simplicity of his life and manners, as well as by his kindliness of nature and humility of person. Dr. Woodlock is of an old and aristocratic family of English descent, who have long been settled in Ireland, and some of whose members have recently occupied high positions here.

MONASTIC INSTITUTIONS OF THE COUNTY.

We will next give a brief glance at the chief monastic institutions which flourished in Longford when Catholicity was the religion of Europe. The principal monastic ruins now to be found are situated in the following places :—Lerha (Abbeylara), Inchmore (Lough Gowna), Ardagh, Abbeydearg, Abbeyshrule, All Saints' Island (Lough Ree), Inchboffin (Lough Ree), and Inisclothraun (Lough Ree). Photographic plates showing the ruins of these ancient religious structures, existing at the present day, are given in various parts of this book. I hope the reader will duly appreciate the effort I have made to give him a perfect picture of these old haunts of sanctity. We will commence with the buildings in the north of Longford.

The Abbey of Lerha.

There are few places in the County of Longford possess such interest for the student of ecclesiastical history as the neighbourhood of Granard, in which was erected the great Abbey of Lerha, which has now given its name to the parish of Abbeylara. It is told by the ancient annalists that one of the first places in Leinster which St. Patrick visited after visiting Tara, was the neighbourhood of Granard, which at that time was one of the chief seats of the pagan worship which then prevailed in Ireland, for here was said to be the " Hill of the Sun," or, in other words, the "Hill" from which worship was offered to the sun, moon, and stars. We may suppose then that St. Patrick, having heard of the fame of this place, made his way thither to teach our rude and unlettered forefathers the history of the birth and death, for our redemption, of our Lord Jesus Christ. It certainly must have been

Q

worth seeing to behold St. Patrick teaching these rude sons of the
forest and of the chase the laws laid down by the Son of God for the
redemption of mankind; for at this time more than half of Ireland was
covered with a dense forest, in which wild boars and even wolves
abounded. St. Patrick preached about the year 440, and his preaching
produced such abundant fruit, that in 460 he founded the Monastery of
Lerha, which he dedicated to the Blessed Virgin Mary, and appointed
St. Guasacht, the son of St. Melchuo, his own old master, to be its first
abbot. No further mention of the abbey occurs until 765, when it
appears that Fiachra, an abbot of the monastery, died. This is the
only mention made of St. Patrick's foundation; but a large number of
the chieftains of Annaly were buried in it.

In 1205, Richard Tuite founded an abbey in Lerha, for monks of
the Cistercian Order in honour of the Blessed Virgin. He brought
several monks from Dublin and placed them in it, so that the abbey
might not lack for priests until it would become a stable erection. In
the year 1231 Nigell was abbot here, and his name is found as a sub-
scribing witness to a grant made by Felix Roache, Archbishop of Tuam,
to the Abbey of St. Mary, in Dublin. In 1315 Edward Bruce besieged,
captured and burned the town of Granard, after which he sacrilegiously
entered and plundered Lerha Monastery. This dreadful act was committed on St. Andrew's Day—the day of all others on which one would
expect a Scotchman not to do any bad act, fearing the anger of the
saint, who is patron of Scotland. For the whole winter of the same
year, Edward Bruce and his army remained in winter quarters in the
ruins of the town which they had destroyed; and the monks, who had
fled to Athlone on the approach of his army, returned in the spring of
1314, when he had taken his departure. In 1320 one William Payne
was made abbot, through the influence of the Tuites, and soon after, a
vacancy having occurred in St. Mary's Abbey, in Dublin, his patron
had him removed to preside there as lord abbot. In the year 1340
it is mentioned that the abbot of this monastery was also one of the
visitors to Dunbrody Abbey, in the County of Wexford. In 1398 the

abbot, an Englishman named Peter, was made Bishop of Clonmacnoise, and in 1447 John O'Mayley, abbot, was made a canon of the same see In 1541 Richard O'Farrell, who was also Chieftain of Annaly, and had been abbot of this monastery for some time, was appointed Bishop of Ardagh, and almost immediately after the monastery was suppressed, when the bishop was seized of land and houses of the yearly value of £6, Irish money.

Of this seizure, Ware says :—

"On the surrender of the abbey, the said Richard was seized of two carucates of land, with their appurtenances, in Olonemore, of the yearly value, besides reprises, of 13s. 4d. ; four *carucates* in *Lerha*, of the yearly value, besides reprises, of 26s. 8d. ; two carucates in Clone-cryawe, of the yearly value, besides reprises, of 13s. 4d. ; two carucates in Tonnaghmore, of the yearly value, besides reprises, of 13s 4d. ; four carucates in Monktown, of the yearly value, besides reprises, of 26s 8d., and the tithes of corn in the rectory of Monktown, of the yearly value, besides reprises, of 40s. ; also of a moiety of the tithes of the rectory of Granard, of the yearly value, besides reprises, of 26s 8d. , a moiety of the tithes of the rectory of Drumlomman, of the yearly value, besides reprises, of 13s 4d. ; and the moiety of the tithes of the rectory of Ballymachivy, of the yearly value, besides reprises, of 10s. ; the rectories of Athlone, Levanaghan, Clonmacnoise, Tessauran, Bally-boughlo and Reynagh (*i.e.*, the whole diocese of Clonmacnoise, were all appropriated to this abbey)."

The present relics of Richard Tuite's foundation consist of a large square tower, in the middle of which is an arched door leading into what was, in all probability, a portion of the dormitory. At the end of this apartment there is a round circular chamber, with a narrow window in it, which I presume to have been one of the cells of the structure. The whole of the tower is covered with ivy, so that it is impossible to clearly note the style of its architecture. From the proximity of the Protestant Church, it was impossible to take a view of it which would show the interior; but I have no hesitation in saying that the place is well worthy of a visit. Here lie the remains of many chieftains of Annaly, as well as the gallant but unfortunate Richard Tuite, its founder, who was killed by the fall of a tower at Athlone in 1211.

Inchmore (Columbkille).

We will next pay a visit to the ruins of the ancient church and monastery which was founded on the island of Inchmore, in Lough Gownagh, about the same time that St. Guasacht was made Prior of St. Mary's, Lerha. This monastery was at one time of very large proportions, consisting of the church and the main building of the abbey. The remains of the latter are very few indeed; yet the visitor can distinctly trace in them the various apartments of the old structure.

Columbkille contains some very beautiful scenery. The parish is cut in twain with the splendid Lake of Gownagh, which stretches far into the County Cavan.

There is certainly no part of the County Longford in which one meets with such romantic scenery as this very spot; and it is recorded that when the great St. Columb determined to undertake the conversion of the Picts and Scots in the fifth century, he retired to Inchmore, in Lough Gowna, where he spent a long time in prayer and fasting preparatory to his journey. Here, too, he raised a monastery for Canons Regular before his departure for Iona, and appointed as its first abbot St. Boodan, who died in 496, or, as some writers say, 476 A.D. In 748 the abbot, Dicolla M'Menidi, passed to his reward, being followed, in the year 800, by M'Laisre, who, for his sanctity and piety, was called *the Excellent*. In 804 the dreaded Danes appeared and plundered the abbey, which they burned to the ground, and for a period of fully fifty years after their visit the place was deserted. The monastery was, however, restored in 860 by Toictuch, who became its abbot, and died in 895, according to the Annals of the Four Masters; and we do not hear of it again until April 27th, 1414, when the abbot, Edmund M'Findbar, died, and was interred in the cemetery attached to the abbey, as were most of his predecessors. Bishop O'Farrell, from whom the Abbey of Lerha had previously been taken, was compelled also to surrender this monastery in 1543. Its remains are yet quite extensive, and are worthy of a visit from any person who desires to visit the haunts of sanctity in the early days of Catholicity in Ireland.

Clonbroney.

We are told, in the Ecclesiastical Records of Ireland, that in the year 460 St. Patrick founded a nunnery at Cluanbronach, over which he placed the two Emerias, sisters of St. Gusacht, Abbot of Lerha, near Granard. It is written of these two sisters that, at the time they received the veil from St. Patrick, they left the imprint of their feet on the spot on which they stood.

St. Attracta was an abbess of this monastery about the year 700 A.D., and was succeeded by St. Samthana, who died on December 19th, 738, on which day, according to Butler's "Lives of the Saints," her feast is celebrated. In the year 760, there died here the Abbess Cealbill. In 771, the death of another abbess, Sithmath, is recorded; and in 775, Forblaith, daughter of Connley, Prince of East Teffia, or East Meath, died, and was buried here. On the 2nd of August, 778, the abbey was destroyed by fire, but this calamity does not appear to have scattered the community founded by St. Patrick; for, in 780, the death of the Abbess Elbrigh is recorded. In 791 the Abbess Learveanvan died here, and was followed to the grave in 804 by the Abbess Finbil. In 810 the Abbess Gormley died in this abbey, and in the year 1107, it is mentioned in the Annals of the Four Masters, from which the above events are taken, that Cosgrach, a daughter of Unon, died here.

After the year 1107, no further mention is made of the ecclesiastical affairs of Clonbroney, and it is presumed by many old writers that the nunnery collapsed in the twelfth century, owing to the disturbed state of the times. After the Reformation and the enactment of penal measures against the Catholic faith, a certain Sir James Ware, who was one of the Government officials in the days of the Restoration, became possessed of a tract of land in this parish, which he left to the Protestant Church in trust for the education of Protestant children; but some flaw having been discovered in* the conveyances, the bequest was a subject of much litigation. In this parish was born, about the middle of the seventeenth century, the Abbé Edgeworth, who attended Louis XV. on the scaffold in Paris in 1789, when the guillotine blade lopped off the head of the unfortunate king, amid the maddened howls of his own subjects; and none was there to comfort him but the heroic priest from Clonbroney.

An inquisition was taken in this parish on January 27th, 1594, when it was found that there had been also in this parish an hospital for the indigent, which was supported by four cartrons of lands. It is not shown where the hospital stood, nor where was the exact site of the nunnery; but it is safe to assume that both existed near the present village of Ballinalee. The hospital mentioned here was a house of refuge for the weak and indigent, whose wants were attended to by two or three monks of the Order of St. Augustine, who acted as physicians and chaplains to their inhabitants. According to Burke's "History of the Church in Ireland," a Gray Friary was erected near St. Johnstown (now Ballinalee) for this purpose, and dedicated to St. John the Baptist. He does not give the date, however, nor are there any remains of either buildings

Clonee.

At a place called Clonee, on the river Camlin, there is recorded to have been founded, in 663 A.D., an abbey; but neither the name of the order which inhabited it, nor the name of any abbot or monk, is given in connection with it. No remains of such a building are to be found at all at the present day.

Longford.

Cotemporary with the foundation of the See of Ardagh, an abbey was founded in Longford by St. Idus, one of the disciples of St. Patrick.

What year this saint lived, or where exactly stood the abbey, it is impossible to tell, but his feast is yet celebrated on July 14th. The reference to this ancient abbey occurs in the Roman Calendar; but whether it continued to exist till the disruption of the religious affairs of Ireland during the Danish invasion or not, is most uncertain

The foundation of a Dominican Abbey, in 1400, by Dhomnal O'Farrell, Prince of Annaly, for Friars of the Order of St. Dominick, was probably the origin of the town of Longford.

In 1429 a great conflagration occurred in this monastery, which was burned to the ground—the monks being left homeless; and such was the distress to which they were reduced that, on March 16th, Pope Martin V. issued a Papal Bull, granting a plenary indulgence to all persons who would aid the monks in rebuilding it. On March 12th, 1433, Pope Eugene IV. granted a Bull towards the same object, which he confirmed by a second one, issued on the 16th of July, 1438. In the year 1448, a terrible disease swept away masses of the Irish people, who were entirely ignorant of its nature, or the remedies for it. Amongst the list of those whom it took away, are found the names of Aedh-buy O'Feargeal, Henry Duffe M'Fedechan, and Diarmud M'Commay, "three righteous monks of the monastery." These men were interred, in all probability, in the precincts of the present ruins, situated in the grounds attached to the Protestant Rector's residence. This place did not exist longer than the year 1530, because we find it recorded that this monastery, with certain lands attached, was granted in the fourth year of the reign of Philip and Mary—that is, about the year 1552—to one Richard Nugent and his heirs, *in capite*, for ever The disposition of the monastery by these royal personages does not seem to have pleased their more thorough-going successor; for, on June 2nd, 1578, Queen Elizabeth granted this friary—after its confiscation the title monastery is not given to it—containing half-an-acre, with a house, cottage, 28 acres of land, six acres of demesne land, and commonage to same, to Sir Nicholas Malby, Knight, at a yearly rent of 16s. per annum. Once again, however, was it destined to a change;

for, in the year 1615, according to Lodge, vol. ii., page 275, on January 29th, James I., who had worked such wonders in and for (of course the good of) the country, made it over to Francis Lord Valentia.

There is a difference of opinion as to the exact site of the old monastery of "Longford-ui-Fearghail." My own opinion is that it existed on the banks of the Camlin, and that its remains are those standing in Templemichael glebe. However, I have seen it stated in an old work, as a matter of known fact, that the present Protestant church is built on the site of the old monastery, and that the old building referred to was the abbey church. Even if this be true, it can in no way detract from the interest that must attach to this latter structure, for, of course, it must be a cotemporary erection with the abbey built in 1400.

The Shannon Isles.

Inisclothraun, or Quakers' Island.

Next in importance to Longford (as the capital of the county), I place the monastic ruins on the Shannon Isles in the forefront. As a living proof of the devotion and the zeal of our forefathers in the cause of religion, they are without equal, except in Clonmacnoise. I have lately visited Inisclothraun, for the purpose of taking the necessary photographs to supply the pictures herewith, and such an impression did they make on me, that I envied the few residents of those islands their calm, peaceful lot. I have conceived a special veneration for the ruins of Inch-Clothraun, which I think are the finest in all Ireland. I hope that the publication of views of those ruins will open them up to the antiquarian in search of a really interesting subject.

In my visit to the island I met the old man whose portrait will be found in the interior of one of the churches. This old man, whose name is Daniel Farrell, is now in his eighty-fifth year, and he told me that his father and mother had been married on that island *one-hundred and twenty-five years ago*. He was the youngest of twelve sons, all of whom had pre-deceased him, and at the time I was

RECTANGULAR VIEW OF THE RUINS ON QUAKERS' ISLAND.

speaking to him he was as hale, hearty and typical an old Irishman as ever I met. In reply to my questions as to the building of these seven churches, he gave a graphic account of them, as he said " by tradition." According to this account the stones that built the churches were taken from the quarry of Blena-Vohr, which lies about three miles distant on the Longford shore of Lough Ree. " They had no boats in those days," said the veteran, " and they used a large flat stone to carry them over the water. This stone lies still down there on the shore." " Oh, but, said I, " surely a heavy stone would not float in the water." " Well, it did," said he, " ever until one day when they were building, and in the morning they found all they had built knocked down. They couldn't tell who did it, and they set a guard at the gate there below. During the night the guard saw a large serpent coming up out of the water and going round the building, knocking it down with his tail. Then they fell on it with weapons and cut it in several places, until it fought its way back to the water, and the next morning they traced it by its blood in the water till they found it went into Blena-Vohr, and so they never took more stones out of that place."

" And where did they find the rest of the stones," said I. " Oh," said he, " they found plenty on the shore after that." " Have you ever heard what kind of monks lived here," I asked. " No," said he, " I never heard their names; but they were very strict men, for do you see that circle all round there " (here he pointed to a circular wall which enclosed five of the churches, and about three acres of land besides). " Yes," said I. " Well," said he, " no woman, on any account or business, was ever allowed inside that wall; and if she came in she was left in one of the churches till she died, which happened very soon, and the church was accordingly called the ' Dying Church.' "

In reply to further questions, he showed me the gate in the circular wall through which the stones were carried to build the churches. About a hundred yards south of this is another gate, which he said was the one in which the corpses for interment in the island were brought to a church which lay *outside* the prescribed circle, and which

R

he said was called "The Lady's Church." Here the interments of all
who died outside took place. "In fact," said he, "there is not a spot
of this island but's full of bones and skulls; and in particular about the
'Dying Church,' a great number of people were interred." In parting
with the old man, I told him my mission to Inisclothraun. "Well,"
said he, "I'm glad to find that the history of our county is going to be
written, and I hope you will not forget to mention in it that you met
the descendant of one of the families that Cromwell banished to hell or
to Connaught." I said I was very glad indeed to meet a true descendant of those people. "Well, sir," said he, "there was a time when
my family were the strongest and richest in the barony of Rathcline;
but when Cromwell scattered us we lost everything, and here you see
the last of the old people." I was much affected with the simple old
man's discourse, and promised him a place in these pages if ever they
were printed. Now for history.

St. Dhiarmuit Naoimh, or the Just St. Dermod, a brother to Felim,
Bishop of Kilmore, in the sixth century, founded an abbey on this island,
in the year 540, where he died a few years later According to Colgan,
the author of "*Acta Sanctorum*," he wrote a learned psalter, which was
in possession of the monks of this abbey until the Danes sacked it in
1089. In 700 A.D. the Abbot St. Sionagh is recorded to have flourished
in this island; and he died, according to the Abbé M'Geoghegan, in
717. In 780 a learned priest, named Eochy M'Fogharty, was made
Abbot of Inisclothran; after which, for a period of one hundred years,
there is no mention of the abbey. In 869 it is recorded that the Abbot
Curoius, who was esteemed as a very learned man, was in the height
of his reputation He died about the year 875. In 1010 and 1016 the
Danes and Munstermen, who had previously visited Inchbcffin, also
sacked and burned this abbey. In 1050 it was again plundered by
them, and, finally, was devastated by O'Brien and the same band of
pirates who visited Inchboffin in 1089. It was restored, however,
about the year 1100; and, in 1136, Aid O'Finn, who was also Bishop of
Ardagh, ruled over it On the 29th of June, 1155, the abbey was

burned to the ground, but must have been again restored ; for, in the year 1160, the death of the teacher of the schools in this abbey—a celebrated poet, scholar, and historian, named Gilda—is recorded. In the year 1170, a refugee prince of the line of O'Carroll took shelter in this island. He had attempted to usurp the kingdom of Ely, which his brother was lawfully entitled to. The latter, however, overcame him, and the former had to fly from his vengeance. He was pursued hither, and despite the utmost efforts of the monks, was slain by his incensed brother, one Rughry O'Carroll, King of Ely, in the middle of the island. The year after, the abbot of the island, one Diarmod O'Brien, died. In 1193 it was again sacked by Gilbert de Nangle, who committed great devastation in it. We read the following extracts in the Annals of the Four Masters about this island :—

" 719. St. Sionach died, April 20th.

" 780. Eochaidh, abbot, died.

" 769. Curoi, abbot and sage, died.

"1015 and 1050. Inisclothrann was plundered by the men of Munster.

" 1089. The fleet of the men of Munster sailed on the Shannon to Lough Ree, and plundered all the islands of the lake, including Innisclothrann. This Rory O'Connor seeing, he caused the fords on the Shannon, called Aidercheach and Rechiath, to be stopped, to the end that they might not be at liberty to pass the said passages on their return, and were driven to turn to Athlone, where they were overtaken by Donnell MacFlynn O'Melaghlin, King of Meath, to whose protection they wholly committed themselves, and yielded all their boats, cots, and ships to be disposed of at his pleasure, which he received, and sent in safe conduct with them, until they were left in their native place of Munster.

" 1136. The Bishop of Breiffny died here.

" 1141. Gilla-na-Naomh O'Fergal, chief of the people of Annaly, the most prosperous man in Ireland, died at a great age, and was buried at Inisclothrann.

"1150. Morogh, the son of Giolla-na-Naomh, the tower of the splendour and nobility of the east of Connaught, died.

"1160. Giolla-na-Naomh O'Dunne, a lecturer of Inisclothrann, and a well-spoken, eloquent man, sent his spirit to his Supreme Father, amidst a choir of angels, on the 17th December, in the 58th year of his age.

"1167. Kinneth O'Ketternaigh, priest of Inisclothrann, died.

"1168. The daughter of O'Quinn, wife of MacCorganma, was interred at Innisclothran.

"1170. Dermot O'Brien, chief, senior of the east of Connaught, died in Innisclothrann in the 95th year of his age.

"1174 Rory O'Carroll, Lord of Ely, was slain in the middle of Innisclothrann.

"1193. Innisclothrann was plundered by the sons of Costolloe, and by the sons of Conor Moinmoy (both of Connaught).

"1232. Tiopraide O'Breen, an ecclesiastic learned in history, died on his pilgrimage on this island.

"1244. Donogh, the son of Fuinghim, son of Torlogh O'Connor, and bishop of Elphin, died here on April 23rd, and was interred in the Monastery of Boyle."

Inchboffin.

Inchboffin is an island in Loughree, in the Shannon. There are many islands in this lough, which extends almost from Lanesborough to Athlone, and is reputed to be in some parts from six to nine miles broad. The name "Inchboffin" is the Gaelic term for the Island of the "White Cow."

According to Usher, an abbey was founded here in the year 520, by St. Rioch, the son of St. Darerca, sister to St. Patrick. The year of the death of St. Rioch is unrecorded; but, in 750, an abbot named Fiengal, who was son of Denchad, of the line of Heremon, died. Twenty years later (in 770), according to the Annals of the Four Masters, the abbey was burned to the ground—the inmates barely escaping with their lives It was rebuilt, however, before the year 800; for the death of Blathmac, the abbot, is recorded by the same writers in 1809. In the year 1010 the men of Limerick and Clare sailed up the Shannon from Limerick, accompanied by a number of Danes, who dwelt in that city, and they sacked all the islands in this lake, including this island and the abbey on it. In 1016 they renewed their acquaintance with Lough Ree, and sacked Innisboffin again. In 1025, the death of the Abbot Chonsal, who originally came from Ulster, is mentioned; and the abbey was finally destroyed by the Danes and Munstermen in 1089, headed by Muirkeartack O'Brien, of Thomond.

Concerning this island we also read the following extracts in the Annals of the Four Masters :—

" 667. Colman, bishop, accompanied by other saints, went to Innisboffin, and founded a monastery, which took its name from that place.

" 674. Colman died.

" 711. Bartan, bishop, died.

" 750. Fiangal, abbot, died.

" 809. Blathmac, Foster-son to the Great Colgan, died.

" 898. Caoncomrag, of the caves of Innisboffin, died. (He was a holy anchorite.)

" 916. Feradhach, abbot, died.

" 1015, 1050, and 1089. The men of Munster plundered and destroyed this monastery."

All Saints' Island and Inch Ainghin.

All Saints' Island is one of the most important islands in Lough Ree, and was the site of a splendid monastery built by St. Kieran, the first Bishop of Clonmacnoise, in the year 544. After founding the monastery, he appointed as his abbot St. Domnan, and then left the island and repaired to Clonmacnoise, where he lived during the remainder of his life.

No other mention is made of it until 1089, when, as well as the other islands in the neighbourhood, it was plundered and despoiled by Murkertach O'Brien and a large fleet of Danes and Ostmen.   In 1272, the death of the Abbot Arectac Y. Fin is mentioned, so that the monastery must have been restored as well as its sister edifices on the neighbouring islands; and in the same year we find it mentioned that Sir Henry Dillon, of Drumrany, who had come into Ireland with the Earl of Morton, erected an abbey on the site of St. Kiernan's structure. There being no mention made of the destruction of the latter, it is difficult to understand how Sir Henry could have erected a monastery, unless he demolished the old one in order to substitute a better one, particularly as the death of the existing abbot is recorded in the same year.   In the year 1405, the Canon Augustine M'Graidan died, and was interred in the chancel of his chapel.   He was a very learned man, and is said to have written the lives of all the Irish saints, as well as the records of the abbey, down to his own time, both of which works are yet preserved in the library of Oxford.   James I. of England granted this island, as well as portion of the islands and land in the lough, to Sir Patrick Barnewall, in the year 1620, but it was again taken from him for his part in connexion with the petition of Catholic grievances in the following reign.

In a small island near Lanesborough called Inch Ainghin, St. Kieran also built a church.

" 894. Inch Ainghin was violated, and persons were wounded in the middle of it, although St. Kieran's shrine and many religious persons, together with Cairbree Cronn, Bishop of Clonmacnoise, were present.

" 895. Toictuch, of Inch Yana, died.

" 1015, 1050, and 1089.   This island shared the same fate as the other islands in Lough Ree."—*Annals of Four Masters.*

Kilglass (Legan).

An abbess named Echea is said to have had founded for her here a convent in the fifth century by St. Mel, Bishop of Ardagh, who was her brother. According to the "Life of St. Patrick," by Colgan, Echea was a sister to St. Mel.

Echea, the virgin of Kilglass, is enumerated amongst the daughters of Darerca (sister to St. Patrick) by Ervinus, in the Scriptural Life of St. Patrick, and by St. Aengus, a scholar of his day, who says :—" The virtuous sons of Darerca were seventeen transmarine bishops. She had two daughters—the devout Echea, who raised the dead and cured lepers, and Laloca of Senlios, behind Mount Badgnah." There is no record preserved of St. Echea's Convent, nor of the length of time it existed ; nor is there anything known in this parish of St. Lupita, who had a convent at the foot of Sheve Goldry about the same time ; and the tradition of both virgins is very dim and uncertain.

Moydow.

The ancient name of this parish was Kilmodhain, or Kilmacdhumha, so called from being the "kil" or cell of St. Modhain, or Modiud the Simple, whose feast is celebrated, according to the "Lives of the Saints," on February 12th. St. Modan lived about the year 591, when he was made a bishop. Previous to this he had erected the Priory of Moydow, no ruins of which now exist. It is said that one Erclaus, a disciple and presbyter of St. Patrick, was a presbyter here for some time after its erection. Mr. O'Donovan says this was one of the oldest priories in Ireland

Dearg, or Abbey-dearg.

Distant about five miles due south from Longford, is the Cemetery of Abbey Dearg, in which stands the crumbling ruins of what was once a priory for Regular Canons of the Order of St. Augustine. This priory was founded about the year 1205, by Gormgal O'Quinn, Lord of Rathcline, and was dedicated to St. Peter ; and in 1217, the first abbot of the monastery, Osin by name, died and was interred here. On the death of Brendan Magodaig, Bishop of Ardagh, in 1255, his remains also were interred in this priory, which continued to exist until 1550, when it was suppressed, and the buildings and land, to the value of £2 annually, Irish money, were bestowed on one Nicholas Alymor, an English soldier.

The existing ruins of the Abbey of Dearg prove it to have been a most perfect monastic structure. The plate which I am enabled to present of it is not a very perfect one, owing to the entire demolition of the main walls of the building, and the complete covering of the walls, showing the eastern and southern window by a thick coat of impenetrable ivy I have examined the ruins minutely, and conclude that it consisted of a main chancel (of chapel), vestry, dining-room, dormitory, and a number of cells. The principal walls of all, except the southern and eastern portion of the chancel, are now demolished to a height of two or three feet, and in this way I have been unable to find a vantage point from which to give a satisfactory picture.

Abbey Shrule.

This abbey was situated near the River Inny, in the barony of Shrule, and its original name was Srohill. It is not stated who was its founder ; but it is recorded that, in the year 901, the Abbot Maelpoil died, and was succeeded by the Abbot Caincomhrac, who died in 952. The old abbey was then destroyed by the Danes, who came up the Shannon from Limerick ; but, in 1340, O'Farrell, Prince of Annaly, raised a monastery on its ruins to the honour of the Blessed Virgin for monks of the Cistercian Order ; and, in 1365, the death of its first abbot, Maceatalius, took place. The abbey then continued to exist until the suppression of monasteries by Queen Elizabeth, who granted it and all its lands to Robert Dillon, Earl of Roscommon, and his heirs male, *in capite* for ever.

This is, next to the ruins in Lough Ree, the best preserved of all our county monastic ruins. In fact, it is really much better preserved than any of them ; but being a more modern erection than they, I do not wish to detract from the merits of "the Seven Churches," or St. Kieran's or St. Rioch's foundations. The Abbey of Shrule is built on a commanding position. At its foot, in a glorious sweep, the Inny

RUINS OF THE TOWER OF THE CISTERCIAN ABBEY, AT ABBEYSHRULE.

flows down to Tenelick, whilst it stands on a gently wooded rising
ground. The existing ruins of this splendid monastery show it to have
been one of the finest in all Leinster. It was built in rectangular
shape, and, after a minute examination, I am of opinion that it contained the following apartments: square tower, with spiral staircase
and numerous small cells; dormitories or cells for monks; chapel, with
magnificent window facing east, vestry, two pantries, dining-hall and
kitchen. The tower faces the south-west, when in a straight line the
cells were ranged to the chapel, into which there were two modes of
ingress. Off the chapel branched a square apartment which, I conceive,
was the vestry, and from this an arched door led into the dining-hall.
From this description and the accompanying plates, the reader can see
that there were few larger abbeys than that of Abbey Shrule.

Ballymacormack.

In the present Cemetery of Ballymacormack, and distant about one
mile from the town of Longford, stands the remains of the old Church
of Ballymacormack, which, I am of opinion, was once a chapel of ease
for Longford. The present remains of the structure consist of a
northern, southern, and western wall, all being in good condition, and
standing at a height of sixteen or twenty feet from the ground. In
the middle of the southern wall there is a low arched doorway, and in
the same wall there are also several well-preserved windows of the
most ancient pattern. In the western wall, which formed the gable-
end of the erection, there are a number of small square holes, resembling,
at a distance, loopholes; and in the northern wall (almost in the very
middle) there has grown up an immense ash-tree, which has dislodged
a considerable portion of the original masonry, but yet affords a very
fair protection to the existing structure. In the middle of the building
there seems to have been at one time a cross wall, as if the church
were composed of two apartments. I have endeavoured to ascertain if
such was the case, and have been told that it was not. I have been

informed that this church was built in the twelfth century by O'Farrell of Longford, and existed until the fifteenth century. No name of abbots or monks is given in connection with it in any monastic record that I have been able to peruse

An old inhabitant of the parish says that at the time of the introduction of the Reformation into this county, the Reformers thought to make a church out of the chapel, and did roof it for this purpose. The next morning the roof was found in a part of the Dash River, called Pullnawatha; and the Reformers did not again attempt to meddle with Ballymacormack Church. In the dreadful days of the mortality of '32, the Parish Priest of Longford used to go out to this old ruin and say Mass in it—the congregation kneeling away from one another, through fear of the contagion Such, indeed, was their fear of one another during those days, that it was with difficulty they could be induced even to enter any church or chapel to assist at divine service.

There is a similar building in the Cemetery of Clondra, beside the Roman Catholic Chapel, concerning which I find an old reference, as follows: "A.D. 1323 Giolla Airnin O'Casey, Archdeacon of Cluanda-rath, died."

PROTESTANT HISTORY OF ARDAGH.

The Protestant Reformation was established in the County Longford by Queen Elizabeth, who joined the Diocese of Ardagh to the Diocese of Kilmore, in virtue of her powers as Head of the Church This occurred about the year 1600 ; and, in 1633, one William Bedell, who had been first Protestant bishop, resigned his appointment, and John Richardson, a native of Chester, in England, and Protestant Archdeacon of Kerry, was advanced in Church preferment to the See of Ardagh. This man foresaw the effects of the constant plundering of the Catholics by the Elizabethan soldiers, parsons, and ruck of followers, which terminated, as history informs us, in the foundation, in 1641, of the Catholic Confederation of Kilkenny. Accordingly, in the summer of 1641, he gathered up all his earthly belongings, folded his tent, and went into England, leaving his flock to take care of themselves. A short time previous to his departure, he had forcibly wrested from one Teigue Roddy, a kinsman of the O'Farrells, some of his hereditary tenements in Ardagh. Teigue resisted the injustice, and applied to the Irish House of Commons for protection; but the members being all of one mind when a native chieftain was to be plucked, declined to interfere on Teigue's behalf. Teigue then applied to the English House of Commons for that which was denied him at home. Thereupon, the Protestant Bishop of Clonfert rose in his place in the Irish House of Lords, and moved that Brother Richardson, of Ardagh, being a member of the Irish House of Lords, was exempt from any jurisdiction possessed by the British House of Commons. He, therefore, proposed that the Lord Chancellor communicate this to the Speaker of the British House, and that a resolution be passed by the House to prevent such "Episcopal grievances" in future. And thus, in obedience to the intolerant spirit of party ascendancy, poor Teigue O'Roddy was denied the benefits of the protection of the law. So much for the justice that prevailed in those days. In 1654 Bishop Richardson died; but his see had been kept vacant by the Cromwellians, from the establishment of the Commonwealth, in 1649, until the restoration of Charles II.—during all which time its revenues had been sequestrated by the Puritans. In 1660 it was reunited to Kilmore; *statu quo* it remained until 1692, when the bishop, William Sheridan, was removed from the see, owing to his Jacobite tendencies, and Ulysses Burgh, an Englishman, appointed in his stead. The union of both dioceses was then broken, and Ardagh was constituted an independent diocese, which it remained until the year 1742, when it was placed under the Archbishopric of Tuam, the Most Rev. Bishop Harte being spiritual pastor of both dioceses. The union between Ardagh and Tuam continued until the year 1840, when Ardagh was taken from the latter and given to Kilmore—the Diocese of Elphin being added to both—and the present bishop is, I believe, the Most Rev. Dr. Shone, his predecessor,

Most Rev. Dr. Darley, having been at one time Rector of Temple-michael, and highly esteemed by Protestant and Catholic alike whilst in the town of Longford. He is now about two years deceased; and although the present bishop may be a worthy successor, yet I think he will never maintain the same place in the affections of his Catholic fellow-countrymen as did the late bishop.

The foregoing historical references to the ecclesiastical history of the County of Longford are, doubtless, amply sufficient to convince the reader of the fact that our county enjoyed the great blessing of the presence of a large number of monasteries, abbeys, and convents in their midst, in the troubled days of the Danish and Anglo-Saxon invasions. During the days of persecution and trouble a good many of these were destroyed by the furious bigotry which then prevailed, and only their ruins now remain to attest that they once existed   Nevertheless, on the ruins of persecution and of trouble, and on the *debris* of religious bigotry and intolerance, are rising up to-day, thank God, convents and colleges in our county which bid fair to rival the cloisters of Lerha and the schools of Lough Ree.

PART II.

GENEALOGICAL RECORDS OF THE COUNTY LONGFORD

The O'Farrells of Annaly.

Although there seems to be some doubt amongst genealogists as to the exact location of Annaly, I do not think there is anyone who will read these lines will doubt that, prior to the English invasion, and long before, the O'Farrells were the Chieftains of Annaly. Any doubt at all which exists on the point seems to rest on the fact that on St. Patrick's arrival at Granard, in the middle of the fifth century, a prince named

Cairbre, who, according to O'Hart, was the progenitor of the O'Kearneys and O'Kearys, lived there, whilst at the same time the posterity of Mann lived in Southern Annaly. It would also appear that the tribe which afterwards conquered Cairbre and Mann's posterity, and in the tenth century assumed the name O'Fearghail, lived more eastward, or nearer to the great heart of Erin at Tara.

Again, recent writers locating the ancient territories of the chieftains of Ireland, have gone the length of asserting that Lower Annaly extended from Longford to the Country of Fenagh, or the MacRannels' country, and Upper Annaly from Granard eastwards to Meath. This would entirely exclude South Longford of the present day, and move Annaly of old more eastward and northward than the dwelling-places of its inhabitants in the tenth and subsequent centuries would warrant.

My own opinion on the subject is, that the O'Ferralls were direct descendants of Mann, who gradually spread themselves by families from the Inny to the Shannon in a north-western direction; and that after the battle of Clontarf they assumed the title of O'Fearghail, by which, as a clan name, they were afterwards known in Irish history. To contend that in those days of rude warfare any sept would be able to dislodge and banish from its country for ever the people whose inheritance it had been, is childish and untenable, whereas the records of the kingdom show that even the Ard-Righ-n'Eirinn was unable to do that, except on very rare occasions. I dismiss, therefore, from argument that uncertain tale; and come to the time when all of the present County Longford was the exclusive patrimony of the O'Ferralls, Princes of Annaly. The most important event in connexion with their rule was that related at page 23, under date 1445. This was the creation of Upper and Lower Annaly, the latter being that part of the present County Longford adjacent to Leitrim, and Upper Annaly almost corresponding to the South Longford of to-day. The chiefs who ruled Lower Annaly were called O'Farrells Bane, and those who ruled Upper Annally O'Farrells Bui or Boy. Coming down to the year 1571, we find that Faghny

O'Farrell Boy of Palles and Mornin, was the Chief of Upper Annaly, and Fergus O'Farrell Bane of Tully, was the Chief of Lower Annaly. In the indenture of surrender agreed upon by the O'Farrells, in 1570, the O'Farrell Boy was made Seneschal of the County Longford, but in the next year his appointment was disputed by Fergus O'Farrell Bane, and the others of that name, including Lisagh O'Farrell, who was the last native O'Farrell, Bishop of Ardagh. This was, of course, the result the English conquerors and diplomatists had in view, and amply was it gained. They played for disunion in the native camp, and they won. The official records presented of the litigation and lawsuits which the O'Farrells revelled in at this juncture, prove most amply the success of the invader. Passing away from that, and coming to look for the descendants of Fergus O'Farrell on one side, and Faghny on the other, we find that Iriell became head of the Bane family, whilst James was the successor of Faghny, as head of the Buidhes. From James the patrimony descended to Roger, of Mornin, whose birth is recorded in 1647, after which it is difficult to trace the main line of the O'Farrell family. It may have been that the Boy line became extinct on the male side, in which case the last living representative of it would be the daughter, Jane O'Farrell, who married in 1660, and of whose issue there is no record. In the subsequent troubles that occurred in Ireland, many of the O'Farrells went to France, Spain, and Austria, where they became military commandants, and raised themselves to places of honour and emolument in their adopted countries. Several of their descendants are living to this day in these countries. I have diligently looked up the family records of the various O'Farrell or Farrell families now living in Longford County, and I regret to express my inability to give a fuller list of direct descendants still living "in the old spot" than the following :—Nominally, Edward More O'Ferrall, J.P., D.L., of Lissard, County Longford, is looked upon by genealogists as the head of the old O'Farrell Clan. Such a claim, if made by himself, could not be upheld. Mr. O'Ferrall's family originally lived in Ballinree, near Edgeworthstown, where they held a farm, and were in comfortable circumstances. By the death of an old gentleman named Roger O'Farrell, who was no relation of theirs, and who owned a large lot of house property in Dublin, as well as landed property in the country, they became possessed of the Lissard estate, which Mr. E. M. O'Ferrall owns at the present day. Their family could not, therefore, be said to occupy more than a sub-chieftaincy in the old days of Brehon laws and tanistry succession in Ireland A very much more ancient family than they, were the O'Farrells of Camliskmore, near Edgeworthstown. [See foot-note, page 147.] They are actually to-day in possession of some of the old patrimony to which Connell O'Farrell was restored by Charles I. in 1660. Quiet, unassuming people, they have not adopted the Anglified manners of their more fortunate (?) former neigh- bour's family, which is now represented by Mr E. M. O'Ferrall. Next in the order of merit I would mention the family of Mr. John Forbes O'Ferrall, of Corbeagh. They are some of the old O'Ferrall Bane stock, who have never parted with the idea of their ancient descent. After them I would put the family of the Farrells of Aghanaspick, who, on the female side, are descended from the oldest family in the barony of Moydow. In " A Registry of Popish Priests, compiled by order of one of the penal statutes of Queen Anne, in 1704, the name of Michael Farrell, of Aghanaspick, appears as security " in the sum of £40, for the good behaviour " of a " Popish " priest, then resident in Longford. At that time this Mr. Farrell was the only native Catholic in the barony of Moydow whose surety for the good conduct of the Roman Catholic clergyman would be accepted. At page 97 it will be seen that the O'Farrell Boy, of Mornin, was granted a number of townlands, which were erected into the Manor of Mornin in 1621. Amongst the town- lands so left is that of Aghanaspick ; and taking into account the near relations subsisting between the chieftains and their feudaries in those days, I am almost certain that this family of Farrells could rightly claim connexion with, if not descent from, the O'Farrells Boy of Upper Annaly.

Another family of the old stock are the Farrells of Lehery and Lisnacusha, in the parish of Rathcline. At page 93 the reader will find refe1 ence to " 60a. of Leary, assigned to Lisagh (Lewis), Oge O'Farrell." This Lisagh was ancestor of the present Lehery and Lisnacusha family. Amongst the families unfortunately extinct are those of the O'Farrells, of Killen-Crubock, in Legan, and that of Mr. Fergus Farrell, who was expelled from the Irish House of Commons for being " an active instrument against the Protestant interest " in 1690. Of the former family, the late Rev. Richard O'Farrell, P.P., of Killashee, was the last representative. Of him there are many strange stories told ; but as they touch on matters religious, I do not deem it prudent to relate them for the sneers of the sceptical or the laugh of the ignorant. The family of Mr. Fergus Farrell became extensive seed merchants in Dublin, where they flourished in the early part of the present century ; but consumption getting in amongst them, they all died off many years ago I will close this lengthened genealogical survey by giving a table of the " old stock," from Ir down to Roger O'Farrell, who was born in 1647, and of whose subsequent career there is so little known :—

SIDE VIEW OF THE RUINS ON QUAKERS' ISLAND, TEMPLE DERMOT.

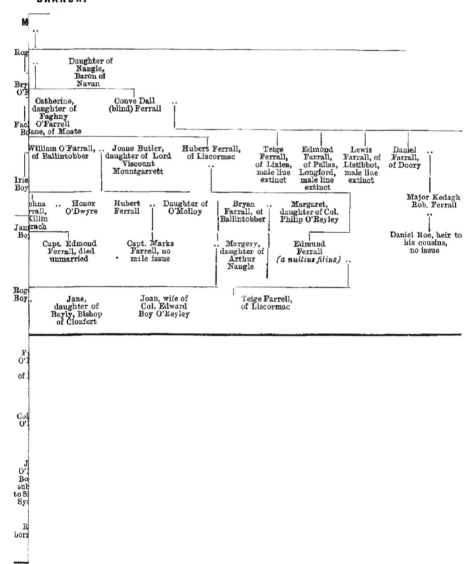

M

Rog

Daughter of
Nangle,
Baron of
Navan

Bry
O'

Catherine,
daughter of
Faghny
O'Farrell

Conve Dall
(blind) Ferrall

Fac
Bo ane, of Moate

William O'Farrall,
of Ballintobber

Joane Butler,
daughter of Lord
Viscount
Mountgarrett

Hubert Ferrall,
of Liscormac

Teige
Ferrall,
of Lixlea,
male line
extinct

Edmond
Farrall,
of Pallas,
Longford,
male line
extinct

Lewis
Farrall, of
Listibbot,
male line
extinct

Daniel
Farrall,
of Doory

Irie
Boy

chna
rall,
Killin

Honor
O'Dwyre

Hubert
Ferrall

Daughter of
O'Molloy

Bryan
Farrall, of
Ballintobber

Margaret,
daughter of Col.
Philip O'Reyley

Major Kedagh
Rob. Ferrall

Jam rach
Bo

Capt. Edmond
Ferrall, died
unmarried

Capt. Marks
Farrall, no
male issue

Margery,
daughter of
Arthur
Nangle

Edmund
Ferrall
(a nullius filius)

Daniel Roe, heir to
his cousins,
no issue

Rog
Boy

Jane,
daughter of
Bayly, Bishop
of Clonfert

Joan, wife of
Col. Edward
Boy O'Reyley

Teige Farrell,
of Liscormac

F
O'

of

Col
O'

J
O'
Bo
sub
to S
Sy

R
bor

Genealogy of the Princes of Annaly.

1. Ir : 37th from Adam.
2. Heber Donn, his son.
3. Hebric, his son.
4. Artreus, his son
5. Artrurus, his son.
6. Sednans, his son, and one of the monarchs of Ireland.
7. Fiachus Fion Scothach, his son, and a monarch of Ireland.
8. Ollamh Fodla, his son, a king of Ireland, and the Solomon of the Irish nation, who first laid the foundation of constitutional government.
9. Carbry, his son.
10. Lauradeus.
11. Brathaus.
12. Finnius, his son, and a monarch of Ireland.
13. Longimanus, his son, a monarch of Ireland, so called because of his long hands, the fingers of which reached the ground when he stood up; slain B.C. 855.
14. Argetmarus, his son.
15. Fomarius, his son.
16. Dubius, his son, so called, because of a hesitating nature.
17. Rossius, his son.
18. Strubius, his son.
19. Indercus, his son.
20. Glassius, his son.
21. Carbreus, his son.
22. Feberdil, his son.
23. Folgenus, his son.
24. Dubuis, his son.
25. Sthric, his son.
26. Rory More, his son, and a monarch of Ireland, who died 218 B.C. He was the founder of the Clan-na-Rory.
27. Rossius, his son, who had a brother called Aongus, from whom descended the Clan MacGuiness.

T

79 Gillacius O'Farrell, his son.
80. Moroch O'Farrell, his son.
81. Charles O'Farrell, his son.
82. Thomas O'Farrell, his son.
83. Charles O'Farrell, his son.

The next family we will turn our attention to will be the Dowdalls, of Ballinamore, in this county. Their family record, procured from a reliable source, is one that tells its own story :—

Pedigree of the Dowdall Family of Ballymahon and Ballymacormack, in the Co. Longford.

Arms.—The arms of this family are a crowned dove and six martlets, and are to be seen on the family vault at Shrule Graveyard.

Motto.—" *Innocentia ut Columba* "—" Innocent as a dove."

Descent.—The Dowdalls are of English descent, having originally settled in Louth, when they became very strong in numbers and wealth. The old saying of " *Hiberniores Hibernis ipsis* " was equally true in their case as in that of the Fitzgeralds, Burkes, &c., for no more sturdy foes confronted English tyranny in Ireland since the twelfth century than the Dowdalls of the County Louth.

Pedigree.

1446. Robert Dowdall appointed Chief Justice of the Common Pleas.

1450. Sir Thomas, son of Sir Robert Dowdall, married Elizabeth, daughter of James, third Baron of Delvin. Issue—An only daughter, who married first Baron of Navan, and then Viscount Gormanston.

1460 Sir John Dowdall, of Newtown and Termonfeckin, near Dublin, was next of the name, and was succeeded by—

1471. Sir Thomas Dowdall, who, in 1478, was created Master of the Rolls in Ireland.

1510. To him succeeded Sir William Dowdall, who had issue three sons—George, John and James. George became Archbishop of

Armagh in succession to George Cromer, but for defending the Catholic doctrine of the Mass had to fly to the Continent. Henry VIII appointed Hugh Godacre as archbishop; whilst Pope Paul III. appointed Robert Wauchop, a man who was blind from his infancy. In 1554, during the reign of Queen Mary, Dr. Dowdall was recalled, and reinstalled in his office by letters patent from the Queen and the sanction of the Pope. In the same year he received a commission from the Head of the Church to depose married and impenitent ecclesiastics.

1540. Sir John Dowdall succeeded Sir William. The youngest son became Solicitor-General, 1554; Judge of the Queen's Bench, 1565; and Chief Justice, 1583. James's issue were—Edward, Patrick, Nicholas, Antony and Jennett, who erected the crosses at Duleek and Baronstown

1570. To Sir John succeeded Sir John, whose children were all daughters, and he made a settlement of his property amongst them. Honor, the youngest daughter, married her relative, Laurence, son to Edward and great grandson of Sir William, thus uniting the properties in Louth County with those in Meath, purchased by Sir James when Chief Justice. To Sir John succeeded Laurence of Athlumny, the grandson of James.

1647. Sir Laurence Dowdal, of Athlumny, was one of the Confederate Catholics who attended the Confederation of Kilkenny. He was on that account deprived of life and estates by Cromwell's Act of 1652. Issue—Luke, who succeeded Henry of Drogheda, John of Glaspistol, Patrick of Termonfeckin, Laurence of Quelca.

1661. Sir Luke succeeded under the Act of Grace of Charles II. He married Mary O'Byrne of Cabinteely, and had three sons—Daniel, who became a priest, James, John.

1691. To Sir Luke, his youngest son, John, succeeded, but only to the name, for there was no quarter for Catholics in those days. He married Margaret Allen, of St. Woolstans, Celbridge. Issue—Patrick, George and James, who came to Ballymahon and remained there.

1750. Patrick (m.) Catherine Tyrrell. Issue—Patrick of Athlone,

James of Mornine. George (m.) Mary M'Loughlin. Issue—Henry, George of Ballymahon.

James Dowdall, born 1702; died unmarried, 1806; lived at Moigh, and purchased Terlicken and Ballyglasson. George of Athlone, son of Patrick (m.) Mary Kelly. Issue—Matilda, who married George Gartlan, Esq, J.P., Newry. William Dowdall (Captain) of Ballymulvy, son of George, (m) Mary Skelton. Issue—Marcella, who (m.) George Fitzgerald, of Bullock, Dalkey.

·1793, born; 1881, died—Henry Dowdall, solicitor, son of Henry, (m.) Anne Coffey. Issue—Anastatia, who married Captain Arthur Croker.

1791, born; 1875, died—George Dowdall (son of Henry and Eliza Cassin), married Anne Agnes Watson, Abbeyshrule. Issue—Henry Francis, James, Joseph, William Laurence.

James Joseph Dowdall, youngest son of George, is a priest, and at present Catholic Curate of Ardagh, the ancient See of St. Mel, which brings down the pedigree to the present day.

We will now give the pedigree of the modern nobility of Longford County.

Pedigree of the Pakenhams of Longford.

The ancient and noble family of Pakenham is of Saxon extraction, and was settled at Pakenham in the County of Suffolk, in England, where William de Pakenham, one of the Judges, resided in the reign of King Edward I. His eldest son, Sir Edmund Pakenham, Knt, in the reign of King Edward II, married Rose, one of the daughters and co-heirs of Robert de Valvines, by whom he had two sons, viz, William and Edmund, which latter died in 19 Edward III. William married, had issue, and was succeeded by Thomas, his eldest son, who died in the reign of King Henry IV.; he was succeeded by his eldest son, Theobald, who died in the latter end of the reign of King Henry V., or beginning of Henry VI. About this time the family changed their place of residence to Lordington, in the

County of Sussex, where Hugh, the eldest son of Theobald, lived in the reigns of King Henry VI. and Edward IV.; he was succeeded by his eldest son, Sir Hugh Pakenham, Knt., who died in the reign of King Henry VII., leaving issue two sons, viz, John and Nicholas, and also a daughter, Anne, married first to Sir Thomas Fitzwilliam, who was slain at Flodden-Field, 4 Henry VIII., and afterwards to Sir William Sydney, Knight Banneret, by whom she had issue, Henry Sydney, Knight of the Garter and Lord Deputy of Ireland; she died in 1544.

John, the eldest son of Sir Hugh, was knighted, and died in the reign of King Henry VIII., leaving issue a daughter, Constance (with whom the lordship of Lordington went at her marriage to Sir Geoffry De la Pole, Knt, second son of Sir Richard De la Pole, Knight of the Garter, and died 5 Henry VIII.), by his wife, Margaret Plantagenet, Countess of Salisbury, only daughter of George, Duke of Clarence, brother to King Edward IV.

Nicholas, the younger son of Sir Hugh, married the daughter and heir of —— Clement, Esq., of the County of Cambridge, and died in the reign of King Henry VIII, leaving issue one son, Robert, who, through the interest of his uncle, Sir William Sydney, chamberlain of the household to King Edward VI., was made Clerk of the Green Cloth, which employment he held to his death, residing generally, when not in attendance at court, at Tooting-Beck, in Surrey; he possessed a very extensive property, which he much improved by marrying Elizabeth, daughter and heir to Sir Maurice Berkeley, of Wymondham, in the County of Leicester, Knight.

Robert made his will, September 2nd, 1552, proved 30th November that year, and died soon after, leaving issue by his wife, Elizabeth (who re-married with Robert Livesey, and had two sons, Edward and Gabriel), four sons, all minors, viz —Robert, Edmund, who married Frances Sackforde, and died in 1601; John of Wimbleton, in the County of Surrey, died 1592 without issue; and Anthony.

The wardship and marriage of Robert, the eldest son, was in the first year of her reign granted by Queen Mary to Sir Henry Sydney;

which Robert married Ursula, daughter of Clement Chicheley, of Worsely, in the County of Cambridge, Esq., and had issue by her, who died before him, two sons, Henry and Clement, and having made his will in February, 1595, died soon after, leaving his said sons minors.

Henry, who resided usually at Northwitham, in the County of Lincoln, was in 1609 made a knight by King James I, and dying unmarried in March, 1620, was buried at Northwitham, and his fortune devolved to his brother Clement, who, being a man of an extravagant disposition, and having no children, dissipated and sold the greatest part, if not the whole of the great estates he inherited from his brother. He died in 1651, was buried 5th July, with his brother, and administration to his effects was granted to Jane, his widow, who died in 1667, and was buried with him, 17th August, at Northwitham.

The elder branch of the family becoming extinct on the death of Clement without issue, we return to the younger sons of Robert, Clerk of the Green Cloth, who died in 1552.

Edmond, second son of the said Robert, accompanied Sir Henry Sydney, in 1576, when he was Lord Lieutenant of Ireland, and was one of his family. He married Frances, daughter of Thomas Sackforde, Esq., who was also one of the Lord Lieutenant's confidential servants; and after the death of Sir Henry Sydney, he settled at Wimbleton, in Surrey, and died there in 1604, leaving issue of five sons, viz., Philip, Henry, Edmond, Thomas and Robert; and one daughter, Mary. John, the third son of Robert, Clerk of the Green Cloth, was educated at Cambridge, he made his will, 24th November, 1601, and died in 1602. Anthony, the youngest son of Robert, died young.

Philip, the eldest son of Edmond, second son of Robert, Clerk of the Green Cloth, was knighted by King James in 1616, and died without issue, as did his three next brothers, Henry, Edmond, and Thomas.

Robert, the youngest son of the said Edmond, succeeding to Northwitham and the remaining part of the estate of Clement, married Eleanor, daughter and heir to Clement, to Thomas Horsey, of Clifton, Dorset, and had four sons, Edward, Henry, Philip, and Robert; the

The Ancient Church of Ballymacormack (See end of "Ecclesiastical History.")

eldest died 1670 ; the others subscribed the greater part of their fortunes as adventurers, and in 1642 obtained commissions and went over to Ireland, each with the command of a troop of horse, among those who were sent on the breaking out of the rebellion of 1641. They obtained considerable grants of lands in consideration of their adventures and services.

The second son, Henry Pakenham, had a grant of the lands of Tullynally, County Westmeath, which he called Pakenham Hall, as also other lands in Westmeath and Wexford, confirmed by patent 20 Charles II.; M.P., Navan, 1661; made his will 16th January, 1690; proved 7th July, 1691; buried at Mayne, aged 80, having married first, Mary, daughter of Robert Hill, of Trim, County Meath; she died 12th June, 1665, having had issue. He married secondly, 1670, Anne, widow of——Bridgewater, and sister of Sir Thomas Pigot, master of the Court of Wards, and a son, Robert, rector of Kilbeggan, County Westmeath. His eldest son, Sir Thomas, knighted by William III., 1692, created Prime Sergeant-at-Law, 1695; M.P., Augher, County Tyrone; died 1706, having married first, 1673, Mary, daughter of Richard Nelmes, Alderman of London, and had issue. He married secondly one Bellingham.

His grandson, Thomas Pakenham, M P , Longford borough, created Baron of Longford, in the Peerage of Ireland, 27th April, 1776; born May, 1713; died 20th April, 1776, having married, 5th March, 1739, daughter and sole heiress of Michael Cuffe, Esq., of Longford (nephew and heir of Ambrose Aungier, second and last Earl of Longford, of the first creation). She was created Countess of Longford, 5th July, 1785; died 27th January, 1794, having had four daughters and three sons—(1) Edward Michael, succeeded as second baron. (2) Robert, M.P., County Longford, 1768, captain, 33rd regiment; born November 1748; died unmarried at Gibraltar, 7th July, 1775. (3) Hon. Sir Thomas, of Colure, County Westmeath, G.C B., admiral of the red, M.P., Longford, 1783, storekeeper of the ordnance; 1788; born 29th September, 1757, died 2nd February, 1836, having

T7

married, 24th June, 1785, Louisa, daughter of the Right Hon. John Staples (Bart.); she died, having had with other issue six sons and four daughters.

Edward Michael, second Baron, post-captain R.N., M.P., County Longford, 1765, P. C. 1777; born 1st April, 1743; died 3rd June, 1792, having married, 25th June, 1768, Catherine, daughter of Right Hon. Hercules Langford Rowley and Elizabeth Viscountess Langford; she died 12th March, 1816, having had, with four daughters, five sons.

(1.) Thomas succeeded as third Baron and second Earl.

(2.) Hon Sir Edward Michael, major-general in the army, G.C.B.; born 19th March, 1778; fell in action, 8th January, 1815.

(3.) Hon. Sir Hercules Robert, K.C.B., lieutenant-general in the army; born 29th September, 1781; died 7th March, 1850, having married, 25th December, 1817, Hon. Emily Stapleton, daughter of Thomas Lord le Despencer; she died 26th January, 1875, having had six sons and three daughters.

Thomas, third Baron and second Earl of Longford (on the death of his grandmother, Elizabeth Countess of Longford); born 14th May, 1774; died 24th May, 1838, having married, 23rd January, 1817, Lady Georgiana Charlotte Lygon, fifth daughter of William, first Earl of Beauchamp, and had seven sons and three daughters.

(1.) Edward Michael, third Earl, major 2nd Lifeguards; born 30th October, 1817; died unmarried 27th March, 1860.

(2.) *William Lygon*, fourth and present Earl; born 1819; succeeded his brother 1860, married, 1862, the Hon. Selina, third daughter of George, third Lord Dynevol; sits in the House of Lords as Lord Silchester, U.K. (cr. 1821); educated at Winchester; is Lord Lieutenant and Custos Rot. of County Longford, a J.P. and D.L. for County Westmeath, a general in the army, and hon. colonel 1st and 2nd Batts. Northumberland Fusiliers; was Under-Secretary of State for War, 1867-8, and formerly Adjutant-General to the Forces in the Crimea and in India. He has three sons and two daughters. Pakenham Hall,

Castle Pollard, County Westmeath, Carlton, White's, and United Service Clubs, S.W.; 24 Bruton-street, London, W.

Heir, his son Thomas, Lord Pakenham; educated at Winchester, and Christ Church, Oxford; born 1864; succeeded to the title on death of his father, in 1888.—Authorities: Lodge, Foster, and Walford's "Peerages."

Descent of the Earls of Lanesborough (from Lodge's " Peerage," Revised by Mervin Archall, 1789).

Ulick Viscount Galway married Frances, only daughter of George Lane, Lord Viscount Lanesborough (who died in August, 1684) and sister to James Viscount Lanesborough (who died without issue the same month in 1724), and by her (who in 1691 re-married with Henry Fox, of East Horsley, in Surrey, Esq., and died in December, 1713) had an only daughter, who died an infant.—Vol I., p. 138.

Dorcas, the second daughter of Sir Anthony Brabazon, in the County of Louth, third Earl of Meath, was married 21st March, 1644, to George Lane, created Viscount Lanesborough, Secretary of State, and Privy Councillor to King Charles the II., Clerk of the Star Chamber, Keeper of the Records in Birmingham Tower, and Secretary at War, to whom she was first wife, and by him, who died 11th December 1683, and was buried at Lanesborough, had two sons and two daughters—James, born 7th December, 1646; Brabazon, baptized 10th February, 1647; Charlotte and Mary; and deceasing 18th July, 1671, she was buried in St. Catherine's Church —Vol. I., p. 274.

Edmond Fitzmaurice, eleventh Earl of Kerry, is said to have a daughter, Catherine, who was grandmother to Emelina or Amy, daughter and heir to Cormac O'Farrell, who was married to Captain George Lane, and was mother of Sir Richard Lane, of Tulske, Knight and Baronet, who died 5th October, 1668, father of George, created Viscount Lanesborough, by his first wife, Mabel, daughter and heir to Gerald Fitzgerald, Esq., who died 10th November, 1630.—Vol. II., p. 190.

Butler, Earl of Lanesborough.

This noble family is descended from John Butler, of Waresley, in the County of Huntingdon, living there in 1376 (50 Edward III.), who married Isolda, daughter and heir to William Gobyan, of Waresley, who by will, dated 19th April, 1371, gave all his lands there to his said daughter, Isolda, and in 1376 bound himself to his son-in-law, John Butler, and Isolda, his wife, in the sum of 20 marcs. He was succeeded by his son John, who, marrying Elizabeth, daughter of Gonnell of Croxton, in the County of Huntingdon, had issue Edward Butler, of Stratford, near Baldock, in Bedfordshire, Esq., who married to his first wife, Etheldred, daughter of Richard Pollard, by whom he had George, his heir; and secondly, Elizabeth, daughter of Sir George Gascoigne, of Cardington, in Bedfordshire, Recorder of Bedford, and by her he had a daughter, Frances, married to —— Molyns of that county.

George Butler, Esq., who succeeded his father at Stratford, was also of Fenny-Drayton, near St Ives, in the County of Cambridge, and of Tewing, or Tewingbury, in Hertfordshire, anno 1575 ; marrying Dorothy, daughter of Stephen, and sister to Sir Stephen Beckingham, of Toleshunt, Beckingham, in Essex. He had issue six sons and four daughters :—

(1.) Beckingham Butler, of Tewing, Esq.

(2.) Sir Stephen, of Belturbet, in the County of Cavan, ancestor to the Earl of Lanesborough.

Daughters :—Elizabeth, Etheldred, Mary, and Rose.

*   *   ⁑   *   *   *   *   *

We shall now proceed with Sir Stephen Butler, of Belturbet, Knight, ancestor to the Earl of Lanesborough. He removed into Ireland in the reign of King James I., being an undertaker in the plantation of the province of Ulster, which that King had greatly at heart, and received a grant of 2,000 acres, called *Clonose*, in the County of Cavan, upon which he erected a castle and bawn of great strength, and in 1618 was able to arm 200 men with very good arms, which he had deposited in his castle, besides others dispersed to his tenants for their security, having then upon his estate forty families, besides under-tenants, who were able to make 135 armed men. And Sir Stephen, with the undertakers of the precinct of Loghtee, being obliged, by their conditions of plantation, to plant a town in Belturbet, for which they were allowed 384 acres of land, and to build a church, Mr. Pynnar, in his "Survey of Ulster," tells us there were built at that time thirty-five houses, all inhabited with British tenants, most of whom were tradesmen, each having a house and garden plot, with four acres of land, and commons for great numbers of cattle.

He married Mary, younger daughter and co-heir to Gervais Brindsley, of Brindsley, in the County of Nottingham, Esq., and by his will, dated 8th September, 1638, ordered his body to be buried in the Chancel of Belturbet Church, and dying 21st April, 1639, was there interred, having issue by her, who re-married with Edward Philpot, Esq., three sons and four daughters, all minors.—Vol. II., pp. 393, 394.

Francis Butler, of Belturbet, Esq., who succeeded his brother Stephen, bore arms in the service of King Charles I. during the course of the rebellion; and with his said brother represented that borough in the first Parliament after the Restoration, but became obnoxious to King James II., and was involved in the Act of Attainder, 1689, having his estate sequestered. He married Judith, daughter of Sir Theophilus Jones, of Osbertstown, in the County of Meath, Knight, Privy Councillor to King Charles II., and dying at Belturbet, 15th August, 1702, aged 68, was there buried, having five sons and five daughters. Brinsley, the second Lord Newtown-Butler, succeeded Theophilus, Lord Newtown, in 1711; in May, 1726, King George II., on his accession, advanced him to the dignity of Viscount of Lanesborough. Brinsley, the second Earl of Lanesborough, who was born 4th March, 1728, on the decease of his father succeeded to the honours, and took the oaths and his seat in the House of Peers, 3rd May, 1768.

His lordship married, 26th June, 1754, Jane, only daughter of Robert, the first Earl of Belvidere, and deceasing 24th January 1779, left issue two sons and six daughters.

Robert Herbert, the third Earl of Lanesborough, was born 1st August, 1759, succeeded his father, and took his seat in the House of Peers, 8th August, 1780. His lordship married, 5th January, 1781, Elizabeth, eldest daughter of the Right Honourable David Latouche, of the city of Dublin, and by her ladyship, who deceased in London, of a putrid fever, in September, 1788, had issue two sons, viz., Brinsley, Lord Newtown-Butler, born 22nd October, 1783; and David, born 27th April, 1785.

Titles—Robert Herbert Butler, Earl and Viscount of Lanesborough, and Baron of Newtown-Butler.

Creations—Baron of Newtown-Butler, in the County of Fermanagh, 21st October, 1715, 2 George I.; Viscount of Lanesborough, in the County of Longford, 12th August, 1728, 2 George II.; and Earl of Lanesborough, 20th July, 1756, 30 George II.

Motto.—" Liberté tout entière "—" Perfect liberty."

So much for Lodge's " Peerage."

Annaly—Pedigree of.

Luke White, Esq., M.P., who had acquired considerable wealth, purchased Lord Carhampton's estate of Luttrelstown, and changed the name of it to Woodlands. He married first Eliza Maziere, and had four sons and three daughters.

I. Thomas, of Woodlands, J.P., High Sheriff, 1840; colonel, County Militia; married 31st August, 1819, the Hon. Julia Vereker, daughter of Charles, second Viscount Gort, and died 4th May, 1847; his widow died 14th February, 1866.

II. Samuel, of Killakee, Rathfarnham, County Dublin, lieutenant-colonel, Dublin County Militia, M.P., County Leitrim, 1842-7; married Salisbury Anne, daughter of General Rothe, Esq., of Mount Rothe, County Kilkenny, and d. s. p. 1854. His widow died 27th Nov., 1880.

' • III. Luke, of Rathcline, M.P., died unmarried, 1854.

IV. Henry, created first Baron, Annaly and Rathcline, County Longford, in the Peerage of the United Kingdom, 19th August, 1863 ; died 3rd September, 1873, aged 83, having married 3rd October, 1828, Ellen, daughter of William (Soper) Dempster, having had with other issue two sons and two daughters.

1. *Luke*, second and present Baron.

2. Hon. Charles William, Lord Lieutenant, County Clare ; M.P., County Tipperary, 1866-73, 1873-5; captain late Scots Guards; born 9th September, 1838.

The Earls of Granard.

In pursuance of the King's Commission of January 29th, 1620, for the "plantation" of Leitrim, Arthur Forbes, Master of the King's Horse, did obtain for ever 500 acres of arable land and 670 acres of wood and bog in the County of Leitrim; and by a Commission bearing date Sept. 20th, the year previous, he obtained 1,268 acres in the parish of Clongish, County of Longford, the whole grant being erected into the Manor of Castleforbes, with all the privileges then existing. All these grants were confirmed to his son, Sir Arthur Forbes, in 1637, by Charles I., and he was then created a baronet of Nova Scotia. Sir Arthur de Forbes spent most of his life, after getting possession of these estates, in foreign countries on active military duty, and was seldom at home. He left the care of his lands to his wife, Lady Jane Lauder, who appears to have been a woman of the most vigorous temperament. She succeeded, in 1624, in building the Castle of Forbes, which was, as will be shown, subsequently burned down; and in 1641 she held the castle against the Irish troops of Colonel Owen Preston, one of the four generals of the Irish Confederated Catholics. As history explains, about that time a vigorous and determined effort was made by the Catholics of Ireland to remedy their miserable condition; and, in order to give force to their demands, the Council of the Confederation, which sat in Kilkenny, appointed four standing armies—one for each province   And it was the Leinster army, under Preston, that entered the County of Longford to dispossess the English garrisons. And they did actually dispossess the garrison at that time occupying the Castle of Longford ; for, on their refusal to surrender, it is recorded that the Irish troops assaulted the castle, in which were quartered a company of English soldiers, and succeeded in capturing it and putting the garrison to the sword, after which they sacked the town and marched to Castle Forbes.

The latter, however, was far better protected than Longford Castle, being surrounded by a good moat and rampart, and being defended by some cannon. Defences are very good when a man's stomach is filled, but in this case the canny Scots, who formed the garrison, had not the wherewith to fill their stomachs, and after a valiant show of resistance on the part of their female commander, they surrendered prisoners of war, and were marched off as such by Colonel Preston to Trim, where they were subsequently released, and whence Lady Jane went into Scotland, where she died. Her husband, Sir Arthur de Forbes, was shot in a duel in Hamburgh in 1632.

Sir Arthur Forbes, his son, was the first Earl of Granard, and gained his honours and titles as well by the force of his ambitious character, as by the allegiance he displayed towards his English masters. In 1641, when only eighteen years of age, he raised a company of men and marched to the relief of his mother, who was then besieged in Castle Forbes, but failed to effect his object. He next crossed over to Scotland, where Oliver Cromwell was beginning to shed the light of his benign gospel, and here he displayed his loyalty to the English Kings, Charles I. and Charles II., and was for it confined in Edinburgh Castle for two years. In 1653 he, in conjunction with some other Scottish loyal lords, attempted to raise a rebellion against the Commonwealth, but was defeated by General Monk; he then returned to Ireland, where, in 1655, he resumed his Irish estates on terms made by him whilst in Scotland with Monk, according to which he was to enjoy his estates in Leitrim and Longford as heretofore.

On March 19th, 1660, Charles II. appointed Sir Arthur Forbes, one

ABBEYSHRULE ABBEY.

of.the Commissioners of his Court of Claims, and in 1661, he was granted the manor and lands of Mullingar for his loyal services to the king, and also received another large slice of the County Longford. In 1663, being then in the north, he discovered what he deemed a great plot against the Crown and Constitution, and immediately pitched upon one Staples, M.P. for Strabane, as the chief conspirator, and had him arrested and confined, through which valour he saved Ireland from a rebellion, and did not fail to duly report same in the proper quarter. Being remembered for this and, doubtless, similar acts, in 1670 he was made a privy councillor and commander-in chief of the British army in Ireland, receiving nearly £700 a year for the post, as well as £600 a year pension, which he enjoyed for certain SECRET SERVICES rendered to the English interests in unhappy Ireland. In 1671 he was a lord justice of Ireland, and in 1672 was ordered to go to the king in England. The Earl of Essex, then Lord Lieutenant, gave him several very flattering letters of introduction, in which his usefulness to the Castle is clearly set out. These letters from Lord Essex had, after some time, the desired effect; and, after several journeys to England, and being again a lord justice of Ireland in 1674, at length, in 1675, he received his nobility from Charles II., creating him Baron Clanehugh and Viscount Granard, of the County Longford. In 1676 his ambition prompted him to lay claim, through a petition, to the lands of Artain, in the County Dublin, but it was proved that they belonged to another, and so his ambition was disappointed. In 1678 he disposed of the remnants of a small estate of his in Aberdeenshire, Scotland, and purchased, in conjunction with one Colonel Alexander M'Donnal, the Manor of Limerick, in County Leitrim, of which, in 1680, they made a division. In the same year he received four other townlands to farm in it In 1684 he raised a regiment of infantry, called the 18th Foot, and on November 29th was created Earl of Granard, which completed the goal of his ambition, and left him one of the most powerful men in the kingdom at that day.

In 1685 the ill-fated and unfortunate James II., the champion of

Catholicity, and yet the cowardly monarch who, by his pusillanimity, lost his kingdom, came to the throne.   He did not ask to disturb the Earl of Granard from his high offices, but appointed him and the Protestant Archbishop of Armagh lords justices of Ireland.   As the year advanced, however, James showed a disposition to confer on the Catholics some of the ordinary civil rights which were so exclusively possessed by the Protestants.   Up to this no Catholic could sit on a jury, possessed a vote at any election, or could hold any position of trust or honour whatsoever, whether in the army or civil ranks.   James, who was a devout Catholic himself, wished to place them on an equal footing with the Protestants, and in attempting to introduce this simple measure of justice in 1685, he met with a most vigorous opposition from all the Protestant Irish, and especially from Lord Granard, whom he had appointed lord justice.   It was in vain that James tried to show him that he simply meant to do justice to the Catholic Irish ; Lord Granard was not content.   And so, in 1686, the king appointed a lord lieutenant for Ireland, making Lord Granard president of the privy council, having previously removed him from the command of the army, to which post he had appointed the noble Duke of Tyrconnell.   Lord Granard refused the proffered post as an unprecedented office in the kingdom, and in 1687 went over to England, where he died some years later

Sir Arther Forbes, second Earl of Granard, succeeded to that title in 1696, being then exactly forty years of age.   His life, previous to his accession to the title, had been spent mostly in foreign countries, where he served, it is said, with distinction in several wars, having taken part against the Turks in 1686, when they besieged Buda, and when, were it not for the bravery of the ill-fated John Sobieski, King of the Poles, Europe would have been overrun by them.

On his father resigning his command of the troop of infantry he had raised, Lord Forbes, as he was called, was made colonel of the regiment, and before he had been any time in this post he was made a brigadier-general   In 1688 he was called upon by King James to serve him with his regiment in England, which he prepared to do, and having sent portion of the troops over before him under the command of his colonel and major, he was very much surprised to find the latter coming back in a few days. They told him that the king had dismissed them because they were Protestants, at which Lord Forbes became very indignant; and bringing them back, he reinstated them in the regiment. When he arrived at head-quarters, King James sharply reprimanded him for this, and Lord Forbes was on the point of resigning his regiment, but was recalled by a remark of the king to a sense of his duty.

When pusillanimous King James at length fled from England without even attempting to strike a blow for his crown, Lord Forbes gave up his regiment, his command being thereupon handed over to his own lieutenant-colonel, one of the Edgeworth family.

Early in 1689 the Prince of Orange, suspecting that Lord Forbes was a partisan to James, committed him to the Tower, where, after spending nearly a year, he was released. Whilst imprisoned the king made, it is said, several covert attempts to bribe him, but to no purpose. In June, 1690, a rumour spread that the country was about being invaded by the French, whereupon the king again committed Lord Forbes to the Tower, from which, however, he was soon released on bail. In February, 1695, he was once more, and for the last time, committed to the Tower, in which he spent a year, through some connexion with a conspiracy on the life of the king.

In 1698 he came back to Ireland, where he found his affairs in a dreadful state of disorder through the mismanagement of a steward to whom he had entrusted them. He set himself to the task of putting them in order again, but only partially succeeded, and in the year 1717 he made them over to his eldest son, on condition that an annuity was settled on him, on which he retired to private life in the suburbs of Dublin until 1734, when he died and was interred in the family burying-ground at Newtownforbes. He had been Lord Lieutenant of the County Longford from 1715, but took no part in the affairs of the county after he had made over his estates to his son.

Sir George Forbes, third Earl of Granard, was what is commonly known as a great man; and few political intrigues in the world of his day went on without his acquaintance. He was born in 1685, and commenced life as a midshipman on board one of his majesty's ships. In this service he was present at several battles, at one of which his brother was killed and he himself promoted for gallantry. Time progressed. The wars of the Continent during Anne and George the First's time took place, in which Lord Forbes took part in Spain with the English army. In 1736 he became Earl of Granard, after which he was made Minister to Russia, and in this capacity, which is represented to have been one of considerable difficulty, he acquitted himself as only an Irishman can, being always polite and deferential to all those he came in contact with. Having in the latter end of his days become eccentric, and, at the same time, disgusted with the disgraceful traitorism at that time a peculiar characteristic of the English Parliament, he retired from public life altogether, and became a student of classical works until his death, which took place in 1765. He was interred at the old Clongish graveyard. His son, Sir George Forbes, who was an army officer of considerable repute, succeeded him, having been born in 1710, and died in 1769, of a sudden attack of scorbutic humour. He had been appointed lord lieutenant of the county in 1756, and this post was conferred on his son, Sir George Forbes, fifth Earl of Granard, immediately on the death of his father. The fifth Earl was born in 1740, and in 1772 was appointed a member of the Privy Council in Ireland. He was twice married, but does not seem to have been in any higher position than lieutenant in the army previous to his accession to the title. He died in 1780, leaving the title to his son, Sir George Forbes, who became sixth Earl of Granard on 15th April, 1780, and who took part in the rebellion of 1798, being present at the "Races of Castlebar" with the Longford Militia, who deserted him and went over to the side of their country It is said that Lord Granard on this occasion endeavoured with all his might to rally his troops, but failed to do so. He subsequently took part in the engagement at Ballinamuck, and for his activity against the rebels is "honourably referred to" in the "Memoirs of Lord Cornwallis." He had a son called Lord Forbes, whose name during the troubled days prior to the Catholic Emancipation Act being passed, was a terror to the poor peasants of the county, whom he mercilessly rode over and hunted down when any chance to do so was given him. He died in 1836, a year before his own father, and so the estates went into Chancery until the coming of age of the late earl, who succeeded to the title in 1854, and died in 1889.

The present Earl is a minor, aged about fourteen years.

PART III·

RAMBLES THROUGH LONGFORD.

We will next read a chapter on the ancient legends and stories told in the different parishes of the county. Nothing, I am certain, reflects so truly the National character as the aptitude of our peasantry for relating at each fireside on winter nights the " *Seanachus*," in which the glorious traditions of mother Erin find so prominent a place. There are few parishes in Ireland in which there are not numbers of haunted places, where the ghosts of the restless dead appear at stated times to remind the unwary of the end of us all. In addition to ghost stories, there is a never-failing supply of stories of the " good people," and the numerous forts or raths scattered about Longford give quite as much food to its people on this matter as there is to be found elsewhere. I do not think it necessary to print these stories. In fact, although the matter that follows is largely a re-print of what I published in August, 1886, I am sure the reader will easily observe that a considerable number of the stories have been omitted. Such has been done because I found so much divergence of opinion on these stories, that I deemed them better omitted altogether. We will commence our ramble in the north, and travel southwards. If the reader takes the trouble to refer to the plates of any of the old buildings met with in his rambles, it will greatly assist him to understand the importance of the places he visits; and now to begin.

GRANARD.

There is no place in the County Longford possesses so much interest for the antiquarian student as the neighbourhood of Granard. In fact, in the old pagan days of our country, and up to 1315, Granard was the only capital of the County Longford, if we are to understand by that the ancient kingdom of Annaly. The word " Granard " was supposed by the learned Dr. O'Connor to be derived from the two Celtic words, " Grain," the sun, and " ard," a high place or hill; so that the proper meaning of the word " Granard " would seem to be " the Hill of the Sun." The reason this name was given to the town would appear to be, that in the early ages of the population of Ireland the people were sun and fire worshippers—that is, they worshipped these things as a deity, potent to relieve them from troubles, and to afford them safety in dangers. It is also said that they worshipped the moon and stars. It is thought that this worship prevailed amongst our pagan forefathers, just as amongst the Aztecs in the days of Montezuma. The usual place from which the people prayed to the sun was off a high hill or emi- nence. At the foot of this hill they stood in a circle, whilst the Druids ascended and offered sacrifice to their deities. Now, Granard is very favourably situated for such worship. On the one side they had the Hill of Granardkill and the Moat of Granard; and on the other side they had the Hill of Carragh, which commands a view of the whole county. An old bard, who sung of the Kings of Conmacne, describes, in the peculiar weirdly-thrilling chant of his profession, the " glories and magnificence " of Granard in these old days. The Granard of to- day is not the actual site of old Granard, which was built about half a mile from the present town, in a somewhat western direction This old town was destroyed by Edward Bruce, in his march towards Dublin, in 1315, having been, it is told, up to then, the residence of King Con

O'Farrell, of Annaly, who lived here in royal splendour at the time. Its destruction is described a little further on. Mr. O'Donovan thinks that the correct interpretation of Granard is, *the Ugly Height,* from the fact that when the father of a king named Carbre was getting it built, he called it *an Ugly Height,* or, in Irish, ᵢᵣ, ᵹᵱᴬɴᴬ, ᴬᵽᵒ, é, meaning, "*it is uglily high.*" Another derivation Mr. O'Donovan gives is, Gran-ard—meaning *Grainhill,* which, he says, would go to prove that there was a great deal of cultivation here for a long period. He subsequently says that the Moat of Granard, or Sheve Cairbhre, in the north, and the River Eithne, or Inny, in the south, were anciently the boundaries of Annaly. Carbre, who gave his name to Sheve-Carbrey, was the eighteenth in descent from O'Catharnaigh, who was progenitor of many families in ancient Teffia, or Meath, including the Foxes, O'Quinns, Carneys, Careys, &c. It is related in Colgan's "*Acta Sanctorum,*" in reference to this Carbrey, that when St. Patrick reached Granard on his apostolic mission, where King Carbre lived at his fortification—the Moat—this monarch refused to listen to his teaching; and some of his chieftains in the then fertile plains of Ballinamuck presented the Apostle with a hound dressed for dinner. The saint, naturally moved with anger at such treatment, pronounced a malediction on the sons of Cairbre, as well as on the land of the place he was in; and, as a result of this malediction, the land became barren, and misfortunes came on the line of Cairbre, from whose race the sceptre passed away. Subsequently, it is said, that his sons received the saint with all honour, and presented to him the beautiful place of Granard. There is another version also given in reference to the cursing of Cairbre, which the following note, taken from the life of St. Patrick, will explain :—" Cap. iv., Part ii.—But on the first day of the week, Patrick came to Taelton, in the County Westmeath, where the royal fair and public games and exercises of the kingdom used to be held yearly; and there he met Carbreus, the son of Niall, and brother of King Laogarious, and like his brother in ferocity of mind and cruelty. When Patrick preached the word of life to him, and pointed out the way of salvation, the man of adamantine heart not only refused to believe the preached truth, but laid projects for the death of him who was propounding the way of life, and caused the companions of the holy man to be scourged in a neighbouring river, called Sele, because Patrick called him the enemy of God. ' Then the man of God, seeing that the man was of inveterate mind and reproved by God, says to him :— ' Because you have resisted the doctrine of the Heavenly King, and refused to carry His sweet yoke, neither shall kings nor the pledges of the kingdom rise up from your stock; but your seed shall obey the seed of your brethren for ever; nor shall the neighbouring river, in which you have whipped my companions, although now it abounds in fishes, ever produce any fishes.' "

These two versions of the same story differ a little as to locality, cause, and effect; but it is certain that St. Patrick did visit Granard on his first apostolic mission and tour of Ireland, because the old town was a place of great natural strength, as well as being an important town in the kingdom in those days.

The Moat of Granard is well known as being one of the largest and oldest of its kind in Ireland. It seems to have been originally cut out of a large hill, because it is situated in such a position that the hands of man could not possibly have framed it. The approach to it is steep, and the visitor comes to a fosse, or trench, which surrounds it, before he can approach the side; after this the ascent has to be made in a zigzag direction, in order to avoid the dangers of a sudden fall; and when we come to the top we find a level and partly hollowed surface, wide enough to support a large body of troops, and partly protected in several places by the remains of what formed the rampart of the original fortification. Mr. O'Donovan says that he was told that an old castle existed inside the moat, to which there was a secret entrance; and that the Tuites and Daltons built it as a protection against the attacks of The O'Farrell in the 13th century; but he thinks it was a storehouse for grain in the days of King Carbre. It is mentioned in the Annals of the Four Masters under dates—236, 476, 765, 1069, 1272, 1275, 1475, 1586. But the events which took place at these dates

INTERIOR OF ONE OF THE CHURCHES ON QUAKERS' ISLAND.

were merely nominal; and it will here serve my purpose just as well to mention them to show the exact amount of importance attached to this old and venerable structure, which I believe can compete with any in Ireland for its antiquity and size. It is not so long since I was upon its top, from whence I could discern the spire of Longford Cathedral, twelve miles away ; Lough Sheelan, in Westmeath ; and Lough Gownagh, stretching away into the County Cavan.

We have referred to the destruction of Old Granard. King Con O'Farrell was a brave soldier, and renowned for the glory of his military exploits. When Edward Bruce landed at Carrickfergus, a number of the native chieftains flocked to his standard ; but a number stayed away also, mainly because they were jealous that a foreigner, as they unfortunately looked on him, should come to rule over them. Amongst those was the King of Upper Annaly (so called by O'Connor ; O'Donovan calls it North Teffia)—perhaps prince would be the better title to give him, he had also another motive in absenting himself, which was, that a neighbouring chieftain, with whom he was at feud, was one of Bruce's strongest adherents. Bruce, as the reader of history knows, first tried to approach Dublin by Drogheda, but subsequently had to fall back on the approach of the Saxon troops. He then determined to go by the midland route, and did penetrate as far as Lough Owel, in Westmeath, in the year 1315, when the severity of the winter compelled him to go into quarters. He had previously been refused admission into Old Granard by Prince Con, who proudly refused to surrender when called upon to do so, and so returning, when he saw further progress was impracticable, he hurled his whole force against the gates of Granard, so that for two days an awful carnage reigned, until the living made a road of the bodies of the dead ; after which Bruce's superiority in numbers prevailed, and Granard, the erection of thirteen centuries, was taken, and was subsequently levelled to the ground by Bruce before he left the spot.

Many old thrilling tales are told of the days when the head of the O'Farrells ruled in royal state in Granard. Thus, it is told of one monarch, named Congal, that his wife, the most beautiful woman in Leinster, was smitten down in child-birth, her demise being so sudden that Congal accused his chief Druid of using some sacred rites to destroy her. It was in vain that the latter protested his utter innocence. The king's ire was raised, and he ordered his execution after one year from the time of his wife's death. In the meantime he shut himself up in his palace, and refused to let anyone even see his face, at which his subjects were very much troubled. The end of the year was drawing nigh, and the chief Druid's day of doom was surely coming. At length his daughter prevailed on him to allow her to intercede with the king for pardon ; and her father consented, believing that, like all his subjects, she could not see the face of her monarch. The maiden, however, disguised herself as a servant, and hung continuously about the royal entrance. In the end her patience was rewarded. One day the king asked for a drink of pure water, which the Druid's daughter immediately fetched to him, and on entering into his presence, fell on her knees and implored the pardon of her father. The king was struck with her singular beauty, which attracted his attention immediately, and he told her that if she attended him every day for twelve days he would give her a decisive answer. Each day, accordingly, she brought him the same drink, and at the end of the twelfth day he not only granted her request, but asked her to take the place of the wife he had lost. This request, according to the laws of the country, she could not accede to, nor could he marry one beneath him in station without the consent of his people, which they refused to him, nor could all his arts persuade them At length he abdicated his throne, and allowed his son to reign in his stead, in order that he might enjoy a peaceful life with the object of his sudden affection.

On another occasion, a King of Annaly, having married a wife whom his brother had previously loved vainly, incurred the mortal hatred of the latter. He collected a large force of the enemies of the fortunate monarch, and one night treacherously surprised the town, putting every man in the king's service, himself and his wife to a cruel death. He then set himself up as king; but the kingdom that had formerly been a model of peace, was now a den of disorder and debauchery. Meantime, Nemesis was approaching in the person of the lawful son of his murdered brother, who, on the night of the massacre, was saved by his nurse, and had since been reared at the house of O'Rorke, in Breffni. Twenty years passed away, and he grew to man's estate, and then, swooping down like the tiger on his prey, he hurled the usurper and his disorderly crew from their ill-gotten possessions, and, ascending the throne himself, commenced a reign which, for prosperity and happiness, exceeded any ever known in the kingdom.

So much for the old traditions; now for a few modern stories.

Of late years the story of the headless horseman occupied a great deal of attention in Granard, where it was almost universally believed that each night a man rode through the streets of Granard on a headless horse, himself being also headless. This story arose from a very singular and unexplained suicide, which occurred in the barracks of Granard during the early years of the eighteenth century. Almost the very first regiment quartered there was one of the most ungovernable corps in the British service. Its captain, one Blundell by name, in dress, manners, sporting propensities, and general recklessness, was the cream of the service. One night a great ball was given in Granard by the officers, at which he was the leading figure; and the next morning, not having turned up at the usual hour, his room was broken open, and he was found lying dead upon the floor, his head being severed from his body. No one could have committed the act, because the captain's door was closed on the inside, and his window barred on the outside. Neither could any motive be ascribed for it; and the matter has remained a mystery ever since, giving rise to the weird story of the headless horseman and his midnight rides. Granard, from its very antiquity, is naturally the spot from which one would expect to hear such stories. I am sure that, could the treasures buried in the ruins of Old Granard be dug up, a fund of fireside lore sufficient to make many volumes would be the result. But, alas! man is made of dust,

and into dust must return; and whether it be on stone or parchment
that man's acts are written, they are equally liable, as he is himself, to
temporal decay   Granard was the scene of very active work during
the Rebellion of 1798, and here were enacted some of the most bloody
deeds history can record.   I have given a history of the momentous
battle which took place at Ballinamuck, in 1798, taken from the Cornwallis Correspondence.   Dark, cruel, and dreadful as were the scenes
that took place at Ballinamuck, they were but mere play towards the
treatment meted out to the "rebels" in Granard.   Thither a small
band of the County Longford insurgents, under the command of
Deniston, of Clonbroney, O'Keeffe, of Prospect, and Pat Farrell, of
Ballinree, "the biggest man in the county," had retreated after the
affair at Ballinamuck.   Above all other places in the country, there is
none so well adapted, in every sense of the word, to warfare as the
town and neighbourhood of Granard.   The town is almost surrounded
on all sides by hills, and on the moat alone a thousand men could keep
a hundred thousand in check, such are the facilities for defence.   The
approaches to it, too, are hilly and inaccessible; and so we can well
understand that, under the command of an able and skilled general, a
small force could keep a much larger one at bay for long enough.

As I have said, to Granard went Farrell, Deniston and O'Keeffe, with
a small force of men, after the route at Ballinamuck.   They found, on
their arrival, the whole place in a state of confusion and uproar.   People
were running hither and thither in the wildest confusion, because every
minute Lake and his bloodstained soldiers were expected from Ballinalee, whilst another squad was said to be on the march from Cavan.   The
appearance, therefore, of the three local and well-known leaders, with
even a small body of men, was hailed with triumphant shouts, and
immediately a council of war was held, at which it was unanimously
resolved to make a bold stand for liberty, and to defend Granard.
Scouts were at once posted on the moat and Granard Kil to watch the
approach of the enemy, whilst all the entrances to the town were bar-
ricaded.   To O'Farrell fell the lot to defend the Finea entrance, to

Deniston the Ballinamuck, and to the approach from Ballinalee the command was given to O'Keefe. The first to appear in sight were the Finea troops under the command of the famous Hepenstal, who had specially gone to Cavan to bring them up in hot haste. O'Farrell was a very tall man, fully seven feet high, with immense breadth of chest and strength of muscle, and during the struggle between both parties it is said the giants met, and O'Farrell, with one ponderous blow of his broken sword-hilt, put Hepenstal *hors de combat,* and his ragged mob of yeomen soon after took to flight. Almost before a pursuit could be made, a messenger arrived from Deniston, to inform him that a large force of the enemy were approaching from Ballinamuck. The brave man at once recalled his pursuing followers, and collected all his forces to oppose the entry of Lake's men into Granard. The three batches were massed on the Barrack Gate road, where a short, desperate engagement took place. By word and act Pat Farrell did all that a brave man could do to animate his sadly-thinned little force; and in this he was ably seconded by O'Keefe and Deniston. Here, there, everywhere he ran; now striking a blow, now parrying one, and again dashing forward into the very thick of the conflict. In the middle of the combat —luckless misfortune—Hepenstal and his Finea yeomen returned to the fight, and finding no opposition to their entry, soon attacked the now jaded Irishmen in the rere. In trying to extricate his force and Deniston's, the two friends became separated. Round Deniston gathered Hepenstal and his Finea militia, whilst O'Farrell was cut off by the Ballinamuck yeomen. Like an enraged tiger, the latter turned in his saddle to relieve Deniston, when a bullet from Hepenstal pierced his heart, and he fell to rise no more. Deniston managed to catch his horse as he was dashing away, and endeavoured with might and main to retrieve the fortunes of the day. But the fall of Pat Farrell had already decided it, and it was no longer a question of fight, but a question of how best to retreat. In this attempt the insurgents were captured in dozens, and Deniston, seeing that to remain were worse than madness, whispered to O'Keefe to mount behind him, and they

would make a bold dash for freedom. O'Keefe had been fighting all
through like a valiant soldier; and he and Deniston escaped in safety,
but were outlawed for three years afterwards, until a general pardon
was proclaimed, when both men returned to their homes, only to find
that the hand of the despoiler had filched from them their lawful possessions, to which they were never restored. The same night Pat
Farrell's mare, Bonnie Bess, galloped home to his house at Ballinree
riderless, and conveyed to his sorrowing family the sad tidings that
Granard was lost, and Pat Farrell had died a patriot's death.

But the darkest scene in this melancholy battle had yet to be enacted,
namely, the executions. As I said before, the effort to make a retreat
had resulted in the capture of the rebels in dozens. These poor men
—most of them country farmers and labourers—were tied hand and
foot, and thrown for a whole night on the streets of Granard, guarded
by a strong batch of yeomen. In the morning a number of yeomen,
who had been sent out during the night to gather cattle for provisions,
arrived with a drove of fat bullocks, and without any ceremony they
drove this herd over the fallen, prostrate Irish, until they trampled the
very life out of them; and such of them as showed any signs of anima-
tion after this brutal treatment, were given over to the tender mercies
of Hepenstal, who swung them out of existence as fast as they were
handed to him. History does not record this horrible British cruelty,
neither does the historian who composed or compiled the Cornwallis
Correspondence; but tradition, the unwritten history of every nation,
does, and it is well known that the whole incidents of the battle have
been carefully suppressed in order to hide these facts. More than once
have I seen references made to the cruelty of the British troops in
foreign countries, but if they could be so cruel at home in Ireland,
what must they not be away! Doubtless, Hepenstal may have insti-
gated the commission of this wholesale sacrifice, though that is scarcely
likely, seeing he was so fond of acting the hangman himself. A fearful
fate overtook this Hepenstal afterwards; for we are told, in a book
called "The Informers of '98," that he was seized with *morbus pedicu-*

laris, with which disease his body was devoured by vermin, and he died after twenty-one days in great agony. He is said to be interred in St. Michan's Churchyard, in Dublin.

Granard, since '98, has been a comparatively quiet and easy-going sort of place, but has managed to keep up in the race with the rest of Ireland, whether in political or commercial matters The accession of the town within the past few years to corporate dignity, is in itself a proof of its increasing prosperity; and whilst there are few places more worthy of the attention of the antiquarian or the poet than Granard and its moat, I regret to say that very few people, even in the place itself, seem to care for its ancient glory. Many respectable families live in its neighbourhood. The Reillys and O'Reillys, of East Breiffny, or Cavan, form a strong element here too, and are mentioned to the number of sixty-two as living in Granard Barony in the year 1659. There is no doubt that this parish was considered in olden days the central parish of Ireland, and that much importance was attached to it by the English of Meath and Leinster. A very well preserved Druidic circle is found near Springtown, within a mile of Granard.

DROMARD—ABBEYLARA—COLUMBKILLE.

I must confess my utter inability to give anything like a connected narrative of the history of these parishes. They formed part of the kingdom of King Lagaorius, the son of Niall, the father of Carbry, who reigned at Granard when St. Patrick visited it, and, beyond that, history tells us little or nothing about them, except that Lough Gowna was invaded by the Danes in 800 A.D , and that there was in the parish of Columbkille a castle on the townland of Rossduff, the ruins of which now form a piggery.

In the parish of Abbeylara, in the townland of Rathbracken, there is a curious and very ancient well, which is said to be the fountain spring of the great Lough Gowna. It is called by the name of Tobhar Gamnha, or the *Well of the Calf;* and, in the year 1837, an old man in the parish, then nearly one hundred years of age, named Farrell Linchy, told the late Mr. O'Donovan that, in the real old times, a well existed here, which was considered to be very holy and possessed of great healing powers. One day a woman in the neighbourhood washed a lot of dirty clothes in the well, and, ere she had done, a large calf came up out of the bottom, who ran off in a zig-zag direction from the place, and who was followed by a gurgling stream, which ran into a valley and formed the Lake Gownagh to-day In the middle of the lake is the Island of Inchmore, on which stands the ruins of Inismore Abbey. Some time ago these ruins were strewn over with skulls and fragments of bones ; and people used to come long distances and drink the water of a neighbouring holy well from the skulls to cure diseases in the head. This custom has now died away ; but there was a stone here, which was called St. Columb's stone, and in which there were the marks of his hand and two knees. From the little cavity so made, people were in the habit of drinking the water for pains and headaches, when any was collected in it In the townland of Ballybay, very close to the boundary of Abbeylara with the parish of Granard, Mr. O'Donovan found, in the year 1837, the sacred well of Tober-reendonny, or, as he translated it, the *Well of the King of Sunday*. This is a very ancient well, covered with bushes and brambles, which grew at the foot of two large trees, at the edge of the fountain. In old times no animal dare drink of its waters save man ; and on one occasion, when the people thought they could draw water from it for their cattle, and wash clothes in it, the cattle died, and the clothes refused to dry, despite all their endeavours. Mr. O'Donovan considered that this was a pagan well, in the dark days of Irish paganism, and its name was never changed, fearing the change would affect the inhabitants' veneration for the first principles of Christianity. He also inferred that there was a sacred well near the Abbey of Lerha, which was called the *Well of the Saintesses*, from which he thinks that a nunnery existed there very early in the days of St. Patrick. In a letter to a friend, which I have seen, he tells him that the present

St. Rioch's Church, on Inchboffin Island, in Lough Ree.

patron saint of the parish of Abbeylara is St. Bernard, but that the oldest inhabitants always venerated St. Kieran, the first Bishop of Clonmacnoise. It is said that there was an old castle, the ancient property of the O'Farrells, near the Abbey of Lerha, where the sons of Iriall O'Farrell lived after their split with the head clans, in 1445. In the year 1478, Melaghlin, son of Hugh Boy MacGheoghagan, Lord of Kinel Fiachra, came to visit the sons of Iriel, at their castle of Lerha; and during the night, whilst Hugh Boy was asleep, three of his attendants fell upon and murdered him in his sleep. They were arrested the next morning, and the crime was considered so inhuman that they were burned to death for it.

Columbkille parish is named after the celebrated Saint Columb, who was said to have lived at one time at Inchmore, and to have made numberless prophecies about the fate and destiny of this country and the world. During the late French war, when people's minds were somewhat excited about events passing round them, a curious phenomenon was witnessed in many parts of Ireland, when, during a fine summer's night, the sky appeared blood red. A great many people thereupon declared that this phenomenon, which was nothing more or less than a phase of the *aurora borealis*, was prophesied by St. Columbkille to be the forerunner of dire misfortune to the Irish race ; and so alarmed did some people become over it, that the clergy had to intervene to allay the general clamour.

BALLINAMUCK AND DRUMLISH.

The word "Ballinamuck" is derived from "Beal-aith-na-muic," which means, "*The Mouth of the Ford of the Pig*," the pig here referred to being no other than the celebrated black pig which rooted up the Danes' Cast in Armagh, and came as far as Ballinamuck, making her famous trench until she arrived at the Ford of Lough Gaun, where a man knocked her on the head with a blow of a stone and put an end to her rooting. The hollow trench extending from Ballinamuck to Lough Gowna, and said to have been formed by

z

this pig, was at one time recognised as the barrier between Ulster and Leinster, and subsequently the barrier between Breiffny and Annaly. The Danes' Cast in Armagh here referred to was a celebrated line of fortifications which extended from near the city to the old ruins of Emania—the residence of the ancient kings of Ulster. The fabulous black pig was supposed to have commenced her operations here, and rooted onwards until she came to Lough Gownagh, where she was killed by a man who had been born predestined to destroy her. The course of her peregrinations was marked by a deep valley, which is plainly traceable from this place to Armagh.

In 1848 the landlords made a desperate effort to depopulate this locality. Such indeed was the venom with which the King-Harman family set about this monstrous task, that the tenants, bad and all as they were with the pangs of hunger, rose up *en masse*, and every attempt at eviction was a bloody massacre, in which the tenants fought wildly and madly for their homesteads; and many of them were sent to their last account by the use of the rifle. The fearful sacrifice of life considerably subdued them, and their vengeance then took the form of midnight attacks on the " planted " families, during which several of them were killed, and one whole family wiped out. A strong police barracks, loop-holed for musketry fire, was then erected by the Harman family, which is the martial-looking building I have referred to at the commencement of this chapter. But after all these determined attempts to exterminate the people, it is gratifying to know that they are still "to the front," and that there are few better men in the county than in this same Ballinamuck.

Drumlish, which is the southern end of the joint parish, extends from the eastern side of the parish of Clongish to a short distance beyond the village of Drumlish, a view of which I give. To say that this portion of the County Longford has anything about it either interesting or uncommonly fertile, would not be to speak the truth, for, as a matter of notoriety, the inhabitants of it are hewers of wood and drawers of water on the worst land in Ireland. Seen as I saw it, in the

dull, drear aspect of a December morning, it was incomparably the
wildest-looking part of the County Longford. But wild-looking and
barren though it is and was, yet it has produced a class of men compared to whom many in the county are, for endurance, long-suffering,
and privation generally, but children. Living, as they are, on the worst
of land, their lives but one continual struggle to eke out an existence,
either in the bogs, or the wet, heavy, unproductive upland, it would be
at all no wonder if some of them "fainted by the wayside." But still
they fight on the battle of life, and when a manly, bold, determined
stand has to be taken, no men step into the gap so readily and fear-
lessly, as the following anecdote will show :—

On January 12th, 1881, a very unwelcome visitor indeed was ushered
into the village of Drumlish, surrounded by a *posse comitatus* of constabulary, who were designed to be his protectors. This was the bailiff,
who came to serve processes for rents which the people of Drumlish
were unable to pay, at the behest of his employer, the Earl of Granard.
Now, at this very time the Land League agitation was in the zenith of
its prosperity; and if a messenger from the lower regions were sent to
those poor people, he would have been more welcome to them than was
this individual. They regarded him in the same light as does the victim
about to be executed regard the hangman, and so they might, for as the
latter takes away the life of the former by the halter, or some other
fearful instrument of his calling, the process-server, ever odious to the
Irish people, takes from them their life when he bids them quit the
homesteads where they were born. It was no wonder, then, that the
people of Drumlish and Ballinamuck prepared to resist the approach
of the process-server to take the bread from the mouths of their families,
when it is considered that for seven months of the previous year they
had been supported on alms, collected for them by their priests, to
sustain them during the terrible distress that prevailed in the year 1880
in Ireland. During that period the reverend and zealous parish priest,
whom God, as if by a special mercy, had placed over the people, found
it on more than one occasion necessary for him to call upon the public

in their charity to prevent famine killing numbers of his flock.   In one
of these appeals he pithily described the condition of his poor people as
follows :—

"There are many houses in this parish at present in which the
last pound of meal has been consumed ; the last bed-covering worth a
shilling has been deposited in the pawn-office ; and the last fire of turf
collected from the saturated heap on the bog has died away upon the
hearth, the last dying embers being the livid emblem of that death
from starvation which is already creeping in upon the threshold.   It
is with a view to avert such a calamity that I am reluctantly con-
strained to ask support for these people."

Such was the condition of the people of Drumlish ; and but for the
exertions of their priests to ward off famine, they would have fared
badly.   Scarcely, however, had famine been put from their door, when
a new danger cropped up to confront them in the person of the
process-server.   They were just after storing the result of their harvest
—the result, after God's blessing, of their own hard work.   But to be
compelled now to pay a rackrent was unbearable, and so, with one
accord, they resolved to resist the process-server's intrusion.   The
latter was to serve the processes on the 12th inst., and in order to
be prepared for him before the morning's sun had risen, the Land
League drums were being beaten on the streets of Drumlish, and the
ringing of the chapel bell announced that something dire in its con-
sequences to the people was about to occur.   To the crowd which the
noise soon collected, the cry of "the process-server is coming" was an
all-sufficient notice—too well did most of them know its meaning—and,
with one accord, every man vowed he would assist his neighbour to
resist the invasion.   At ten o'clock in the forenoon a vast crowd had
assembled on the road leading to Newtownforbes, on which, in a short
time, they saw the unwelcome visitor approaching, surrounded by a
small force of Royal Irish Constabulary.   The latter were unprepared
to meet such a large crowd, and fixed their bayonets when approaching, until they were stopped in their march by these instruments of

·death touching the breasts of some of the stalwart men who formed the advanced guard of the contingents. The latter, however, never flinched, but shouted defiantly that "not a process they would allow to be served." The process-server cried out that he had no processes for them ; but, not believing him, they demanded why he came there if he had not ? After some parley, however, they let the police and their *protegé* get into the barrack. Immediately a telegram conveying news of the resistance was flashed into Longford, whereupon all the available police there hurried off to the scene of the row, in charge of the kind and humane Resident Magistrate of Longford at the time, H. W. Rogers, Esq. The police were in charge of District Inspector Horne. Immediately on their arrival a hollow square was formed, in the centre of which was placed the unlucky process-server, who was fairly shivering in his clothes with fright. The whole force then marched to the house of a man named Rogers, who was the first on the list of intended victims ; but the crowd dashed on ahead of them, and surrounded the house in so complete a manner, that the police could not even get into a small field in front of the house. Here were three thousand determined men, armed with sticks, stones, scythes, &c., who defied the police to get near the house they wanted. In vain the magistrate cursed, raved, and swore at them ; in vain he read the Riot Act ; in vain he lathered them with soft soap—all was useless ; for the sturdy defenders refused to budge one inch. The latter received fresh encouragement every minute, for from all directions, across hedges and ditches, came running men and women, armed with every available weapon. It was, therefore, useless to attempt to serve any processes that day ; and after a consultation, the magistrate and his forces determined to retreat to Drumlish and await further reinforcements. The retreat was not as pleasant, however, as they would wish, for they were followed by a mocking crowd, who mercilessly pelted the jackdaw process-server with jeering remarks the reverse of complimentary to his personality. The magistrate, however, warned the people that he would return next day and complete his work. To this they replied that they would meet "force with force;" and they prepared to carry out their promise. During that night horsemen were sent in various directions to summon forces to repel the invaders; chapel bells rung, and drums beat the whole live-long night, and the result was that by morning's dawn 20,000 men had been drawn together about the village of Drumlish. In the meantime the landlord element had not been idle, and, by permission of the Government, one troop of cavalry, three companies of infantry, and 120 police, were placed at Lord Granard's disposal to assist him in insisting on his LEGAL right.

But what a strange sight met these soldiers' eyes on the morning of the 13th January, 1881. Far as their eyes could reach were to be seen men with deep-knit brows and flashing eyes, in whose hands were grasped the ever handy *loy*, the scythe, the blackthorn, billhook, &c., &c. These brawny, sinewy, determined men sent up a chorus of defiance as the long file of infantry and cavalry approached them, and formed into line for forcing their way through the dense mass that choked up the road. The whole military and police force—I should have mentioned that the latter had arrived in the village mostly during the night of the 12th—was under the supreme control of Mr. Rogers, mentioned above. This gentleman had some experience of battles in India; and, well knowing the fearful carnage that would result that day from the loss of a drop of blood in Drumlish, hesitated before resorting to extreme measures. One of his first acts was to address the people at some length, pointing out to them the folly of resisting the law, and asking them, for God's and their own sake, not to force him to use the power vested in his hands. The people were somewhat mollified by his kindness, and even cheered him, I am told; but they refused to leave the way unless a promise would be given that no processes would be served. This promise Mr. Rogers could not give, and so the whole cortege of infantry, cavalry, and police—followed, preceded, and surrounded by the crowd—moved again towards the scene of the preceding day's operations. Who, it will be asked, directed the movements of what might be called the GRANDE ARMEE—the people?

Who controlled and guided such a mass? It was no other than the venerated and much-beloved parish priest of the place—Rev. Thomas Connefry. Father Connefry, a nephew to the late Most Rev. Dr. O'Higgins, was a native of the parish—a *Soggarth aroon* in every sense of the word—and the man to whom, under God, the people on that day owed their salvation. To him the people looked for guidance; him they obeyed; and he it was that, through the most superhuman exertions, saved Drumlish from being another Mullaghmast. Should I say Mullaghmast? No; because the tragedy there was but a painted picture towards what would have been the result if one drop of blood had been spilled in Drumlish. An old and experienced inhabitant of the parish, who had seen the Tithe riots of 1832, told me that they were but child's play to what was nearly occurring that day However, to proceed. The military and police marched to Rogers' house again, and here a halt was made to enable the miserable minion of the law, who was the cause of all the hub-bub, to drop his precious missive; but no—the people were determined no such service should be performed. Immediately the house was surrounded, and the crowd defiled into a BOREEN leading to it. Up this the military endeavoured to force a way, but failed; and suddenly, trying a feint, debouched into a field on the right, with the object of coming to the rere of the house. But the people were before them, and in the twinkling of an eye, the field was packed with men, whilst the threatened dwelling was surrounded back and front, being filled inside with armed men and women, who had hot water ready to fling on the advancing host. Here the Riot Act was again read and defied, as on a former occasion, whilst the Rev. Father Connefry flew about from one to another, remonstrating, entreating, and commanding in turn, in order that no chance would be given to the authorities to draw blood. After many attempts to carry out their mission, a conference took place between the priests and Mr. Rogers, with the result that the forces of the Queen were withdrawn until negotiations for a settlement with Lord Granard could be entered into; and once more the process-server retired, foiled in his object.

He never served the processes, simply because a settlement was arrived at between the Earl and his tenants; but for fully a month the forces of the Crown held Drumlish in a state of siege, until about fifty men, who had taken a prominent part in resisting the law, were bound over to the peace, after a week's imprisonment in Mullingar Jail

In reference to this famous period in the history of the Irish land agitation, the following scrap is taken from the issue of *The Tablet*, of January 22nd, 1881, on a question asked by Mr M'Carthy in the House of Commons:—

"THE EARL OF GRANARD AS A LANDLORD.

"Mr. Justin M'Carthy having alluded on Monday to a tumult caused by the serving of certain processes of ejectment on behalf of Lord Granard, Mr. Errington, on Tuesday, vindicated the character of that excellent nobleman as a good landlord. These remarks were warmly received by the House, as was also Mr. Errington's testimony to the pacific influence of a Catholic priest on this occasion, and to that which the Catholic clergy in general might be expected to exercise. 'There was another point also,' continued the member for Longford, 'to which he wished to allude. He meant the conduct on the occasion in question of a priest who was present. He believed it was due mainly to the Christian and manly behaviour of the parish priest, under difficult and dangerous circumstances, that, if not bloodshed, at all events serious disturbance was avoided. His name should be mentioned here. It was the Rev. Father Connefry, P.P., of Drumlish. The House would agree that his conduct was that at once of a good priest and a brave man. As to the connection of this episode with the main question, the House would hardly consider the fact that even so kind and indulgent a landlord as Lord Granard was reluctantly compelled to invoke civil and military aid to preserve order, was a logical reason for suspending the employment of such forces throughout the country. With reference to what fell from the hon. member for Carlow, he agreed with him that the Catholic clergy had found that

The Village of Ballisamuck, showing Fortified Barracks on extreme right.

the present agitation was going too far for them to support it; but whatever the result might be, of this he was confident, that in the future they would show themselves as they always had in the past, ministers of peace, opposing any movement, however popular, as soon as it went beyond the strict limits of justice, of religion, and of honour.' "

Mr. Errington's sense of the " limits of justice, of religion, and of honour " in those days was rather undefined, I think.

At the Longford Spring Assizes, on the 8th of March, 1881, ten young men were indicted before Lord Justice Deasy for conspiracy, and on the occasion of addressing the grand jury, his lordship fully described the offence committed.

Lord Justice Deasy, addressing them, said " he was sorry their county was not in as satisfactory a condition as to tranquillity as it was when he had the honour of presiding at last assizes The number of offences had increased very considerably. Some of the cases had been disposed of at the winter assizes, but a number still remained undisposed of, and bills on them would now be sent up by the Crown. He was very glad to say that no case had occurred involving the loss of human life, and there would, therefore, be no bill sent up for murder or manslaughter. The principal case or cases arose out of an unfortunate affair at or near the neighbourhood of Drumlish, which was made, according to the depositions, the scene of great disturbances, which continued for a period of three days. The disturbances appear to have been of a serious character, in some respects amounting, as they did, almost to an insurrectionary movement against the law. He sincerely hoped that such a state of things would not occur again. Bills in the case would be laid before them (the grand jury), who would give the evidence in support of the charge the best consideration they could. The bills charged ten persons with participating in the riots which unfortunately occurred at Drumlish, and which, as he had said, lasted three days. Perhaps it would be con-

1 A

venient to give a short outline or general statement of the facts for the
consideration of the grand jury. It appeared from the facts, as they
appeared on the face of the depositions both of the resident magistrate
and sub-inspector, that Lord Granard employed a process-server named
Murphy to serve processes for rent on some of his tenants in the
neighbourhood of Drumlish, and in order to enable the process-server
to discharge his duties, he sent his bailiff, who was acquainted with the
tenantry, to point out the persons upon whom the processes were to be
served. It was apprehended, and not without reason, that there would
be resistance to the service of the processes on the part of the tenants
and those who sympathized with them, and accordingly, the resident
magistrate and two sub-inspectors went with a force of 100 policemen
to protect the bailiff and process-server. And having got to Drumlish
they found that the place was crowded, and that the people attempted
to obstruct the passage of the bailiff and process-server through the
village to the scene of their intended operations. However, the police
forced their way through the crowd, and got to the police barrack, and
there the resident magistrate and sub-inspectors left fifteen men, and
proceeded with the remaining eighty-five constables to the residence of
a man named Thomas Rodgers, about half a mile from Drumlish. The
crowd accompanied them, and along the road the numbers of the crowd
were considerably augmented by various contingents. Having proceeded some distance, the police found that there was a lane leading
from the road to Rodgers' house, and from the aspect of the people,
which was very menacing, the resident magistrate and the officer in
charge of the police thought that it would be inexpedient to proceed
through the lane, which was, of course, flanked by ditches and hedges
which would afford cover to the crowd in the event of any disturbance
occurring. They then made a detour or flank movement through the
fields, and by pressure of the eighty-five men with their swords on the
crowd, they succeeded in approaching the house. When they got to
the wall near it, they saw that the house was deserted, and as they had
no authority to break open the door, the service of the process was

on that occasion ineffectual. The resident magistrate thought it would be inexpedient to go further, and he fell back upon Longford, taking with him the process-server and bailiff, to protect them from the violence of the mob, for the threats of the mob against the process-server were of an exceedingly violent character. They declared they would have his life, and it was probable that if he had not been protected he would have met with serious violence at the hands of the mob, and serious disturbances would have taken place. That was on the 12th of January. The police, seeing the threatening attitude of the people, came back to Longford, where they were reinforced by two more magistrates, and, what was perhaps equally important, they were joined by a number of extra policemen, thus bringing the force of constabulary then present up to three hundred men, and with this additional force the parties returned to Rodgers' house, where they saw a crowd of about five hundred persons, and a band came apparently to join them from Mohill. The police returned to Drumlish, having with them the bailiff and process-server, and protecting them in what was called 'a hollow square.' Another attempt was made on the 14th of January with a like result. It was right to state that but for the exertions used by the parish priest, the Rev. Mr. Connefry, there might have been serious disturbances. He got in among the crowd, and disarmed some of the men by taking their bludgeons from them, but, of course, in a crowded assembly he was unable to do more than take a few of them; and there was nothing wanting on his part to prevent acts of violence and breaches of the peace. Whether the people took the priest's good advice, he (his lordship) was unable to say. The state of things disclosed by the depositions appeared to be lamentable, and amounted, as he had said, on a small scale, to a sort of insurrection against the law, and, unfortunately, so far with temporary success. Ten persons would be charged with participating in these riotous proceedings, and it would suffice to say that if the prisoners were aiding and abetting, although they did not strike a blow, they would be guilty of taking part in a riot. Evidence of overt acts on the part of the several defendants would be given, and that being so, the duty of the grand jury would be very plain. He (his lordship) understood the accused parties would be positively identified, that overt acts would be proved against them, and that being so, the duty of the grand jury would be to find true bills, leaving it to the parties accused to defend themselves before a petty jury in this court. Though the language of the mob was violent, and their disposition towards the bailiff and process-server hostile, through the intervention of the police no violence was inflicted upon anyone."

Three of the ten men indicted were sentenced to short terms of imprisonment, and so this interesting episode in the history of the Irish Land Agitation terminated; but it is only fair to add, that ever since the people of Drumlish have been the bone and sinew of the land war in Longford.

EDGEWORTHSTOWN—CLONBRONEY—KILLOE.

Edgeworthstown, or the parish of Mostrim, has a population of about 3,000 souls, nearly all Roman Catholics, of which the town absorbs fully 1,000. It is so called because of its being the residence for the past two hundred years of the Edgeworth family, of which another branch lived in the parish of Clonbroney, the present representative of the former being Antonio E. Edgeworth, a gentleman who has, I am told, lived a considerable time in Italy. The little town of Edgeworthstown is pleasantly situated enough, and a considerable portion of the land about it is the very best to be found in the County Longford. Like all other places though, the landlord is disinclined to give it at a moderate rent; and quite recently a very animated dispute took place between him and his tenants, during which he invoked the power of the law and held a sheriff's sale in the town.

Edgeworthstown House, beautifully situated a short distance from the town, is the birthplace of the famous Maria Edgeworth, daughter of Richard Lovell Edgeworth, who died in 1817, and whose remains are interred in the cemetery of the place. Maria Edgeworth was born in 1770, and died in the year 1849, at the ripe old age of eighty. Her long and useful life was chiefly passed in Ireland; and many of her earlier works were produced by the aid of her father, who was a man of very eccentric character, but great intellectual activity in devoting himself to educational experiments and the improvement of society. Miss Edgeworth was a novel writer, who in her works endeavoured at once to please the taste and educate the mind; and the most valuable series of her early educational stories were the charming tales entitled "Rosamond," "Harry and Lucy," "Frank," published under the title of *Early Lessons*. These tales are written in the simplest style of language, and are both intelligible and interesting to the youngest readers; whilst the knowledge of character they display, the sound practical lessons they convey, and the naturalness of their incidents, make them *morceaux choisis* to the adult reader. In a work called the *Parents' Assistant*, Miss Edgeworth endeavoured to teach people of a more advanced age the very lessons contained in the previous sketches; and she next tried, in a short series of stories, such as *Simple Susan*, which is a masterpiece of grace and style, to combat the follies and prejudices of youth. Her best novel was a story entitled *Castle Rackrent*, in which the miseries and wretched state of poor Irish tenants, and the tyranny and hardships to which their landlords subjected them, are vividly sketched; and a defence of the badly vilified Irish character makes Maria Edgeworth do for the Irish what Sir Walter Scott did for the Scotch. Her other literary efforts included two very good stories—*The Absentee* and *Patronage*, in both of which she endeavoured to correct other social errors, and not unsuccessfully either, for she has done more good in the cause of common sense than any other similar writer in the ranks of British literature. Her father, brother, and some of her cousins were decidedly noted for their literary propensities; and whilst none of them showed the same rare gifts and talents as did herself, yet the family deserve specially to be complimented on their literary ability. Their exertions, too, in the cause of education deserve well for them from the people of this county; for, during the lifetime of Richard Lovell Edgeworth, prior to the passing of any edu-

cational measures, he patronized no less than eight different schools in
the town, which was noted amongst surrounding towns for the excellency of its teaching and general proficiency of its scholars.   In the
year 1740 a Latin School was taught here by the Rev. Patrick Hughes,
at which Oliver Goldsmith spent two years; but, strange to say, despite
his descriptive ability and general references to places he met with, he
makes no mention either of the size or population of Edgeworthstown.
It, however, appears to me to be about 200 years erected, during which
it has undergone vast improvement for the better.   About the year
1800 a great part of the town was rebuilt, owing to roof dilapidation
and other causes, and at this time it is said to have consisted of 145
houses, which was by no means a small number for those days.

The only historical reference I can find made to this parish is under
date—

"1430.   Owen O' Neill, accompanied by the chiefs of his province,
marched with a great army into Annaly   He went first to Sean Loug-
phort, and from thence to Caoillseallach (Kilsallagh), where he resided
for some time "

The Edgeworth family settled early in this place, to which they gave
their name, the old name being Mostrim.   The district which they
obtained at the time of the plantation of Annaly previously belonged
to the O'Farrells of Camliskmore.

The ruins of an abbey existed on the lands of Cullyvore, in this
parish, in 1837.   Very little more than the foundation-stones of it now
remain, although it was in a tolerable state of preservation then.   There
can be no record of its existence found in any ecclesiastical work I have
seen.   The patron saint of the parish of Mostrim is unknown; but Mr.
O'Donovan believes, from the fact that a well called Barry's Well was
lying almost beside the old ruins, that the ancient patron of this parish
was St. Bearach.   The present patron is the Blessed Virgin Mary,
whose feast is celebrated by the people on August 15th.   At a place
called Noghaval, some distance from this parish, in the year—

"1462.   O'Farrell of Annaly was defeated by the sons of Con

O'Melaghlin, Laviseach, the son of Ross, and the Dillons of Westmeath. Edmund O'Ferrall, and eleven men who were descendants of Murtogh Oge O'Ferrall, were taken prisoners, after a loss on their side of seventy men in the battle."

During the visit of O'Neill in 1430, his army fell short of provisions, and a bull having been procured, it is said that O'Neill had him roasted alive. His roars were so great that all the kine in the country ran towards him, and O'Neill, putting an end to his sufferings, captured all the other beasts Portion of the parish of Streete which is cut off by the boundary of this county from Westmeath, adjoins the mearing of this parish. Mr. John O'Donovan believes that it should be dedicated to St. Fintan, because there is a holy well here in the townland of Queensland; but he makes no historical reference to that part of the parish in this county.

Clonbroney.

This is an extensive parish, generally low and flat, lying to the north-east of the parish of Mostrim, and directly between Longford and Granard In the middle of the parish is the pleasantly-situated town of Ballinalee, which up to the year 1800 was known as the Corporation of St. Johnstown, and returned two members to the Irish Parliament. No doubt, the existence of such a place as a borough would create considerable feelings of risibility were one to visit it as such to-day. It was created, however, in the year 1680, for the purpose of being a convenient and handy "pocket" from which to return two upholders of "law and order."

Between Ballinalee and Edgeworthstown is the celebrated Moat Ferrall, and also Charlton's Folly, both relics of a past age, worthy of the attention of the historian, poet, or painter. Moat Ferrall is about the same size as the Moat of Lisserdowling, but more elevated and ancient-looking. A tradition is preserved amongst the people that the interior of it is hollow, and that in old times there was a private entrance to it by which the O'Ferralls entered when they were fleeing from their enemies, and remained in concealment here until danger was passed. Another story I have heard of it was, that here were inaugurated the ancient chieftains of Annaly prior to the dissensions which occurred amongst them in 1445. The ceremony of inauguration was a curious and solemn one. When the ruling chieftain died, or was killed in battle, as most often happened, his remains were borne on a bier to the moat, on the top of which they remained for one whole day and night, his people meantime keeping watch over the body in respectful silence. At the expiration of the appointed time for waking it, the body was removed, and the new chieftain, who had been selected in the meantime, ascending the moat, took an oath to observe the customs and laws of his country; and a white wand being presented to him, he thus assumed the lordship of his chieftaincy. Two hundred years ago the lands of Moat Ferrall belonged to a Mr. Charlton, who at his death willed them and his estates in Longford, Meath, and Westmeath to be divided in certain sums of money between young married labouring couples. This will has been a subject of much litigation. In order to spend as much money as he could, he built in this neighbourhood a rambling old structure, now in ruins, which, from the lot of money expended on it, and the way it is built, is called Charlton's Folly to this day. Both these places are well worthy of a visit from any person. In the year 1798, there encamped in the village of Ballinalee the blood-stained soldiers of Lord Cornwallis, who hanged more men during his three days' stay in it than ever were known to be executed at one period in the county before. If the reader refers to Part I. of this work, he will find full statistics given of the men who represented St. Johnstown in the Irish House of Commons.

At a place called Firmount, in this parish, was born the celebrated Abbé Edgeworth, who attended Louis XIV. on the scaffold at his execution in Paris in 1789. He belonged to the Edgeworth family; and was at the time of his death esteemed a very learned and holy man. He was converted to the Catholic faith whilst travelling in France in his young days.

DRUMLISH, AT A DISTANCE.

· Generally speaking, the parish of Clonbroney is one of the most fertile and pleasing-looking to be met with in the county. I am not very well versed in the topography of the parish; but I know that not far from the town of Ballinalee the Camlin takes its rise; and into the Camlin the surplus waters of the small lake of Gurteen discharge themselves by a natural underground sewer, forming one of the most curious phenomena to be met with in any part of Ireland. On the slope of Cornhill, and to the west of the town, there is also some splendid natural scenery in a place called the Glen, well worthy of a visit from any person—even the tourist who has visited the hills of Switzerland or the Lakes of Killarney. This beautiful place, which has not been at all improved by the loss of some trees lately cut down by the landlord, consists of a fairy dell, through which a tiny rivulet runs, falling in its course over a succession of natural cascades, in one of which there is formed a regular pot and pan, out of which the water dashes and forms a miniature fountain, very pretty to see on a fine day. On the whole it is the most beautifully fairy spot in the County Longford.

Killoe.

The parish of Killoe, which is bounded on the north by Cornhill, on the east by Clonbroney, west by Drumlish, and south by Longford, is, according to Mr. O'Donovan, a wild parish generally, low, flat, and boggy, and on the whole far from fertile. Nevertheless, the men of this parish have been at all times good stout men, ever in the breach when the call of duty required their presence. I have referred to Cornhill, which is so called because of the existence on its top of a large cairn, or huge pile of stones, which marks the last resting-place of some of the Irish kings. It is questionable if any relics of the monarchs could be discovered were search made beneath the cairn, but I have no doubt that an interesting *suite* of martial weapons would be discovered. It was on this hill that the beacon was lighted which proclaimed to the people that the Rising of '98 had been accomplished, and O'Rourke, ın his march to Ardagh ın 1172, stayed at the foot of the hill for one night. I am sorry to say that, except for these few and uninterestıng records, I have found no other references to these parishes.

CLONGISH AND KILLASHEE.

Clongish.

The parish of Clongish extends in an oblong direction from the brıdge of Clonart to the cross roads of Kilmore—a dıstance of about four miles, its greatest breadth not exceedıng three. It is entirely flat and unınterestıng, except that in the very centre of ıt almost stands Castle Forbes, the residence of the Earl of Granard, a costly fabric of recent erection, standıng between the village of Newtownforbes and the Shannon. The castle is erected about one mıle from the main entrance to the demesne, which ıs about a mile square ın cırcumference, the entrance opening into the single street of the vıllage itself. It consists of a minaretted tower of solid and substantial proportions, attached to whıch is the main or house portion of the buıldıng, five storıes high, erected of purely-dressed limestone. At right angles to this buildıng ıs another similar building formıng a triangle wıthout a base, the apex of which is the tower At the base of this trıangle a line of stables runs parallel to the northern wıng of the buılding, ın which the carriage and other horses belonging to the Earl of Granard are kept; and were a comparıson to be ınstıtuted between them and the wretched dens in which some of his lordship's tenants are forced to live, a very fair idea would be gaıned of the fetid passıon which often ımpels human beings to fondle a pug dog and spurn a Chrıstıan from their doors at the same tıme.

There are inside the walls of the demesne, and behind Castle Forbes, the remains of a graveyard in which, prior to the year 1800, all the people of the parısh had leave to ınter deceased relatives. But the fourth Earl of Granard, havıng spent much of hıs tıme ın fencing in the demesne with walls and palings, determined to close this graveyard against future interments, except of members of his own family. When this became known it aroused a great deal of anger and discontent in the parish; so much so that many persons had recourse to burying their friends in the graveyard at night sooner than forego their right to interment in it. This Lord Granard always resisted, by having the remains lifted and deposited outside the castle walls as soon as he discovered that an interment had taken place. There lived in the parish at this time a notorious prize-fighter and village Sampson, whose prowess with the fists had gained for him the pugnacious title of the "Bulla-watha." This man fell sick in the course of time, and, when dying, called his sons to his bedside. "Bury me," said he, "in the graveyard in the demesne, where my father before me rests; and put a good blackthorn stick at my right hand in the coffin, for if anyone disturbs me you'll hear something." The man died soon after, and the directions he gave to his sons were faithfully carried out; and at midnight his remains were placed in a grave in the forbidden burial-ground. Next day the earl came to hear of it, and ordered the removal of the remains. His orders were promptly obeyed, and poor "Bulla-watha" was left on the road side; and the people of Clongish heard next morning that Lord Granard was dead

There is a good story told of the wife of Sir George Forbes, fifth Earl of Granard. She, it seems, was a very benevolent lady, who recognised that "those who give to the poor lend to the Lord." One day she was walking in the demesne of Castle Forbes, accompanied by her husband, the earl, when they were accosted by a poor mendicant, who craved of them an alms. Lady Granard immediately put her hand in her pocket, and took from her purse a guinea, which she handed to the poor man. The earl, who was rather "tight" in money matters, expostulated with her on such extravagance, and said guineas were not so plenty as to be given away at random. Her ladyship requested him to lend her half-a-sovereign and she would exchange it for the gift she had just made; and having called back the mendicant, she said, "Here, poor man, his lordship desires to add a donation

to my small gift " She then gave him the half-sovereign, and, having
rejoined her lord, informed him what she had done. It is needless to
say that his lordship did not again interfere with his lady's bequests.

About the year 1780 an innocent man was ordered to be executed
in Longford Jail for the crime of sheep-stealing. In vain the poor
fellow protested his innocence of the crime with which he was charged;
there was no mercy for him, and when the day appointed for his execution had come, he was brought out to a large tree in the neighbourhood of Longford Jail, and there publicly strung up like a dog. In those
days a man's friends obtained his body after death, and in this case, as
soon as the officials of the jail had departed, the body was cut down and
borne off by the relations. When bearing it away some of them
observed that it was very warm, and that the tongue did not protrude
as in the ordinary case where a man's neck is broken by a fall; and
having applied restoratives they had the satisfaction of seeing the apparently dead man come to in a few hours, an injury to his spine being
the only serious result of the hanging. The truth was, that in those
days hanging was an every-day occurrence almost, and in this instance,
the officials had been so careless in performing their ugly task, that they
had not carried out the sentence of the law. From the effects of the
injury to his spine, the man was hunched during after-life. His friends
succeeded in conveying him away in secret to the woods of Castleforbes,
where they built for him, in a secret place, a small hut. Here he lived
in privacy for about five years, never daring to go out except after dark.
One day, however, a frolicsome boy ran into his hut, and shouted to him
that the soldiers were coming, and the poor fellow got such a fright
that he dropped dead on the floor.

During the stormy days of '98 and 1803 this parish was the scene
of very active work. Lord Forbes, son to the Earl of Granard, was then
about in his maturity, and his father, the earl, in virtue of his command
of the Longford Militia, had at his back a company of about 120 yeomen.
With these men the young viscount was in the habit of sallying out and
searching for rebels, as he was pleased to call any person who had

rendered himself obnoxious to the ruling powers. On one occasion intelligence was conveyed to him that a rebel who held a command at Ballinamuck, was concealed in a house in his father's bog Immediately the young lord and his minions dashed out and scoured the whole country, but without avail. It was afterwards known that the hunted patriot had lain in a boghole whilst the yeomen searched the bog, and these gallant sons of Mars never thought of looking in such a place for him.

His father, the Earl, who had a seat in the Irish House of Lords, opposed the passing of the accursed Union; and it is said of him that neither bribery nor offers of promotion could induce him to give his assent to it. When the union was passed, he, in company with twenty-eight other peers of Ireland, entered a written protest in the most solemn manner against it. He is said also to have invariably supported Charlemont, Grattan, and Curran in their Irish policy.

It is gratifying to find that in so important a matter Lord Granard took the right side; and it would, in my opinion, do a great deal for his grandson to-day in the estimation of the people of Longford, if he could bring himself to support the policy of the great statesman who is endeavouring to undo the chains which have bound Ireland since 1800. I have at some length previously referred to Lord Granard's action at Ballinamuck in no very complimentary terms. At that time I was not aware of his other action in 1800; and whilst I am most willing on all occasions to show up the bad acts of men in power, I would not wish to be understood as a partial critic who looked but to the one side of a picture.

In Lord Granard's demesne there is a kind of old stone pier, with a curious inscription in Latin carved upon it. This inscription is supposed by Mr. John O'Donovan to be dedicated to Barbacela, "*the guardian of the spring*," a well that once bubbled forth from the root of an ash-tree in the vicinity. I have never seen the inscription or the monument myself, but I take the liberty of attaching hereunto Mr. O'Donovan's translation of it. He says that the people of Clongish call this monument Granuewael's Tomb, but in this they are, of course, mistaken.

He also says that the parish of Clongish was originally founded by St. Eilether, according to Colgan; but the name of the saint, or when he lived, is no longer even remembered by the present inhabitants. In a previous notice of the Earls of Granard, I have given the recorded events that took place during the Irish Confederated Catholic War in 1641, and also the events of the War in 1690. I will now conclude my notice of this parish with a word about

THE BARBACELA MONUMENT.

O'Donovan's translation of the inscription on this monument is :—

> " O Polycletes, tell why has old fame
> Extolled thy arts and raised on high thy name,
> When the fair figures fashioned by thy hand
> Can ne'er the wasting power of time withstand
> Why boast of Phydia's nobly sculptured forms,
> As they have not defied the rage of storms
> But look at me with artless native face,
> Sit here, eternal vigil of the place;
> For snows and storms may rage
> In vain to strike me with the marks of age
> I still retain the beauty of my prime,
> And bid defiance to the hand of time
> Good friend, whene'er thou travellest this way,
> Shouldst thou be thirsty from a sultry day,
> Consulting for thy stomach and thy head,
> Drink freely of this well—'twill serve instead
> Of wine and all such artificial drink,
> Which cause the body and the mind to shrink.
> But when thou travellest here some offering bring
> To Barbacela, goddess of this spring "

Killashee

The word " Killashee " means " the wood of the fairies," and this parish is so called because of the number of forts which are to be found in,it, and which, some hundreds of years ago, were covered with trees. This is an uninteresting parish, free from many historical reminiscences. It is mostly composed of low land and bog, which, except for some fertile and productive spots, is generally of a very inferior quality.

It is said that at the old graveyard of Ballmakill there stood in ancient times a monastery for Grey Franciscan Friars, the remains of which are still plainly to be seen in the old graveyard, which is nearly midway between the villages of Killashee and Clondra, and is very picturesquely situated. In reference to this monastery, I find that there were fifteen Franciscan convents founded in Leinster, and that in

"1302. The Convent of St. John the Baptist, near Killashee, in the County of Longford, was founded by Dhomnal O'Farrell, Chieftain of Annaly."

Dhomnal O'Farrell is mentioned as 76th on the O'Farrell pedigree from Ir, the founder of the Iran Monarchy. The date at which the Convent of Killashee was destroyed or deserted is not given; but we may reasonably suppose that in the reign of Elizabeth it shared the same fate as the other monasteries and abbeys in Ireland. An old story is told in reference to it, which is the most interesting about this parish. This is, that at the time of its suppression there was a splendid musical bell suspended from an ash-tree beside the old monastery; and the soldiers who demolished it took away the bell, and set it up on the belfry of a church which they had erected for their own use, near the Shannon. The bell, however, was not disposed to call to prayers people to whose religious feelings its own were not consonant; and the Sunday following its removal, when the time came for Mass, the bell sprung from the belfry on which it had been placed, and, flying back through the air, clanging aloud to the people to assemble for their ancient worship, once more become settled upon the tree, from which it fell to the ground and was broken. This beautiful legend in reference to the sound of the bell in the air is yet told amongst the people of this parish, and many of them will also tell the querist of their having heard it themselves—*auribus ipsis* There is in Killashee, as well as in every other place, a holy well called by the name of *Ardneeves Well*, to the waters of which certain miraculous powers are attached.

Rynmount House is a very old erection near Clondra, and was at one time the residence of a family of Montforts.   The little village of Clondra, at the upper end of the parish, is an ancient place, and was the head-quarters of all the grain merchants of the county prior to the introduction of the canal into Longford, in 1826.   A tremendous traffic was carried on between this place and Dublin at or shortly before the time of the Union, which was subsequently transferred to Longford, and carried on there for years.   There was a distillery here in those days, too, which carried on a large trade.   Many accidents, too numerous to record, have occurred about the canal and locks which open into the Shannon.   Unfortunately, the trade done on these high-ways of traffic has largely decreased.

In the graveyard of Clondra there stands the ruins of what the inhabitants of this parish call " Cromwell's Church," which is one of the strongest-looking structures I have seen, and is certainly in a state 'of great preservation.   Inside and outside the walls are surrounded with bushes and brambles, which add a good deal to its ancient appearance ; whilst the long, narrow slit windows testify to its undoubtedly strong claims to antiquity.   I have made a careful examination of the ruins, and my own belief is that this place was once a friary chapel of some sort or other, in which the clergyman who officiated lived.   My reason for believing that the latter lived here is, that at the rere of the building there is a kitchen-like apartment, the roof of which is composed of small stones, arched and grouted together.   A flight of stone steps leads on to this roof, which is thus made a gallery of.   Probably the whole building was roofed in like manner in the good old days gone by.   The walls of this priory chapel, which is exactly similar to Abbeydearg, Ballymacormack, and Longford, are very thick ; and in the graveyard itself there is to be seen more than one old stone carved in raised Irish letters.   Irish scholars should note this fact, and pay a visit to Clondra graveyard.

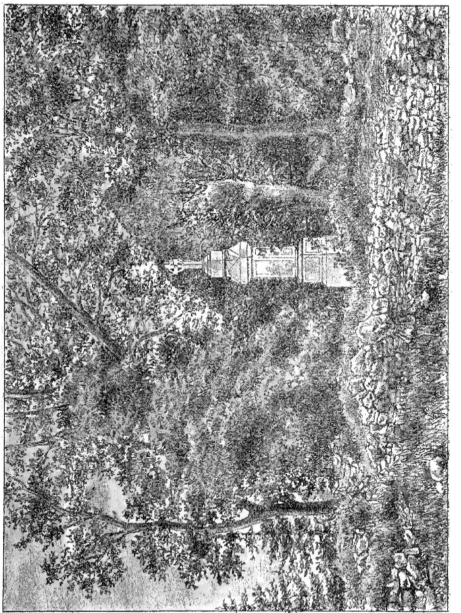

The Ruins of the Abbey of Deirg (See "Abbey Deirg," in "Ecclesiastical History.")

. I have been told that almost at the edge of the Shannon, and in a bee-line south-west from this old ruin, there was erected a castle, the remains of which are now scarcely discernible. I have found no historical mention made of it. Coming back to the village of Killashee, we pass, on our way into Longford, Ballyclare Castle, reference to which will be found in the extracts from the Patent Rolls of James I.

LONGFORD.

The parish of Longford is at the present day made up of the parishes of Templemichael, Sraid, and Ballymacormack, and numbers 7,000 inhabitants, of whom 4,000 live in the town of Longford. The town of Longford is incorporated under the Towns' Improvement Act, 1854, and is represented in the Town Council by fifteen Town Commissioners, of whom one is borough magistrate and holds a Court of Conscience once a week; whilst the electorate is divided into two wards, called respectively the Longford and Abbey Wards.

The Upper Barracks, built about the year 1790, was used as the depot of an artillery regiment, and possessed many more attractive features about it than a mere outside inspection would attach to it.

The Lower Barracks, which was built about the year 1815, has served for the head-quarters of a cavalry regiment up to within a few years ago, when, contrary to the wishes of a large number of the people of the town, whose trade was benefited by the presence of the soldiers, the head-quarters were removed, and have not since been restored. Among the other buildings in town worthy of notice, are—the county jail, the county infirmary, the Roman Catholic Cathedral, St. Mel's College, St. Joseph's Convent of Mercy, and the Protestant church. The county jail is a comparatively new erection of very formidable proportions, and capable of holding 150 prisoners.

Up to a recent period it was the jail in which all prisoners from the county were confined; but owing to the diminution of crime in Ireland, as well as to the paring economy of our rulers, the county jail of Longford is now an empty building, in which no

prisoners are confined.   After its erection, a practical system of remu-
nerative labour introduced at the time into Irish prisons was carried out
here with great success, and starch and Indian meal was ground by the
prisoners on the treadmill ; whilst female prisoners were employed in
sewing sacks and other useful articles of house use ; and so very eco-
nomically was the business managed, that the governor at the time,
after feeding his prisoners and paying them 1d. per day, had a profit
to balance his accounts with.   Now all this has been changed, and the
prisoners, instead of being employed at some useful work, are sent
down to Sligo to break stones for road contractors, and to cost the
cesspayers in railway fares more money than if they had been left in
Longford.

The county infirmary was erected in 1848, and is capable of holding
about sixty patients, whose wants are attended to by a staff of nurses,
a doctor, and an apothecary.   The present doctor is by repute a
clever surgeon ; and very few cases of death have occurred under his
hands, although it is not to be expected that there are the same
appliances, medical and surgical, here as one meets with in a city.   It
is a great pity that the Government do not empower their universities
to place such hospitals as these on the list of those places from which
students could obtain a medical degree; and I am sure that if such
regulations were put in force regarding county infirmaries, the result
would be to greatly assist the doctors and to tend to the general welfare
of the patients.

With regard to the County Longford Infirmary, a good story is
told of its first doctor.   This was a Frenchman named Dubedat, who
exercised all the medical and surgical skill the patients needed at that
time, and is said to have been a wondrously clever man.   Be that as it
may, after his death it was rumoured among the patients that they had
" seen " Dr. Dubedat, or rather his ghost, and forthwith it was ordained
as an unwritten law that Dr. Dubedat's appearance meant the death of
the patient whom he visited ; and up to a few years ago Dr. Dubedat's
visits were almost as regularly reported as the advent of a new moon.

The Roman Catholic Cathedral of Longford is the largest building of its kind in Leinster. For the stupendousness of its proportions, the height of its tower, the massiveness of its columns, and its gorgeous interior decorations, the Cathedral of Longford can vie with any other in Ireland. The first stone was laid on the 19th of May, 1840, by the then bishop, Right Rev. William O'Higgins, and it was completed and opened on 29th September, 1856, by the Right Rev. John Kilduff, his immediate successor, than whom no greater benefactor of the Church ever lived. The cathedral is cruciform in shape, consisting of a nave, two transepts, two aisles, and a spacious chancel. In the aisles and round the whole church, at a distance of some twelve feet from the ground, there are niches placed between each window, in which the present illustrious and saintly bishop has erected costly statues of the saints and the Holy Family; and in recent years a large sum has been expended in the interior decoration of the church. The roof is supported by more than 24 large columns, massively thick, and cut out of a limestone quarry in the parish of Newtowncashel. Underneath the floor of the church are vaults for the interment of priests, and there are also here interred the remains of the founder and opener of the cathedral. The erection of this stupendous building cost £60,000, and the high altar (which is cut out of French marble) and the grand organ cost £10,000. The collection of this vast sum to erect a fitting temple for the Catholics of the centre of Ireland surely reflects credit on those who undertook the herculean task; and the writer is fully sensible that he is unable to do sufficient justice to the result of their labours. The architectural beauty and finish of the mouldings of the ceiling are alone worthy of the greatest praise; but it would require a more skilled and experienced writer than I am to adequately describe the whole building, a personal visit to which will amply repay the stranger.

St. Mel's College is nearly twenty years doing practical good for the Catholic youth of the county, and already it has passed through its portals some eminent men, including Joseph R. Cox, Esq., M.P. for East Clare, and his brother, Dr. M. F. Cox, a distinguished man in the medical profession in Dublin.   The number of priests who have been educated in St. Mel's College is beyond reckoning, and a good many of its students at the present day occupy high places in the various professional ranks of our country, whilst not a few have obtained creditable places in the Civil Service.   St. Mel's College is built in a north-eastern direction from the town, and presents to the eye all that is needed to make a college a healthy home for students.   The teaching staff is large, the curriculum varied, every subject necessary to a man's present day education being taught by it   Not the least attractive feature is the foundation of a number of valuable bourses by the present bishop, which are offered for competition each year to the students ; and every care and attention is bestowed by the authorities on the latter.

St. Joseph's Convent of Mercy is a recent building which cost a large sum of money, and is admirably fitted for the wants of the large community that dwell within its walls.   The community is under the spiritual care of the Rev. Mother Mary Joseph Howley, and the patronage of the Lord Bishop of Ardagh.   To the convent are attached the young ladies' and other schools, in which a very good education is given to the Catholic female youth of the town.

The Protestant Church of Longford is built in the same style as nearly all such churches are built throughout the country, and there is nothing peculiar about it except that it is said to be erected on the site of the old parish church of Longford.   The present church is not more than eighty years erected, having superseded an old and shaky building which had stood in the same place from the reign of Queen Anne.   The building of to-day is the plainest of the plain—neither pretentious in its outward nor (we believe) interior appearance.

There are also in Longford a Methodist chapel, opened in 1843, a Presbyterian church, and what is called a Bartonite meeting-house ; and we have national schools to correspond to all these persuasions.

Coming to historical matter, I may be permitted to say that never have I ever experienced more difficulty than to discover the origin and history of the town of Longford.   The name Longford, however, gives us a clue to the origin of the town. We are told in an old record that the Gaelic name of this place was Athfada, which means the long ford—*ath* being the Gaelic for ford, and *fada* long. Our forefathers had a curious fashion of calling every place by its peculiar natural characteristic, and when the Saxon came, in order to name places he simply translated the Gaelic name, and gave himself no more trouble about it. Thus, by the translation of Athfada, we have Longford, the name we know to-day.

The Castle of Lios-ard-abhla, erected at the Moat of Lisserdowling, and now represented by a few crumbling old walls at the foot of the moat, is within the parish boundary of Longford, and is well worthy of a visit from the people of the town, who do not seem to know that such a place exists at all. The ruins of the castle, as shown in the old walls, prove it to have been a large and important erection ; but I have been told that nearly all the main portions of the structure, which was in a tolerable state of preservation up to some short time ago, have been removed. The people who live in the neighbourhood tell that the moat is hollow within, and that they remember the time when a chimney-shaft was open on the top of it. They also say it was believed by many old people that the owners lived within and had underground passages from it to escape through in case of attack or surprise. I am inclined myself to think that, like the Moat of Granard, Lios-ard-abhla was used, if for anything, as a storehouse for grain, but as nothing else than that.

The first mention that we find of the existence of such a place as Longford, occurs in the year 1400, when we find that Dhomnal, or Donnell O'Farrell, chieftain of Annaly, founded a monastery which continued to flourish for more than one hundred years, until the suppression by Elizabeth. The next thing we know is that Longford became a borough, and was represented in the Irish House of Commons by two members of Parliament from the year 1613 to 1800. The whole county was, during this time, represented by ten members—not a few of whom were celebrated men—such as Sir John Parnell, John Hely

Hutchinson, Arthur Gore, &c. It was during those days that the Aungiers became Lords of Longford, having obtained large grants of land about the present town in these days; and they, in my opinion, erected the present old Castle of Longford.

Perhaps it would be well now to say a few words about the Castle of Longford. This castle consists at present of a large tower and a square building attached, the whole forming a large and comfortable dwelling-house, which is let out in tenements to the wives of the soldiers of the adjoining barracks. The tenement rooms are large and airy; so large, indeed, that some of them would make a very good little dwelling-house in itself. In this respect alone they show their age and antiquity, for, together with the old houses built round them, they are now in use more than 200 years. The Castle of Longford was built by Lord Aungier, the first Lord Longford, about the year 1627. Lord Aungier, in building the castle, attached to it a keep for soldiers, and surrounded it with a fortification, which extended in parallel lines from the back of the jail to Mullagh Bridge, thence across to the River Camlin, which formed the southern and eastern fortification to the castle. The River Camlin at this time flowed in a straight line from the Bridge of Longford until it joined its small tributary at a point midway between the railway and Mullagh Bridge, whence it swept round to the north and flowed by an at present clearly defined channel into its present course. The old course of the river will be plainly seen if the reader takes the trouble to walk from the end of this old channel towards the Lower Barrack back gate, when he will find a green track leading him straight till he strikes the river at the point where the present new cut was made for it. The track of the old fosse or fortification will be also plainly discernible if the reader draws a straight line from the wooden bridge to the end of Abbeycartron lane, and thence across to the north side of the present barracks. The space inside and outside this old boundary is called The Demesne, and has never lost the title bestowed on it by the first owners, who in those good old days had it planted with fine oak and birch-trees, which are now all cut down, but traces of which are yet plainly to be seen in the number of little mounds that now cover the whole flat pasture of this portion of the land.

The Castle of Longford remained in possession of the Aungiers as long as they continued Lords of Longford, and passed from them to the Pakenhams, when they obtained the title (which was about the year 1765), who continued to reside in it until the year 1816, or thereabouts, when, owing to the suicide of one of the family in it, they abandoned it for good as a residence, and went to reside near Castlepollard, where they still live. The Pakenhams are first mentioned in connexion with the county about the year 1730, on 6th October, 1747, Thomas Pakenham being elected M.P. for the Borough of Longford His son, Edward Michael Pakenham, was created first Viscount Longford, and the present earl is the fifth of the name who holds the title

Many and thrilling are the stories which could be told concerning past events in the town of Longford. It is built on the Camlin, which, many hundred years ago, was a wide and shallow stream, flowing by an irregular and zig-zag course to the Shannon. Its course at present is very irregular, it is true ; but then efforts have been made, and not without success, to build up proper embankments, &c , to repress the overflow of the river ; and in many places are to be found traces of an old and (now) disused course such as I have described. The peasantry of the county have always told that there was a prophecy made by St. Columbkille about this stream. The prophecy was to the effect that it would be seen to run red with blood on three different occasions, the last being a warning of the approach of the end of time. The people aver that already this prophecy has been fulfilled twice, each fulfilment having occurred during times of sore trial to the Irish people. On the first of these occasions the river was reddened by the blood of the men slain at Ballinamuck, which a body of soldiers washed off their garments in the river at Ballinalee. The second took place when, during the great cholera epidemic of 1832, a butcher in Longford killed a number of sheep on the banks of the river. If the prophecy ever was made, and that its fulfilment was of such direful moment to the people, it is no harm to say that we hope the third fulfilment will not occur, at least during the present generation.

Several very cruel events occurred upon the advent of the satellites—lay and clerical—of Queen Bess in Longford. One of the stories told of it is, that on their arrival they found three monks of the Order of St. Dominick in the old parish chapel. The times these men lived in were times in which a man's life was held at very little value; and, of course, everyone is aware that, as well as Mahomet in Arabia, Elizabeth in England and Ireland "made men's consciences by the sword." Thus it came that the discovery of the poor Dominican friars was somewhat like a godsend to the soldiers, who immediately led them out to execution. Two of them were strung up at once to a large elm-tree that grew near the present church entrance. The third, a venerable grey-headed old man, was offered his life and liberty if he would renounce his faith and lay aside his Dominican habit The old gentleman calmly listened to the proposals made to him by his enemies, and then he said : "In these garments I have lived my life—in them I will meet my death" The words were scarcely uttered when he fell to the ground, pierced to the heart by the sword of the Elizabethan officer in command of the soldiers, whose bloody act was loudly applauded by his coarse-minded, vulgar soldiery. This story is probably an unauthorized version of the martyrdoms related at page 181.

Some time previous to 1798, a poor man was one fine morning going to the fair of Ballymahon to sell a cow, and in walking along the road he met a party of four men carrying the bleeding corpse of a fifth, whom they were after murdering. Naturally the poor man was very much alarmed at meeting such persons, for it is an old saying that " he is a wise man who never finds a dead man;" but there being no hope for it, he boldly advanced towards them. One of them ran away, but three remained, and, in order to shut the new arrival's mouth, they made him take the place of the man who had fled, and assist them to

RUINS OF THE "LADY'S CHURCH," ON QUAKER ISLAND.

cast the dead body into a boghole. He did so in fear and trembling, and then went his way. A short time afterwards he was tried for the offence, and, although the authorities knew well that he had no further act, part, or knowledge of the brutal affair than what is related, he was condemned and executed in Longford Jail, despite the loudest protestations of innocence, whilst the real murderers escaped. Shortly after the Battle of Waterloo, a double execution took place within the same walls for wife murder, the sufferers being brother and sister, who had combined to murder the wife of the former. The female prisoner on this occasion must have been of a very hardened disposition, for she insisted at her execution on being dressed in the most fashionable style; and such was the disgust her action created, that a peculiar cloak then in great vogue was, after the execution, never again worn by the women of the county. In the year 1799 twelve men were hanged in Longford Jail for various offences, many of them for murder, of which all the Irish insurgents of '98 were accused.

About the year 1792 there officiated in Longford two brothers as clergymen—one Father O'Beirne, P.P., of Templemichael, and the other the Rev. D. O'Beirne, Protestant Rector of Templemichael, and afterwards Bishop of Meath. In a book called "The Sham Squire" there appears the following reference to this Mr. O'Beirne :—

"Of Bishop O'Beirne much has been written, but we never saw in print some curious details embodied in a letter dated April 22nd, 1857, and addressed to us by the late Mr. Wm. Forde, Town Clerk of Dublin :—'I can furnish,' writes Mr. Forde, 'an interesting anecdote of the early history of that gentleman, which I learned when very young, living within two miles of the See-house of the diocese of Meath. Dr. O'Beirne was never ordained a Roman Catholic priest, but was educated at the Irish College of Paris, with a view to his becoming a priest. His brother, Rev. Denis O'Beirne, was educated at the same time and in the same college, and died parish priest of the town of Longford, of which his brother was rector. The name of the parish in the Church is Templemichael. The history of the bishop in early life

was, that having suspended his studies owing to ill-health, he returned
home for a couple of years, and was returning to college when the
following incident that altered his life occurred to him   He was travelling on foot through Wales, when the day became very boisterous and
rainy, and he had to take shelter in a wayside inn.   Having ordered
his dinner, he went into a little sitting-room, and in some time afterwards two gentlemen, who were of a shooting-party, came in also for
shelter, and asked what they could have for dinner   The woman said
she could give them nothing, as the only piece of Welsh mutton she
had was down roasting for an Irishman.   They said they would take
it, and Paddy might go hang ; whereupon O'Beirne walked in and
asked who was hanging Paddy, told them they could not take his
dinner by force from him, but if they would take it by invitation they
were welcome.   The invitation being accepted, they began to speak
in French, when O'Beirne began to speak in it too, as he was a
perfect master of it ; and in the course of conversation he told them
who he was and what he was going to be.   This led to a confidence, and
the result of it was, that on his way to Paris O'Beirne passed through
London, where he called at a house named on a card given to him
by one of the gentlemen ; and there he learned that he had become
acquainted with the Duke of Portland, who subsequently introduced
him to Lord Howe, with whom he went to Canada.   Here he became
an apostate and Church of England Minister , and, on his return,
through the influence of the Duke of Portland, then Lord Lieutenant of
Ireland, he became first Rector of Templemichael, and afterwards
Bishop of Meath, in which position he died in 1822.   He married Miss
Stuart, niece to the Earl of Moray, and wrote a comedy entitled " The
Generous Impostor," which was performed six times.   During this
man's stay in Longford as rector, he usually walked and talked and was
on the best of terms with his brother the priest ; and after his removal
to Meath he lived beside Dr. Plunkett, the Catholic bishop, with whom
he kept up all the usual courtesies of life.' "

About the year 1740 there lived in Longford a butcher named Paul

Reddy, whose grave is yet plainly to be seen in Longford graveyard, with the date of his death marked on it, 1763. Paul did a large trade, particularly with the gentry, but was much annoyed to find that a certain clergyman was a bad pay. At last Paul refused point blank to give his reverence any further credit, much to the disappointment of the latter. One Sunday, however, he sent to Paul to inform him that if he would oblige him with a joint of beef for dinner, he would pay him all he owed him in a few days. The servant-boy who brought the message was immediately hunted by the butcher, who told him he would give it when he was paid for the last. The boy returned and, entering the church, found his reverence preaching from the Epistle of St. Paul to the Romans.

"And, dearly beloved brethren," said he, "what did Paul say?"

"He said," answered the servant boy, mistaking the question, "that he would give you more beef when you paid for the last."

The situation created by the servant-boy's answer, and understood at once by the congregation, was so awkward for the reverend gentleman, that he hastily wound up his discourse and descended from the pulpit.

About the year 1795, a Hessian regiment was stationed in Longford, the men of which were so extremely sensitive to the least rebuke or reprimand, that suicides were every day occurring in the barracks. One morning alone there were found no less than fifteen dead men after the night, all of them having destroyed themselves for frivolous excuses. The fifteen men were brought out and stretched side by side on the grass, where hundreds of people came to see the bodies; and they were all buried together in a large hole, at the back of the barracks, at the foot of three large trees. This occurred at the Lower Barracks, which was then much smaller than it is now. The regiment is said to have contained a number of Catholic men, who, when the Elevation of Mass took place, always stood up with drawn swords, and remained standing whilst the Sacred Host was exposed. The suicides having become so notoriously numerous, the regiment had to be disbanded and sent home.

Amongst the clergymen whose names are familiarly known to every

Longford man who loves his country and his religion, there is one that stands out in bold relief from the rest as a patriot, priest, and scholar. This was Father Richard Davys, who died in America, in the year 1846, whilst engaged there in the arduous task of collecting funds for the completion of Longford Cathedral. This reverend gentleman was —for gentle blood, high-minded patriotism, and nobleness of soul—one of the brightest ornaments of the clergy of his diocese of that day, and many good and touching stories are told concerning him.

During the great Repeal movement in 1843, Father Davys was one of the most well-known and familiar faces on the Repeal platforms of the county; and was second only to his bishop in his ardour in the cause. Thus, it is told of him that he never preached a sermon without some political reference in it ; and so famous did his habit become, that the Government of the time stopped sending their Catholic soldiers to twelve o'clock Mass, and sent them instead to ten o'clock, lest their loyalty to the crown would be corrupted by listening to the patriotic eloquence of Father Davys   On the other hand, it was always remarked that when it was his Sunday to preach, a great many more people went to twelve o'clock Mass than was customary, in order specially to hear him.   On one occasion, during an election—and elections in those days meant something more than what they mean now—Father Richard heard that a party of Tories, who came in to vote for the Government candidate, were in danger of being attacked when leaving the courthouse; so he hastened down town, and was just in time to witness the exit, under guard, of the unpopular voters.   They were immediately surrounded by an angry crowd of the opposite political belief, who cheered, groaned and flung missiles at them ; and into the thick of the crowd the priest threw himself, with a view to restrain their somewhat inflamed passions.   The Tories meantime marched up towards Killashee-street, in a house in which they stopped ; but when nearing the crossing at Dublin-street, a stone was flung which floored one of the loyal minority. Just then the priest was in the act of exhorting the crowd, for God's sake, to be calm, when one of the Tory party, turning sharply, caught him by the shoulder, and, wheeling him suddenly to the right, almost pressed a revolver to his forehead, whilst he swore an oath that were another stone thrown he would blow his brains out The crowd was thunderstruck at the scene, which did not occupy a minute; and before they could recover their senses, the Tories had vanished into their domicile, which the presence of a large constabulary force alone saved from being wrecked. They dispersed, however, at the wish of Father Davys, who did not seem the least disturbed by the threat that had been made use of to him The last, and decidedly the most touching story I have heard about him, occurred during his travels in America. In company with another young priest, he went there to collect funds for the cathedral; and on landing at Boston both separated—one to go northwards, and the other south. Father Davys went to the north, and in the course of his travels visited the City of Montreal, which was famous for the number and opulence of its Orangemen. During his stay he met with very little support, principally because those who had the heart to help him were poor, whilst those who could, and would not, were rich The night before he left, however, he heard there was to be a great Orange dinner given in one of the leading halls of the city, and he determined to go there and ascertain for himself if his mission were to be a complete failure. The entrance of a Catholic priest into such a place was, the reader may be sure, the signal for much surprise and astonishment; but when he unfolded the cause of his entrance, the surprise was turned into ridicule. Some laughed, some mocked, and even some made insulting remarks to him ; but to all Father Davys had a ready answer, and finally appealed to them as Irishmen to help him, the majority present being Ulster Protestants. One of the members said he would give him a subscription if he would sing for them a song about Ireland, which suggestion was immediately loudly applauded by all present. The reverend gentleman said he had no objection, but asked if there would be any musical accompaniment. A piano standing in a corner of the room was pointed out to him, and at this he took his seat. I have said he was a scholar ; but if there was any one thing he excelled in, it was music. His voice, too, was beautifully soft and clear; and so, having tested the instrument, and found it to be one of the best of its kind, he began the plaintive air of "*The Exile of Erin*," accompanying it with that splendid song. It was in vain those who were merry tried to laugh—gradually, slowly but perceptibly, a solemn stillness pervaded the whole assemblage; and as he proceeded, handkerchiefs were brought into requisition, and hard-hearted, iron-willed men of business hid their faces, to conceal the blinding tears that stood in their eyes, until, by the time Father Davys had concluded, a single dry eye was not to be found in the audience. Protestants and Orangemen have often been taunted with their religious intolerance and Irish-hating propensities; but here was an instance where men in a distant land, and immersed in foreign pursuits, had their souls stirred to the very depths by a simple Irish ballad, recalling to many of them the happy days of childhood, when they had wandered carelessly by the Foyle or Bann. Father Davys' simple, artless appeal to their Irish sympathies went home to their very hearts, and, in a pecuniary sense, was the very best one he made whilst in Canada on behalf of our cathedral. He died of heart disease in Boston, on July 4th, 1846, having been three years collecting in America; and the light of a noble, generous heart and patriotic soul went out with him   But thus it is ever—blessed be the will of an all-wise Providence   The best and purest are taken, and the inferior remain to rough it with a hard world. To Irishmen and Longford men, who have ever heard of Father Davys and his patriotic sermons, it is a reproach that his grave abroad and his memory at home are alike forgotten and unmarked. I hope it will never fade from sight, until a fitting monument can be erected to it in a regenerated Ireland, which he so longed to see!

ARDAGH AND MOYDOW.

Ardagh and Moydow, which formerly were distinct parishes, are now united, and form one parish, of which Very Rev. James Canon

Reynolds is parish priest.   There are two chapels in it—Ardagh and Moydow, the former being a beautiful new building, which was consecrated in 1882 by Most Rev. Dr. Woodlock, assisted by the Most Rev Dr. M'Gettigan, of Armagh, and at the grand foundation ceremony of which the late great orator, Father Tom Burke, O.P., preached one of his finest sermons.   The church, which is cruciform in shape, and has a splendid front entrance, is built of fine dressed stone, nicely ornamented with brown and white marble, whilst the interior decorations, both of painting, plastering, and wood-carving, are of the most costly and fashionable description   It has been named " St. Brigid's Church," and is well worthy of being the church of a diocesan parish.   The other is situated in Moydow, and is a plain, unadorned country chapel, of an old pattern in building.   The Roman Catholic element in this parish is decidedly strong, although their ranks have been sadly thinned from time to time by eviction, emigration, and reverses of fortune.

Of the local families which claim aristocratic descent in this parish, the principal is Fetherstone of Ardagh.   The present representative of the family is Sir George Fetherstone, who is fifth baronet of the name. He is an absentee landlord who resides in Wales, and draws a princely income from his estates in this parish.   His residence, called "The Big House of Ardagh," is situated on the north side of the village, and is approached by a long avenue, lined with noble trees hundreds of years old.   It was in this mansion that the amusing incident occurred to Oliver Goldsmith, which is told further on

Another family worthy of notice, in days past, were the Jessops, not of Doory Hall, but of Mount Jessop.   They were owners of a fine tract of ground in Moydow, which they lost by their inveterate passion for gambling about forty years ago.   They are said to have become possessed of the estate in a curious way.   It is told that one day, during the plantation *regime*, there came a discharged soldier to the town of Longford, who asked to be shown certain portions of land in Moydow which he was after being granted for his services to the Parliament.   The man that met him was a butler in the local inn in

Longford, who was possessed of some money; and he volunteered to show the discharged trooper the lands. He conducted him up to the top of Castlerea, or Slieve Golry Mountain, and pointed out to him the bleakest and most uninviting portions of that sterile hill The man was much disgusted with the prospect before him, and said if he saw any man who would give him £5 and a horse to carry him to Dublin, he would sell him his right to the lands. The butler took him at his word, handed him out the money, and got him a horse, and in return received the title-deeds of a property which he converted into the Mount Jessop Estate, being the first of its owners himself. "Ill got, ill gone," is, however, an old maxim, and the last owner of the lands put them beyond his reach for ever, by risking them on a game of cards at a ball in the Military Barracks of Longford, and losing them, as well as every penny he was possessed of, in one night.

One of the oldest gentlemen's residences in the County Longford is Bawn House, in the half-parish of Moydow, and distant about a mile from the chapel This old house is now shut up, and presents, as it stands away down in the fields, to the eye of a person standing on the road, a forlorn and deserted appearance; and yet there are many weird stories in connection with it.

Immediately behind Bawn House stand the ruins of the ancient Castle of Moydow, or Moydumha. Some people suppose that these ruins formed the old Priory of St Modiud the Simple. Such is not the case. Anyone can see that the ruins now standing were surrounded by a deep fortified moat, and that the building itself consisted of the usual tower and square keep. This, in fact, was the ancient Castle of the Lord of Moydumha, which was sacked in the thirteenth century at the time that Barry and Camagh Castles were levelled. I am sure that if any expert in antiquarian matters visits these ruins, he will agree with me as to their original purpose.

There is a very tragic story told in connexion with Bawn House. In 1770 the "Whiteboys" were very strong in numbers and very determined in action all over Ireland As history tells, they were

BAWN HOUSE, MOYDOW.

first called " Levellers," from the fact of their assembling at night and levelling the fences with which the landlords endeavoured to enclose certain commons that had previously belonged to the people. But the pent-up agony of a long persecuted race having once found vent, was not to be easily crushed, and for a period of twenty years the " White-boys " were the only protection the unfortunate Catholics had in their troubles. These men, most of whom banded themselves together for the one noble object—to relieve their distressed condition—when going to do any act of violence, blackened their faces and put on a white shirt over their dress as a disguise, from which they were called " White-boys." For many years they, by the very terror of their name, imposed a restraint on the landlords and agents who were inclined to oppress the people—which was most essential to the very existence of the latter, and when they were at length condemned by the priests of the Church, it was because unscrupulous persons had, by bloody acts, turned the association to their own base purposes

About the year 1780 there lived in Bawn House a certain Captain Barnes, agent over several estates in the neighbourhood of Moydow, and famed among the people as an uncompromising exterminator of the tenants, whom he ruled with a rod of iron. On a certain November night he was after collecting the rents of his estates, and was engaged upstairs with his clerk in counting up his money and making out his accounts. While thus engaged, a thundering summons came to the front door, and immediately divining the cause, Barnes and his clerk piled up a lot of furniture on the main stairway, first locking the room in which the money was left. The summons to open the door not being answered, the men, who were Whiteboys that had previously committed several acts of violence in the neighbourhood, burst it in with a log of a tree, which they used as a ram, and were about to rush upstairs when Barnes fired down on them. The shot did not kill any person, and the leader of the party, seeing Barnes about to fire again, immediately took aim and shot him dead on the top of the stairs. The rest of them then ran up and knocked the clerk on the head, leaving him

senseless, whilst they entered Barnes' office and abstracted every penny
he was after receiving that day. The military authorities hearing of
the attack, turned out next day from Longford and captured a dozen
of men, of whom several were hanged on the evidence of an informer,
who did not receive any of the money taken from Barnes, and turned
king's evidence on that account.

In reference to the Jessop family, the old house of Mount Jessop is
at present extant in which one of them, who was just after succeeding
to the estate, committed suicide. It occurred about the year 1820, and
caused great comment at the time. He was an officer in the army, and
had a fine prospect before him, but desired to marry an inferior in rank
to himself, with whom he was in love. This, his guardian, Sir George
Fetherstone, of Ardagh, would not allow, and the young man grew
melancholy thereon, and died by his own hand. When the news of the
deed was conveyed to Ardagh, Sir George galloped over to Mount
Jessop, caused the body of the young man to be dragged out on the
lobby, turned out all the servants, and sealed up the whole house. The
body was buried at night—none knew where. This melancholy occurrence happened about ten years prior to the family losing their property
by gambling.

A horrible tragedy was enacted in the Fetherstone mansion at
Ardagh. The circumstances of the case forcibly point the moral
that "mocking is catching." About that time the then baronet
kept a large retinue of servants and workmen of all descriptions.
Among the latter there were a carpenter, and a gardener who
was deaf and dumb. The carpenter was in the habit, as he deemed
it, of playing with the dumb man—throwing pieces of wood at him, and
in various ways annoying him. Frequently his fellow-servants and
tradesmen warned him that some day or other the victim of these jokes
would resent them, and bring him to an account for them; but he dis-
regarded their warning and continued his pranks. One day in summer,
the weather being very close and sultry, he fell asleep in his workshop,
with his head resting on his own block. The dummy, in passing to his

work, happened to look in to see was John inside, and beheld him in the position described. Instantly the treatment he had for so long a time endured at his hands, and the awful temptation to rid himself of such a nuisance, flashed across his mind, and, with the cunning of such persons, he crept into the workshop. Here he searched till he found the carpenter's own hatchet, the poor fellow unconsciously sleeping all the time; and, with one blow of this murderous weapon he severed his head from the body. The wretched man (now a maddened murderer) then rushed out into the country, where he roamed at free will for many days, until captured by the authorities, when he was sent to Maryborough Lunatic Asylum

It was in Ardagh House that, in 1744, the celebrated scene took place between Miss Fetherstone and Oliver Goldsmith, which subsequently led him to write his famous comedy of "The Mistakes of a Night." Goldsmith was at school at the time with a classical teacher named Rev. Patrick Hughes, of Edgeworthstown, and, in his biography by Irving, the following account is given of his experiences in Ardagh House :—

" An amusing incident is related as occurring on Goldsmith's last journey home from Edgeworthstown. His father's house was about twenty miles distant; the road lay through a rough country, impassable for carriages. Goldsmith procured a horse for the journey, and a friend furnished him with a guinea for travelling expenses. He was but a stripling of sixteen, and being thus mounted on horseback, with money in his pocket, it is no wonder his head was turned. He determined to play the man, and to spend the money in true traveller's style. Accordingly, instead of pushing directly for home, he halted for the night at the little town of Ardagh, and, accosting the first person he met, inquired with somewhat of a consequential air for the best house in the place. Unluckily, the person he accosted, one Kelly, was a notorious wag, who was quartered in the house of Mr. Fetherstone, the local gentleman of fortune. Amused with the self-consequence of the stripling, and willing to play off a practical joke at his expense, he directed him to what was literally 'the best house in the place'—the family mansion of Mr Fetherstone. Goldsmith accordingly rode up to what he deemed to be an inn, ordered his horse to be taken to the stables, walked into the parlour, seated himself by the fire, and demanded what he could have for supper. On ordinary occasions he was diffident and even awkward in his manners, but here he was at his ease in his inn, and felt called upon to show his manhood and enact the experienced traveller. His person was by no means calculated to play off his pretensions, for he was short and thick, with a pockmarked face, and an air and carriage by no means of a distinguished cast. The owner of the house, however, soon discovered his whimsical mistake, and, being a man of humour, endeavoured to indulge it, especially as he accidentally learned that his intruding guest was the son of an old acquaintance. Accordingly, Goldsmith was 'fooled to the top of his bent,' and permitted to have full sway throughout the evening. Never was schoolboy more elated. When supper was served, he most condescendingly insisted that the landlord, his wife, and daughter should partake, and ordered a bottle of wine to crown the repast and benefit the house. His last flourish was on going to bed, when he ordered a hot cake for breakfast. His confusion and dismay on learning the next morning that he had been swaggering in this free and easy style in the house of a private gentleman, may be easily conceived. Goldsmith, who had flirted to his heart's content during the evening with Miss Fetherstone, who personated the servant-maid to obtain his attention, went away from Ardagh very crestfallen; but, in his usual good humour, he turned the whole affair into a joke, in producing from it the play of 'She Stoops to Conquer, or the Mistakes of a Night,' years after, when he became a famous man."

An anecdote is told of Sir Walter Scott in reference to a visit he made to this parish. It is told that when he was visiting Maria Edgeworth, about the year 1800, he drove with her to the house of Sir George Fetherstone. In passing along the road, they met a little boy minding a sow and her little pigs, who were actively engaged in rooting up the ground in all directions. Sir Walter, as became a canny Scot, when he came as far as the boy, asked, "Who owns the pigs, boy?" "The sow, sir," promptly answered the boy, which so pleased Sir Walter that he produced his purse and gave the youngster a guinea, much to the latter's delight.

In the parish of Ardagh occurred many strange things, but none more strange than the libel of St. Brigid. It is told that in the days of St Patrick, St Brigid paid a visit to Ardagh, where she was received with profound respect; but, as usually happens everywhere, some person told some lying story about her, which reached her ears, and was such a source of annoyance to her, that she went to St Patrick and complained to him of the scandal given her. St Patrick, too, was profoundly annoyed that one so holy and so good should be scandalized; and, in order to prove to the world that she was innocent of the lie told about her, he ordered her to place a flaming live coal in her bosom, and carry it from the Cross of Ardagh to the Pound of Killen, a distance of about three miles. St. Brigid did so, and threw out the coal at the end of her journey as fresh as ever, and without the smallest burn being inflicted. She returned then to St. Patrick, and related to him the result, whereupon he became very vexed, and prophesied that the parish would never be without a rogue or a liar. This much is told in tradition; and the shrewd inhabitants, watching the different townlands from time to time, have pitched the onus of the prophecy on different places, according as the course of events verified it. The whole thing, however, may be as mythical as the story of the old woman and St. Patrick, for all that I can prove *au contraire*; but on many occasions I have heard it, not from outside authorities, but parishioners themselves.

The Pound of Killen seems to have been an important part of the parish in old times. There is a tradition amongst the people that, some two or three hundred years ago, the broken bottom land on the right side of the road, as one goes from Longford to Ardagh, was covered with a large sheet of water, which was called St. Brigid's Lake, and which gave rise to two streams running counter to each other—a phenomenon not every day witnessed. The land does look certainly like as though once covered with water, for flaggers, rushes, and other watery plants, cover its broken surface in profusion. In Cromwell's Survey of Ireland, it is mentioned that in the year 1651 there stood at the head of this lake the ruins of an old castle, the property of O'Farrell of Ballynesaggard. But of this structure none now remain at all; and the deserted Pound of Killen testifies that

" Past are all the glories "

of this once memorable spot.

In the townland of Cross, in Ardagh, there is the remains of an old cross, on which people were accustomed formerly to do stations of penance, and at Glenn there was an ancient graveyard well worthy of a visit. St Brigid's Well and Sunday Well, in this parish, have at all times been considered by the people to be very holy places.

About Castlerea Mountain is told a very old legend. This mountain is also called Slieve Golry. Mr. O'Donovan tells it as follows .—

"The mountain in the parish of Ardagh, now called Slieve Golry, was anciently called Brigh Leath, and a legend is taken, in reference to it, from the Book of Tara. In this Book it is related, in the old Irish style, that a comely chieftain's son, named Leath, loved Bri, the daughter of a powerful chief who lived on this hill, then called Tully-na-hearinaghtrihi; and, coming with his servants to Midir, her father, asked the beautiful Bri as his wife. Midir refused to give her, whereupon a fight ensued, and the result was that Leath was vanquished. Bri then returned to her father's house, from which she had fled, and died of a broken heart, the mountain ever after, until the last century, being called Bri Leath. It is now called Castlereagh Mountain, or sometimes Slieve Golry."

The Fetherstones of Ardagh received their baronetcy about the year 1780, the first baronet being Sir Ralph Fetherstone, who entered the Irish Parliament as a representative of the county on October 22nd, 1765. They have held the title of baronets since, and Sir Thomas, who sat in the Irish Parliament during the days of the Union, was one of the rotten members who, for bribery and corruption, sold the liberty of their country; and, as far as we can find out, the succeeding generations of this family are true to the traditions gone before them. Ardaichaidh of the days of St. Patrick has many ancient historical facts to recommend it; and not the least of these is, that in the days when to be a Catholic was to be an alien almost, the thought of ancient Ardagh buoyed up many a wayfarer's heart to struggle on for his faith and his country

CARRICKEDMOND.

This parish corresponds to the Protestant parish of Taghsheenod, and its capital is the village of Tashinny. The small village of Barry is also within its parochial bounds. Barry is called after St. Barry, or St. Bearach, an ancient saint held in great veneration by the people of Longford and Roscommon. Outside the village of Barry are to be seen the ruins of Barry Castle, levelled to the ground in 1295 by Geoffry O'Farrell, Chieftain of Annaly, to avenge an affront offered to him by the Chieftain of Magh Breaghagh At the same time O'Farrell demolished Moydow Castle. Mr. O'Donovan thinks that this parish should be dedicated to St. Senecha; but he says that such a saint is not now remembered amongst its inhabitants. The Castle of Mornine, formerly the inheritance of Sir Matthew O'Farrell, and erected by the O'Farrells in 1400, stands near Barry, in this parish.

CLOUGH.

The parish of Clough corresponds to the Protestant parish of Kil-commick, and is placed under the patronage of St. Dominick. Mr. O'Donovan says this is wrong, and that the rightful patron of Kilcom-mick is St. Da-Camog, who was an Irish saint of much celebrity. The following historical notes are given by him in reference to the parish of St. Da-Camog :—

"1476. Jeffry, son of Siacus, Prior of Abbeyderg, died, and was interred in the monastery bearing that name.

" 1519. Mavilin, son of Torna O'Mulconry, ollave to Sil Murray, an exceedingly learned man, selected by the Geraldines and others to be their ollave in preference to all others. died at Mainster Derg, and was interred there "

A holy well exists in this parish, which is dedicated to St. Dominick.

Legan.

This parish corresponds to the Protestant parish of Kilglass, and was the place where dwelt St Echea, in the days of St. Patrick

In the parish of Legan is the old cemetery of Kilglass, which is reached by means of a small bridle-path across the fields, and is now almost entirely closed, except to those who have the right of interment in it. Very old headstones stand in this cemetery, which, I have been informed, was once on a time the burying-place of the O'Farrells of Ardan-dragh. In reference to this family, it is told in tradition that they owned Legan, and that part of the parish near Ardagh called Rath-reagh. The last of the name who possessed this property took into his household a valet named Fox, who, in addition to being of comely person and attractive figure, was a smart scholar He pretended to O'Farrell, his master, that he was in love with a beautiful girl near Mullingar, whose hand he was sure of winning, could he but show her that he was a man of property. He, therefore, begged that he would be given the loan of O'Farrell's deeds for a short time, to enable him to gain his ends. O'Farrell, foolishly enough, gave them to him, and when he asked them back again, instead of receiving them, he was told by this gentleman that if he dared say anything except that he had purchased them from him, he would turn him out of the place altogether ; and thus O'Farrell lost his estates and Fox got them This is a tradition about the Fox family handed down in this parish ; but I think it is more or less incorrect, and that the property of O'Farrell was at an early date confiscated, and handed over to the Foxes. Of course, were we allowed to peruse the family papers or deeds of these people, we could then give a true account of how their forefathers became landowners,

RUINS OF THE CASTLE OF RATHCLINE, BUILT IN 1667.

RATHCLINE

According to O'Hart, the parish of Rathcline, and part of the parish of Newtowncashel, in olden times formed the inheritance of the O'Quinns, who were styled Lords of Rathcline, and had their castle, the ruins of which were very extensive, a very short distance from the present town of Lanesborough. But Mr. John O'Donovan thinks that Granard and the northern portions of the County Longford was the location of the Muintir Gilligain, or the country of the O'Quinns, whilst the ancient name of Rathcline was Caladh-na-H'Anghaile, or, as we might translate it, "the Callows of Annaly." Now, whilst I cannot pretend to deal with such a vast subject as the ancient topography of the County Longford—a subject requiring deep research and a thorough mastery of the old Celtic tongue—yet I am inclined to believe that the parish of Newtowncashel formed the ancient tract of Caladh-na-H'Angaile, whilst the territory of the Lords of Rathcline extended from Rathcline Castle, which had been built beside Lough Ree to guard against invasion, to the bridge of Ballyclare, in the parish of Killashee, and southwards as far as the present town of Kenagh. In this belief I am borne out by the *Clan Map of Ireland*, which marks the Castle of Rathcline as existing near Lanesborough ; and by O'Harte, who says :—" O'Cuinn had his Castle at Rathcline, in the County Longford," and "the Muintir Magellan (Magillan), whose Castle was at Rathcline, were located in the territory of Muintir Eoluis, in the northern portion of the County Longford, and their chief was O'Quinn."

The town of Lanesborough is built on the Shannon, and the parishes of Rathcline and Newtowncashel (the latter including the isles of Inisboffin, Inchyana, Inisclothran, and All Saints' Islands) also extend along by the Shannon. Both of them border on Lough Ree—the great "king of lakes"—which, in the days of the Pagan Invasion of Ireland, was the scene of many bloody encounters between the Danes and the Irish, as well as the Irish themselves.

l F

The ruins of Fermoyle House lie a short distance from the present town of Lanesborough. It is said by some people that this old house is not more than one hundred years deserted, and that its last occupiers were a band of travelling tinkers. When the castle was given up as a dwelling-place, it belonged to a lady who lived in Dublin, and is since deceased She took no particular care of it, and soon it became the residence of every tinker, piper, and stray traveller in the country. At length the people of the locality declined to have their hen-roosts visited and robbed at night, and some of their sheep cooked in the large hall of Fermoyle House; and they complained to the agent of the owner of the nuisance to which they were subjected. He came down like a wolf on the fold, expelled the invaders, and stripped the roof of the building, which has since remained a smouldering ruins. I insert here the following further historical notes I have collected about these parishes:—

The Callows.—The district in the County of Longford and parish of Newtowncashel, now called The Callows, was anciently called Caladh-na-H'Angaile; and the following references are quoted in a manuscript I have seen about it:—

" A.D. 1411. Mortogh Midheach, the son of Brian O'Farrell, Lord of Caladh-na-H'Angaile—a man who was never censured—died.

" 1486. Giolla-na-naomh, son of Donnell, son of Mortogh Midheach, Lord of Caladh-na-H'Angaile, died.

" 1572. The sons of the Earl (of Roscommon, I think) next plundered the district lying between the River Suck and Shannon, and pillaged every person who was on friendly terms with the English as far as the gates of Athlone. Afterwards, keeping the Shannon on the right hand, they marched directly outwards to Sheve Baghnad-tuath, crossed the ferry of Anghaile, and burned Athleague "

The place in which dwelt these lords of Caladh-na-H'Angaile is now represented by the ruins of Elfeete Castle, in the townland of Elfeete, on the shores of Lough Ree. The old castle consists of a very high tower and some old walls, and is in a tolerably good state of preservation, being built of large blocks of stones firmly bonded together with the ancient compound known as grout. This old castle, and the height on which it is erected, as well as the wild scenery about it, is very well worthy of a visit, indeed, from any person who would like to enjoy the antique and picturesque in combination; and although its distance from Longford and other towns renders it somewhat difficult of access to persons unacquainted with the locality, yet I am considerably surprised that travellers do not frequently visit it.

There are but few stories available in reference to these parishes; but, taking them in their present-day appearance, I am forced to the belief that ancient Caladh-na-H'Angaile, or the parish of Newtown-cashel, was at all times a legend-giving locality. One of the stories I have heard in connexion with it is in relation to Saints' Island. In this island there is a graveyard where a large proportion of the inhabitants of Newtowncashel are interred. Up to about fifty or sixty years ago there was a remarkable flat stone in this island, which was said to be possessed of a very unwonted power. This was, that when a funeral arrived at the shore of the lake, preparatory to being transmitted to its last resting-place, the stone was always standing still on the surface of the water, waiting to carry across to the island the remains of the deceased. Incredible as this may seem, it was, nevertheless, a fact. The coffin was placed on the stone, which was elongated and slab-like, and, in the twinkling of an eye, had cleft the waters and deposited its burden on the shore of Saints' Island, whilst the friends followed in their boats, and the stone returned to its resting-place. One day a certain family went to bury a friend in the island, and, either on their return from or entry to it, one of their number committed a nuisance on the stone, which immediately sank to the bottom of the lake, nor could the person who committed this sacrilege ever lift his eyes from the downward position in which they were at the time he did the deed.

There was another tradition in reference to this island, which shows the sacred feelings with which it was regarded by the people. Men or women, when they wanted to protest the truth in a very solemn manner, always swore—" By the Crineeve ;" or called that word to witness the truth of their assertion. Their reason for this was, that there was a stone figure on this island representing a man's head ; and the people believed that if they took an oath in the presence of this figure, and that the substance of their declaration was untrue, the result would be that their own heads would be turned on their bodies.

During the Cromwellian visitation of Ireland, it is told that there lived in Clonbonny House one of the descendants of the O'Farrells of Annaly, with his two daughters. This man was old and feeble, and fearing he would not be able to defend his daughters in case of attack, he resolved to go into an island in Loughbonny. He did so, and lived there for some time in perfect security ; but one day, when fishing in the lake, one of his daughters was seen by two Cromwellian troopers. The soldiers hallooed to her to come to land ; but she, not minding their menaces or their threats, rowed beyond the island out of sight. Here she pulled a plug out of her little boat, which sank to the bottom of the lake, and she scrambled on shore. At first the soldiers seemed inclined to go away, but after some time they began to fire shots at the island, on which was her sister and father. Seeing their conduct was likely to bring more soldiers on the spot, her father took aim at them, and missed, whereupon she rested the gun on his shoulder and fired, and killed both men at the same discharge. She and her family sub-sequently lived to enjoy the reward of their courage.

Lough Bannow, which is on the right-hand side of the road from Lanesborough to Longford, is so called because, when the road to Longford was but a bridle-path, a large lot of pigs coming from fairs used to be drowned in the lake, which is of a marshy, boggy bottom, but not deep—hence the name Bannow, which means " little pigs."

A writer on " The Beauties of Ireland " says :—

" The town of Lanesborough, seated on the River Shannon, derives the first part of its appellation from the family of Lane, formerly proprietors of this place, and ennobled by the title of Viscount Lanesborough.

This small town consists of no more than about sixty houses, and affords few objects to interest the traveller The River Shannon is here crossed by a substantial bridge, erected in the year 1706, towards the expense of which £100 was contributed by James Viscount Lanesborough. The parochial church is formed from the nave of an ancient structure, traditionally termed an abbey, having some remains of a square tower at the west end. No monastic foundation of this place is noticed by any historian, but some traces of such an institution may possibly still be discovered, on a diligent investigation of the records. Several of the noble family of Lane are buried in a vault beneath this church.

" On the failure of heirs male in the family of Lane, in the early part of the eighteenth century, Brinsley Butler, Baron of Newtown-Butler, was (August 12th, 1728) created Viscount Lanesborough; and Humphrey, the eldest son of that nobleman, was, in 1756, raised to the dignity of Earl of Lanesborough, which titles are still enjoyed by his descendants. At the distance of about two miles from Lanesborough are the ruins of *Rathline,* or *Rathcline Castle.* These vestiges are situated at the base of the hill of Rathline, and on the margin of .the River Shannon. The situation is extremely fine, and the ruins are picturesque and interesting. This castle is said to have been first erected by the family of O'Quin, and many sanguinary contests for possession of its embattled walls are still remembered by traditionary records, although unnoticed by the regular historians of the country. The fortress was dismantled by Cromwell, and was afterwards reduced by fire in the wars of James II. It is observed by Seward that ' a very ancient inscription, cut in the Irish character on a marble slab, and fixed in the wall of one of the rooms, was removed or destroyed by a gentleman who lately resided in the modern house, built close to the castle from its ruins.' In the vicinity of the castle are the remains of a church, evincing considerable antiquity, with an attached cemetery, still used as a place of burial for Catholics. The town of Lanesborough is situated in the parish of Rathline.

" At the distance of one mile from Lanesborough is the residence of Captain Davys, agreeably situated on the eastern banks of the Shannon.

" On the south-west border of this county the River Shannon expands into that noble spread of water, which has been already noticed in our account of Westmeath, under the name of *Loughree*. Such parts of this Lough as are contiguous to the County of Longford are interspersed with various islands, and afford some of its most pleasing features to a district little indebted to nature for picturesque charms. On several of the islands in Loughree, monastic institutions were founded at early periods "

James Stephens, the celebrated Fenian Chieftain, says, in a publication of his in the columns of the *Weekly Freeman*, that the County of Longford can compare favourably with any county in Ireland for the number, variety, and beauty of its legends, as well as the vividly-narrative style in which they are told by the peasantry; and I believe he quotes more than one legend about the parish of Rathcline in reference to a white mare that (as tradition told) used to come up out of Lough Bannow and eat a poor man's vegetables, until by some potent means he managed to " settle " the noxious visitor.

The Town of Ballymahon.

Ballymahon is a small town consisting of about 1,200 inhabitants, situated on the main road between Longford and Athlone, and about midway between both towns. Consequently the reader will admit that if the town of Ballymahon existed in the stormy days of the thirteenth, fourteenth, and fifteenth centuries, it would have been an important post between Granard, in the north of Longford, and Athlone, on the borders of Westmeath. But we have no positive information that Ballymahon did exist in those days ; and it is more possible than probable that, situated as it was, if it did exist, there would be historical reference made to it somewhere. The earliest mention recorded of this neighbourhood is the year 1578, being the year of the suppression of the Abbey of Shrewle, when it is recorded that certain houses and lands adjoining in " the town of Ballymanaghe " were conveyed to Robert Dillon, his heirs and assigns, for ever.

What occurred next in the history of the little town is best told in a tradition handed down among the people in the neighbourhood, and immortalized in the " Poem to Gracie," by " Leo." This has reference to the present owner of Ballymahon, and is to the effect that when De Ginkle invested Athlone, there came in his train an old fellow named Molyneux, who was after obtaining a grant of the lands of Ballymahon, for his services to William III.

This old man, when he came to take up his residence in the old mansion at Ballymulvey, found there three Dominican monks, who were, it seems, hiding. At the end of this house there was a fish-pond, round which grew a number of crab-apple trees. The house was built, as is the present one, almost on the banks of the Inny. Old Molyneux was an ardent hater of monkery, and his immediate action, on finding the poor men, was to have them hanged out of the trees over the fish-pond. It is told that when the poor men were dead, each of them was observed to point the index finger into the water ; and it was not long until it was known that whenever Molyneux went to drink out of any vessel, three index fingers were pointed up to him, as if it were the monks were pointing out their murderer. This visitation continued to annoy Molyneux for many years, until at length it became intolerable to him. It is said that he repaired to a holy bishop then in Dublin, through whose intercession for him the ugly reminder was removed. All this is, of course, mere tradition.

Ballymahon has in its day produced two ornaments to Irish literary character, whose names will be remembered in the locality as long as the Green Isle peeps above the Atlantic. The first of these was Oliver Goldsmith, the celebrated London poet and writer, and the second was John K. Casey, the life and soul of the Fenian movement in his district in the days of '67. To Oliver Goldsmith I do not know is it necessary for me to refer at any length, for I am sure that in those days of enlightenment and education every schoolboy is acquainted with the life, times, and writings of the author of "The Deserted Village." However, as a portion of my original plan of this work purports dealing with "the illustrious sons of Annaly," amongst whom I reckon Oliver Goldsmith, I will quote his life from a contemporary literary critical writer, after which I will relate some anecdotes illustrative of his good-humour and good-nature.

"1728-1774. One of the most charming writers of the eighteenth century was Oliver Goldsmith, whose works are stamped with gentle grace and elegance. He was born in the village of New Pallas, in the County Longford, and in 1745 entered Trinity College in the humble capacity of sizar. Here his career was eminently strange, and after failing to take out a medical degree, he at length went to Edinburgh with the same object; but having failed there also, he was sent to Leyden, in Holland, where he took out some kind of a diploma. He then started on a tour on the Continent on foot, and visited in his travels France, Switzerland, Italy, and parts of Austria, returning to London in 1756. Here he began life as an usher in a school; then as an apothecary; then as a tutor; and finally began to practise medicine. Whilst assisting to teach school he became acquainted with a Mr. Griffiths, proprietor of the *Monthly Review*, who engaged him to contribute pieces to his periodical in the capacity of (at that time a very common employment) literary hack. This laid the foundation of Oliver's future literary career—a career pursued amid all the poverty, misery, and uncertainty of a man's life who depends upon his wits or the produce of his pen to make a living; and after a hard struggle with adversity he died in 1774, having established for himself the name of being the most generous alms-giver, the best poet, the most pleasant prose writer, and the most genial companion of his day."

Oliver Goldsmith's works include—"Letters from a Citizen of the World," "Life of Beau Nash," "History of England," "The Vicar of

RUINS OF CASTLEREAGH, MOYDOW.

RUINS OF CASTLE MORNIN, CARRICKEDMOND.

Wakefield" (1766), "History of Rome" (1768), "The Deserted Village" (1770), "The Traveller," "She Stoops to Conquer," "Retaliation," "The Haunch of Venison," "The History of Greece," and "The History of Animated Nature" Some of these works rank as first-class masterpieces of their style, such as the poems, "The Traveller" and "Deserted Village," and the comedies of "She Stoops to Conquer," and "The Good-natured Man." "The Vicar of Wakefield" and the "Letters of a Citizen of the World" also rank as some of the best and purest of good English compositions.

Oliver's mistakes and mishaps in this life have often enough been the subject of laughter to all those who have read of his chequered career; and it seems to me that in attempting, as it were, to rip up the ground afresh, I would be doing that which would neither reflect credit on me nor on the subject of my pen; therefore, I will simply cursorily refer to these stories, lest, perchance, I might offend the susceptible or irritate the critic Oliver's purse and friendship was ever open to the needy and distressed, as I have said before. Thus, when appealed to by either a professional beggar or a fitting subject of charity, he never refused a gift. Whilst in Trinity College, he was one day during the middle of winter, and whilst himself suffering from extreme poverty, accosted by a poor woman, who told him that her husband was in prison, and she and her children were starving for want of food. Oliver had not tasted food for twenty-four hours at the time. However—

"His pity gave ere charity began"

in this case; for, remembering that he had at home on his bed a good blanket and coverlet, he brought them to the poor woman and gave them to her, telling her to sell them for food for her and her children. Next morning when a friend went to call Goldsmith, he could see nothing on the bedstead but the bare mattress of feathers After calling some time, however, a head was popped up out of a hole cut in the cover, and Oliver announced to the astonished visitor that he would be with him directly. Goldsmith, having no other shift to make for a bed

1 G

after his extravagant gift, cut a hole in the feather tick, and slept in the feathers all night.

The death of Goldsmith's father in 1747 rendered his condition at college so precarious, that in addition to receiving gifts from his friends to support him, he was often compelled to pawn his books for a support. It was then that he began first to scribble verses, which he used to sell privately to a small shop for five shillings a piece. He would then stroll out of an evening to listen to them being sung by ballad-singers in the streets of Dublin, and to observe how the crowd received them.

After an attempted attack on Newgate Prison, made by the T.C.D. madcaps, in which several of the warriors came to grief, Goldsmith gave a feast in his rooms to make up for the disgrace which he, as one of the rioters, suffered. He had just won one of the minor prizes of the college, value thirty shillings, and thought by him to be a little fortune. He forthwith gave a dance and a supper in his rooms to several persons of both sexes from the city, which was a flagrant violation of the rules; but the sound of the fiddle reaching poor Noll's tutor's ears, he rushed to the room, inflicted corporal punishment on the father of the feast, and turned the astounded guests out of doors.

Goldsmith's description of his life in Edinburgh, to which he had gone to study medicine and to take out a degree (in both of which he, as usual, failed), is witty and laughable. Describing the hostess's method of making up a hocus-pocus mess for him, he wrote:—

"A loin of mutton would serve me and two fellow-students for a week. A brandered chop was served up one day, a steak another, collops with onion sauce a third, and so on until the fleshy parts were quite consumed, when finally a dish of broth was manufactured from the bones on the seventh day, and the landlady rested from her labours."

En route from Edinburgh to Leyden, in Holland, to study medicine, the ship was forced by stress of weather to put into Newcastle. Here Goldsmith and other voyagers went on shore to refresh themselves, but were taken prisoners, on suspicion of being French spies. This arrest saved Goldsmith's life, for the vessel sailed without him, and was lost, with all hands, at the mouth of the Garonne, in France. On his arrival in Holland he wrote home the following description of a Dutchman :—

"The modern Dutchman is quite a different creature from him of former days; he in everything imitates a Frenchman but in his easy way. He is vastly ceremonious, and like a Frenchman in the days of Louis XIV. Such are the better bred; but the downright Hollander is one of the oddest figures in nature. Upon a lank head of hair he wears a half-cocked, narrow hat, laced with black ribbon; no coat, but seven waistcoats and nine pairs of breeches, so that his hips reach almost to his armpits. This well-clothed vegetable is now fit to see company or to make love. But what a pleasing creature is the object of his appetite ! Why, she wears a large fur cap with a deal of Flanders lace; and for every pair of breeches he carries she puts on two petticoats."

On his travels through the Continent, during which he picked up the materials for his splendid poem, *The Traveller*, Goldsmith became travelling tutor at Geneva to a mongrel young gentleman, son of a London pawnbroker, and himself an attorney's clerk before a legacy left him plenty of money, of which he was a pettyfogging miser. Goldsmith describes their connection as follows:—"I was to be the young gentleman's governor, with the proviso that he should always govern himself. Avarice was his ruling passion, and all his questions on the road were, how money could be saved, and whether anything, if bought on the way, could be turned to good account in London. Such curiosities as could be seen for nothing, he was ready enough to see, but if the sight of them was to be paid for, he usually asserted that he had been told they were not worth looking at. He never paid a bill that he would not remark how amazingly expensive travelling was, and all this, although not yet twenty-one. Arrived at Leghorn, as we took a walk to get a view of the port, he inquired the expense of a passage by sea home to England; and finding it was but a trifle compared to his return by land, he paid me the small part of my salary that was due, took his leave, and departed, with only one attendant, for London."

After Goldsmith's return to London, in 1756, he became usher in a boarding-school, his career in which may be pretty well understood from the following extract from one of his works :—

"This is, indeed, a pretty career that has been chalked out for me. I have been an usher at a boarding-school myself, and may I die by an anodyne necklace, but I had rather be under-turnkey in Newgate! I was up early and late, browbeat by the master, hated for my ugly face by the mistress, worried by the boys within, and never permitted to stir out to receive civility abroad. But are you sure you are fit for the position ? Let us examine you a little. Have you been bred apprentice to the business ? No !—then you won't do for a school. Can you dress the boys' hair ? No !—then you won't do for a school Have you had the small-pox ? No !—then you won't do for a school. Can you lie three in a bed ? No !—then you will never do for a school. Have you a good stomach ? Yes !—then you will by no means do for a school. The truth is, in spite of all their efforts to please, the tutors are generally the laughing-stock of the school."

After trying his hand at medicine for some time, he had again recourse to the schools as a method of earning a living; and here he met the editor of the *Monthly Review*, who gave him his first task in literature; and after some time he began to sell literary productions to a Mr. Thomas Newbury, a bookseller in St. Paul's Churchyard, whom Goldsmith subsequently described as follows, in his own work, the "Vicar of Wakefield ":—

"This person was no other than the philanthropic bookseller in St. Paul's Churchyard, who has written so many little books for children ; he called himself their friend, but he was the friend of all mankind. He was no sooner alighted than he was in haste to be gone, for he was ever on business of importance, and was at that time actually compiling materials for the history of one Mr. Thomas Trip. I immediately recognised this good-natured man's red-pimpled nose."

At this time he became rather well known, which soon enlarged the circle of his acquaintances ; and the report of his greatness soon travelling to Ballymahon, his friends thought he could do anything for them They accordingly wrote to him to ask him for his patronage ; and in reply to the letter he received from a Mr. Hodson, he wrote, *inter alia* :—

"I suppose you desire to know my present situation. As there is nothing in it at which I should blush, or which mankind could censure, I see no reason for making it a secret.   In short, by a very little practice as a physician, and a very little reputation as a poet, I manage to live.   Nothing is more apt to introduce us to the gates of the Muses than poverty ; but it were well if they only left us at the door The mischief is, they sometimes choose to give us their company to the entertainment, and want, instead of being gentleman usher, often turns master of the ceremonies."

Soon after writing this letter he obtained an appointment as surgeon on the coast of Coromandel, but failed, from poverty, to appear either in fitting garb or with accurate ideas before the Examining Board of the College of Surgeons.   He was examined in December, 1758, but was rejected on account of inefficiency, and his spirits were soon after still further damped by the threat of the editor of the *Monthly Review* to have him committed to prison, if he did not pay the debt he owed him for a proper suit of clothes in which to appear before the Examining Board of the College.   Bishop Percy, of Dromore, called on him during those days, and thus describes his abode :—

"I called on Goldsmith at his lodgings, in 1759, and found him writing his 'Inquiry' in a miserable dirty room, in which there was but one chair, and when, from civility, he resigned it to me, he himself was obliged to sit in the window.   Whilst we were conversing together some one tapped gently at the door ; and being desired to come in, a poor, ragged-looking little girl, of a very becoming demeanour, entered the room, and dropping a courtesy, said : 'My mamma sends her compliments, and begs the favour of you to lend her a chamber-pot full of coals.'"

After the publication of his " Inquiry into the Present State of Polite Learning in Europe," a furious onslaught was made on him in the *Monthly Review*, with the editor of which he had the quarrel about the suit of clothes. In this unjust and unnatural attack, poor Goldsmith was described as " labouring under the infamy of having forfeited all pretensions to honour or honesty;" but the attack was universally condemned as malignant, and was never replied to by the author.

In 1761 he met and made the acquaintance of Dr. Johnson, who quickly introduced him to the host of celebrated men who formed the Literary Club of those days ; and soon after he was on intimate terms with Garrick, Boswell, Sir Joshua Reynolds, and others. In 1763 he published the beautiful story of the " Vicar of Wakefield," which he followed in 1764 with the poem which made his reputation—" The Traveller "—and which was dedicated to Rev Henry Goldsmith, rector of Lissoy. This poem raised him at once, in the opinion of the public and of his competitors for literary fame, to the level of the greatest living poet, and added most considerably to his circle of acquaintances, which now consisted of wits, scholars, authors, artists, actors, and states-men, amongst the latter being the great orator, Edmund Burke.

Boswell recorded several of the conversational disputes that occurred at the Literary Club between Johnson and Goldsmith. Johnson was somewhat of a bully in conversational matters, and could ill withstand contradiction. One day, when Goldsmith was going to speak, Johnson interrupted him. " Take it," said Goldsmith, angrily. " Sir," said Johnson, angrily, " I was not interrupting you; I was only giving a signal of attention. Sir, you are impertinent." The same evening he met Goldsmith in company with a friend, to whom he said he would make Goldsmith forgive him. " Doctor Goldsmith," said he, " some-thing passed to-day where you and I dined ; I ask your pardon." It would be much from you, sir," replied poor Goldsmith, " that I would take ill," and so the angry feelings were at once allayed. On many occasions he had to do the needful for distressed countrymen of his own. One time a fellow named Glover lived on his bounty for some weeks, ánd thus described Goldsmith : "Our doctor, as Goldsmith was called, had a constant love of his distressed countrymen, whose wants, as far as he was able, he always relieved ; and he has often been known to leave himself without a guinea in order to supply the necessities of others "

On May 26th, 1770, he produced his poem, "The Deserted Village," which he followed by producing the Histories of Rome, Greece, and England for the use of schools, which contain a good deal of matter and some literary merit ; and he took a voyage to France about this time. In 1772 he wrote a play, "She Stoops to Conquer," which was produced in Drury-lane Theatre, and had a triumphant success wherever it was performed, and still retains its place amongst the pieces on the stage. Goldsmith's life was now drawing to a close, and his end was not happy. He had for some time suffered from an ugly complaint, which the extravagance he plunged into from his sad and pensive moods greatly aggravated, and on 4th April, 1774, he expired of a slow fever, having some time previously retired to live in the suburbs of London. He was interred in Westminster Abbey, in the Poets' Corner, and the following inscription in Latin stands over his remains .—-

This Monument is raised
to
OLIVER GOLDSMITH,
Poet, Natural Philosopher, Historian,
Who left no species of writing untouched
or
Unadorned by his pen,
Whether to move laughter or to draw tears
He was a powerful Master over the affections ,
Of a genius sublime, lively, and versatile ;
In expression noble, pure, and elegant
His memory will last
Whilst society retains affection,
Friendship is not devoid of truth,
And reading is held in high esteem
He was born in Ireland, in the Parish of Forgney,

County of Longford, at a place named
Pallas,
29th November, 1728.
He was educated in Dublin,
And died in London,
4th April, 1774

John Keegan Casey, who wrote some of the most charming and
patriotic verses to be found in the whole range of Irish poetry, was
born at a place called Castletown Geoghegan, in the County Westmeath,
on the borders of the County Longford, about the year 1845. Whilst
the future poet was still a mere child, his father obtained the appointment of schoolmaster in the village school of Gurteen, about two miles
distant from Ballymahon, and between that town and Kenagh. Here
young Casey was reared, and here, in the neighbourhood of Ballymulvey
and the Inny, he inhaled, as it were, the first inspirations of poetry.
As soon as he was able to do so, he was called upon by his father to
assist him in teaching his school; and at this occupation he spent
nearly ten years. About the year 1860, he first began to write pieces
of poetry, which from their beauty and style, as well as lofty conception,
soon obtained a prominent place in the columns of the *Weekly News*
and *Nation*. Previous to this, poor Casey, whilst yet a mere boy, had
been in the habit, even when teaching a class for his father, of falling
into an abstracted mood, out of which he would start by repeating some
lines of poetry audibly, which he was thinking how to put together ;
and this habit obtained for him the very uncomplimentary title of
"Shawn the Rhymer." Between the years 1860 and 1864, Ireland's
intense curiosity was aroused by the gigantic struggle which convulsed
the United States; and during those days, too, "Leo's' mind (for
"Leo" was the *nom-de-plume* he wrote under) was actively engaged in
pouring forth abundant stores of patriotic verses, so that not a ballad-
singer in Ireland but was acquainted with him. In 1865 "Shawn the
Rhymer" had grown to be "Leo the Poet." Everyone is acquainted
with the initiation in that year of a great political movement—a move-

BALLYMAHON,

ment set on foot by one man, and a movement which struck terror into the hearts of our British rulers. During its early stages, John K. Casey became accidentally acquainted with a prominent Fenian in his neighbourhood, and was easily and soon converted to the doctrine for which Tone, Emmet, and Fitzgerald died. He was so enthusiastic, too, in the cause he had espoused, that he was at a loss how to propagate its doctrine. It is easy, however, to find a way when there is a will. There was at this time in Ballymahon a real true-hearted *Soggarth Aroon*, named Father Lee. To him Casey applied for permission to start a Purgatorian Society in the parish. Father Lee knew Casey well—knew him from his boyhood—and readily gave his consent to the formation of a society for so charitable an object. The society was easily formed—everyone knew and everyone loved " Leo "—and ere long he had all the young men, and some of the staid men too, in his Purgatorian Society. But after each night's meeting, the scholars used to wonder how it was that the seats would be piled up in a corner, and the floor cleared. They thought that if the " *Dies Iræ* " was being chanted, the society should be seated, or if the Rosary were being recited they should kneel—for neither of which positions would it be comfortable to have the seats piled in a corner ; and so gradually it came to be tacitly understood that whilst "Leo " and his brother-members were doing good for the souls of the dead, they also were thinking of doing good for those who were living—in other words, " Leo " was a Fenian organizer ; and what safer way could he take to make converts ? As for poor Father Lee, he never found out that " Leo " was doing a corporal and spiritual work of mercy at the same time, in holding Purgatorian and Fenian meetings together.

Towards the end of '65 he obtained an appointment in the town of Ballymahon as assistant school-teacher and clerk in the Roman Catholic chapel, and was next given a school of his own in the parish of Newtowncashel. During this time he was engaged writing anti-Saxon songs, a number of ballads which, under the title of the " Wreath of Shamrocks," were published in leaflet form, and took a prominent place in the homes and at the firesides of the peasantry of the County Longford.

He does not seem to have liked school-teaching as a profession, for, having been offered an appointment by the Murtagh Bros. as their agent in Castlerea, he resigned his school in a few months, and went to reside there.   During all this time he had continued to pour forth, week after week, songs, poems, and ballads of all descriptions; and he and another contributor to the *Nation*, who wrote under the *nom-de-plume* of the " Bard of Thomond," had more than one controversy such as pressmen often engage in.   At the close of '66 he repaired to Dublin to live.   Here he became a miscellaneous writer, and was attached to the editorial staff of the *Irish People*, in which position he, his editor, John O'Leary, and many others were arrested after the Fenian rising early in '67.   After that he was imprisoned for nine months in Mountjoy Prison, where he fell in love with Mary Briscoe (who, some said, was the daughter of a respectable Castlerea merchant, where, when in the service of the Murtagh Bros., he met and wooed her), and married her privately at Marlborough-street Cathedral on November 20th, 1867. He had been released from prison on condition of leaving Ireland for good; but how could he leave his young and dearly-loved Mary Briscoe just after the sacred link that bound them inseparably together had been fastened?   " Leo " resolved not to leave Ireland, and for this purpose disguised himself as a Quaker, and took up his residence near Cork-hill, and in fact, in the very vicinity of the Castle.   Here, disguised as a Mr. Harrison, he lived in seclusion from November, '67, until March '68, when, throwing aside all fear of further arrest, he came forth from his hiding-place on St. Patrick's morning, and was never afterwards disturbed by the Goverment.   During the remainder of '68 and '69 he contributed a number of short spicy tales to the *Shamrock* and *Young Ireland*, the best of which were : " Ella, the Dancing Girl," " My Aunt Tommy," " Marion," and " The Green Flag of France."

At the same time Casey made several lecturing tours in the South of Ireland and England, the subjects of his lectures being—" The Influence

· of National Poetry," "The Irishwomen of Letters," and the "Orators Letters;" and a lecture delivered in Dublin and Cork on the first-named subject, gained for him a round of congratulatory critiques on his oratorical powers.

It was during those days that the election of Dungarvan took place, which fairly covered him with glory, when, by his burning appeal to their patriotism, the men of Dungarvan hurled Sergeant Barry—the foul libeller of the Fenian Brotherhood, whose conduct during the State Trials of '65 was condemned as an outrage to Irish feeling all over the world—from his position as M.P. for that borough, and adopted in his stead an Englishman and a lawyer, named Mathews, in pre-ference to the traitor Irishman. Poor Casey and Rev. Father Anderson, O.S.A., harangued the people, and roused them to a sense of their duty to their country, and "Leo's" burning speeches largely influenced the election and its result. It will not be uninteresting to some of my readers to know that this same Mathews is, as I write, Home Secretary for England.

In March, 1869, the firm of Cameron and Ferguson published the copyright of some hundreds of his poems, including the "Wreath of Shamrocks," which he already had issued before his arrest in '67, and their publication, under the title of "The Rising of the Moon and other Poems," was highly applauded by critics of all shades of religious and political feeling. His death was tragic almost in its suddenness. For sometime he had suffered from that dread and terrible disease, a bad chest and affected lungs, but, under the skilful care of the Dublin physicians, was rapidly improving. Early in March, 1870, he was driving down by the quays in Dublin, when a dray came in collision with the cab he was seated in. He went to jump out of the cab, when he fell heavily to the ground, the shock stunning him almost to unconsciousness. He recovered, however, but on next evening when crossing O'Connell (then Carlisle) Bridge, he was attacked with a vomiting of blood which almost killed him on the spot. He was conveyed home in a very weak state, and lived for a week; and on St. Patrick's morning, in 1870, after

vomiting blood for almost five hours, he expired in his wife's arms,
fortified by all the consolations of the Holy Catholic Church, of which
he was a faithful son during life.

His poems were collected afterwards, and, from the profits raised
by their publication, the publisher has just succeeded in raising a hand-
some tomb to commemorate the virtues of him who sleeps beneath.
Cut off, as he was, in his very prime, regretted by all those who knew
him as a pure-souled lover of dear Ireland, how great and how honoured
might he not be to-day, had it pleased the Almighty to spare him!   But
it was not to be; and the heartfelt wish of many a patriotic Irishman
will be echoed when I say—May the clay rest lightly o'er him! may the
grass there be ever greenest! and may the soul that dwelt within him
rest for ever in the mansions of eternal bliss!

" Leo's " Poems.

Casey's poems may be classed under three headings—Legendary,
Patriotic, and Amatory. Of these, very few, with the exception of
"Shawn O'Farrell," are at all known to the people of the County
Longford. The people about Lissoy and Pallas delight in repeating
Oliver Goldsmith's verses; but the people of the same neighbourhood
seem to know nothing about J. K. Casey's patriotic verses, written at
a time when all Ireland was in a blaze of patriotic ardour, and when
the dearest hopes of a struggling nation were being slowly undermined
by false friends and open foes. It is, in my opinion, a stain on the
literary escutcheon of the people of Longford that they do not get a
copy, and devour with all the ardour of their souls the verses of " The
Wreath of Shamrocks " or " The Rising of the Moon ;" and I promise
any young man or young woman in our county that if he or she read,
even in the most passing manner, poor " Leo's " patriotic, amatory, and
legendary poems, their love of country and love of Erin's ancient and
modern minstrelsy will in nowise suffer.

PATRIOTIC.

DUNGARVAN JAMES.

Written at the Dungarvan Election

Vote for him, slaves, take his hand as a brother;
Shout for him, people, his heart is your own
To the hustings, good patriot, the country's in danger,
And Barry will save it, he swears by God's throne

Tho' the gold that he flings so profusely around him
Has been won by the blood of the brave that he sold,
Tho' the tongue that you hear bears the slime of soul murder,
Vote for him ! cheer for him ! pick up the gold !

He has hunted your kin from their home to the dungeon;
He has spat on the name and the fame of your land;
With the hate of a demon he spied for his master—
Then raise up a chorus for Barry the grand.

How blandly he smiles with his Hacketts around him !
How sweetly he bows to the men at his side !
How blandly he smiled when he strangled the hero
Who died for the cause for which Emmet had died !

For the sake of his saintship let mankind be sullied,
And all that is glorious dragged into the dust.
Shut your eyes to the dock—to the bench be they lifted,
As he adds one more link to the fetters that rust

He comes, the Apostle, his deacons around;
Even you must forget all the things of the past—
The tongue of the serpent, the scent of the bloodhound,
The coil that was woven, the nets that were cast.

YES, HAUGHTY LORDLING.

Yes, haughty lordling, I am poor ;
    I'm low-bred, if you will—
A thing mayhap to please thy sport,
    And prove thy tyrant skill
But proud's the blood that fills my heart
    And sets my breast aglow—
No bastard blood, proud Saxon lord—
    Though humble, I'm not low.

[*5 Verses.*]

THE BOLD RAPPAREE

And I'll ride to the north in the morning,
And I'll ride to the north in the night,
Till I come to brave Redmond O'Hanlon,
And give him a lift in the fight
'Tis then I'll be sporting and courting ;
It's then I'll be riding full free,
With an eye on the black undertaker
Who plundered the bold Rapparee.

[*2 Verses*]

OUR TOASTS

Air—THE MINSTREL BOY.

To be learned by every Longford man

We drink a toast to the brave old land—
    To the land that we love dearest ,
We drink a toast to the men who stand,
    Who cling to our cause the nearest
Our flag is raised to the rushing wind ,
    No foe can stain its colour—
O Ireland ! soon thy sons shall find
    Thou'rt freed from chains and dolour.

We drink a toast to the men who died
  For the cause of our olden Nation,
We drink a toast to the men still tried
  In the hulks for our land's salvation.
And as we clasp each brother's hand,
  With the eyes of our sisters shining,
There's more than hope for our own dear land—
  There's more to do than pining

LOVE POEMS

AMONG THE FLOWERS.

Every proper name used here has reference to the neighbourhood of Ballymahon

In leafy Tang the wild birds sang—
  The brown light lay on Derry's heather;
But years have pass'd since we the last
  Sat courting in the summer weather
The tender light of stars at night,
  That soothes the wanderer so weary,
Could only show the silvery glow
  That lit your glance, my darling Mary!

The Inny's shore, and tall Rathmore,
  The sunlight on the trembling meadows,
The pastured lea by fair Lough Ree,
  Are now to me but fading shadows
Two eyes of blue still keep their hue—
  Two lustrous eyes that never vary,
And on me shine with love divine—
  Those eyes are thine, my darling Mary!

In summer hours, among the flowers,
  The wandering west wind found thee lonely,
In autumn time the streamlet's rhyme
  Appeared to chime unto thee only
By wildwood side, by Shrughan's tide,
  You wandered like a gladsome fairy—
No winds can tell the airy spell
  That floated round thy presence, Mary!

O loved and lost ¹ tho' tempest tost,
   The exile's track is mine for ever ;
Far o'er the sea, astor machree,
   I stray to thee and Inny's river—
For by its side I'd call thee bride,
   But fortune of its gifts was chary ,
A sunlit gleam—a passing dream,
   And all is gone for ever, Mary !

I have, doubtless, taken an unwarrantable liberty in culling these few verses from an old coverless copy of the "Wreath of Shamrocks," which a friend lent me ; but I am chiefly anxious to show, if possible, the beauty and patriotic fire of poor "Leo's" pieces. I was never poetically inclined myself, nor could I put two lines of poetry together ; but I can conscientiously declare that if ever I did think of attempting to soar into lyrical regions, it was when I read the songs of the dead "Leo."

Ballymahon and the parish of Shrewle possess very little further interest for us, if we except the interest attached to its legendary tales, some of which are given in Casey's legendary poems, the beauty and simplicity of which will be apparent on perusal.

One of those that I have heard referred to a giant who lived in ages past in the parish, and who was in the habit of exercising himself every morning and evening in throwing a large rock, about twenty tons weight, from beyond the Curneens River into Ballymahon and back again. History does not record this wonderful man's name, but he must not have been the fabulous Finn MacCoul, because Finn never did such foolish things. Another legend referred to the city supposed to be buried beneath Lough Drum, and which a diver, in searching for the lost body of a child, discovered. The diver brought up a pan from the town, and was told by a priest standing by not to attempt to see who called to him for it. He broke the command, however, and got his eye poked out for his pains. A third legend relates to St. Patrick's Well, a holy well about two miles from Ballymahon, the waters of which,

Rere View of Ancient Churches on Quakers' Island, in the Shannon (See "Ecclesiastical History.")

when put on a roaring fire, never boil, no matter how long they are left on, nor how strong may be the blaze Outside Ballymahon is New-castle, the seat of Col. King-Harman, a local aristocrat, to whom I shall probably again refer.

Forgney.

A small portion of the parish of Forgney, which belongs to the diocese of Meath, comes into the County of Longford, and in this small portion is Pallas, the birth-place of Oliver Goldsmith, and not the town of Ballymahon, to which I have given credit. Pallas was anciently called Baile-atha-na-Pailse, where the following historical event took place —

" 1462 Thomas, the son of Cathal, who was son of Cathal O'Farrell, tanist of Annaly, was slain at Baile-atha-na-Pailse (Pallas) at night, whilst in pursuit of plunder which a party of Dillons—the Clan Eonchobhar and the sons of Murtogh—were carrying off They carried away his head and his spoils, having found him with only a few troops—a circumstance that seldom happened to him "

In this parish there were the ruins of an old church which Mr. O'Donovan believed should be under the tutelage of St. Muniseps, and stood in the townland of Forgney. He also found that there was an ancient holy well, dedicated to St. Patrick, who, he says, was not its rightful patron, but no person in the parish knew any other. Those details are all that I can give of this parish.

A Personal Memoir.

Before I conclude this volume, I would like to say a few words regarding a gentleman to whom I can trace back my first love for history. I refer to my old teacher, Mr. Thomas M'Geoy, whose lectures about Irish history, at school years ago, first awoke in my heart a love for that study. Of Mr. M'Geoy's services to national education, it is perhaps unnecessary to speak; but I am one of those who believe that in the dark days, before Irish education was a

1 I

department of State, Mr. M'Geoy rendered yeoman service to the cause of Irish education here. Regarding his ability to do so, Assistant-Commissioner Harvey, in his evidence given before a Royal Commission, which presented a report to Parliament in 1870, says:—

"Passing from external details, I come next to the teachers and scholars in ordinary National Schools. The teachers may be divided into two groups—trained and untrained. Were I called upon to characterize these two groups, I should describe the trained teachers as good, and the untrained as indifferent, and sometimes bad. It would hardly be fair, however, to speak in this way without reservation. Amongst the trained teachers I met several whom I could not rank above fair, and among the untrained there were some who by natural aptitude were good. In my district the numbers in the two classes were nearly equally divided. In a list of forty-three, whose schools I examined, there were nineteen who had been six months or more in the Dublin Normal Institution, and twenty-four who had had no such intermediate training. Of these, half-a-dozen or more had enjoyed the benefit of district or minor model schools; but in order to avoid unnecessary and minute sub-divisions, I shall confine the designation of trained teachers to those who had been educated in Dublin. Without reference to their training, but solely by examination, and under regulations of the Board as to the numbers of their scholars and other matters, the teachers were arranged in three classes—first, second, and third. These again were subdivided into grades, so that altogether there were seven steps from the highest to the lowest—the highest being a teacher of the first division of the first class, and the lowest a probationer. Of the nineteen trained teachers mentioned above, five were in the first class, eight in the second, and six in the third; and of the twenty-four untrained, there was no one in the first class, eleven in the second, ten in the third, and three were probationers. Of the whole number I met only one who had attained the highest possible rank, whose name and school, *honoris causâ*, I may be allowed to mention—Mr. M'Geoy, of Longford."

Mr. M'Geoy is now considerably over ten years retired from active service as a teacher, and, with his worthy son, Rev. Thomas M'Geoy, Adm., Ballymahon, enjoys in a ripe old age the pleasures won in his long and well-spent life. I trust that many more years will pass before he is called to that reward which we expect to be the lot of those who fight for faith and fatherland to their latest breath.

Conclusion.

We have now come to the conclusion of our County history. Nothing that could be done to make it instructive and interesting has been spared by me. I trust that the reader will do all he can to make allowance for anything he meets that may jar on the feelings or sensibilities of anyone. I have endeavoured to the utmost of my ability to give a true narrative, from the most reliable sources, of all the important events that have ever occurred within our borders; and if one result of my labours will be, that Longford men in exile will find their hearts warmed anew to the land of their birth, and that Longford men at home shall esteem the blessing of being able to live at home as one of the greatest pleasures of their humble lives, because of the traditions of their native county, then I shall be amply rewarded and satisfied

The End.

Dollard, Printinghouse, Dublin.

Milton Keynes UK
Ingram Content Group UK Ltd.
UKHW020225211223
434752UK00004B/88

9 781015 520226